Suba of Kabul
Under the Mughals:
1585-1739

Suba of Kabul Under the Mughals: 1585-1739

Kabul Under the Mughals

FARAH ABIDIN

PARTRIDGE
A Penguin Random House Company

To order additional copies of this book, contact
Partridge India
000 800 10062 62
orders.india@partridgepublishing.com

www.partridgepublishing.com/india

Contents

Acknowledgement:

I would like to acknowledge and extend my heartfelt gratitude to the people who have made the completion of this research possible.

I must express my deep sense of gratitude to my supervisor Professor Shireen Moosvi for her vital encouragement, support and the much needed motivation. In spite of being so preoccupied, she devoted considerable time in checking my draft and made valuable suggestions and corrections in it. Her constructive criticism all through this period has been very useful.

I owe much to Professor Irfan Habib for his guidance and assistance. His useful suggestions practically at every stage and the valuable time he spent in going through some portions of the thesis have been of immense help to me. He has also taught me Persian.

I am indebted to Dr. Farhat Hasan, Prof. in the Department of History, University of Delhi, for his deep involvement in the preparation of this work at the last stage.

I am very grateful to Mr. Faiz Habib, Cartographer, who has drawn all my maps. He was always very generous to me, both with his time and attention. His senior colleague Mr. Zahoor Ali Khan has also helped me in this task. I should also thank Professor S.P. Verma, who has helped me in locating reproductions of relevant Mughal miniatures.

I am much obliged to the ICHR and UGC for granting me scholarship which provided necessary financial backing.

I am also grateful to the staff of the Research Library, Department of History and Maulana Azad Library for their cooperation.

My parents Mr. Azfar Husain and late Mrs. Asma Husain have always been my source of inspiration. My sister, Mrs. Shaheen Akhtar and my brothers, J.A. Nasir, Rashid Akhtar, Khalid Akhtar and especially, Hamid Akhtar have been a source of extraordinary support to me. I owe my deep gratitude to my family Mr. Nurul Abidin, Mrs. Nighat Abidin, Yasser Abidin and Yusuf Abidin without their love and support it could not have been possible.

Finally, I must acknowledge my deepest gratitude to my husband Saif Abidin for his indulgence and patience during the drafting of this work. He did some of the corrections and, on top of all this, always remained a loving companion.

Needless to say that any shortcomings and errors that remain are mine.

Aligarh   **(Farah S. Abidin)**

Abbreviations:

A N	*Akbarnåma*
Bib. Ind.	Bibliotheca Indica.
Bodl.	Bodleian Library, Oxford.
Br. Mus.	British Museum.
EFI	The English Factory in India.
I.O	India Office
IESHR	The Indian Economic and Social History Review, New Delhi.
IHR	Indian Historical Review, New Delhi.
JASB	Journal of Asiatic Society of Bengal, Calcutta.
JIH	Journal of Indian History.
M A	*Ma'asir-i-'Alamgiri*
M U	*Ma'åsiru-l Umara*
M.A Library	Maulana Azad Library.
MS	Manuscript
Or.	Orient
PIHC	Proceedings of Indian History Congress.
R	Rotograph
Tuzuk	*Tuzuk-i Jahangiri*

Introduction

Kabul was an important part of the Mughal Empire. It formally became a *suba* of the Mughal Empire in 1585, when Akbar annexed it and remained a part of Mughal India till 1739, when it was lost to Nadir Shah. It was strategically located and control over Kabul was viewed by the Mughals as quite necessary for the security of the empire from incursions from the powers in Central Asia.

Despite its economic and strategic significance, it has not yet received the deserved attention by the historians. Irfan Habib's *Atlas of the Mughal Empire* provides an almost exhaustive geographical and economic information about Kabul.[1] He has also done some work on the tribal system of the Afghans.[2] M. Athar Ali is another important historian who has studied the political process in Kabul.[3] Some other important works in a trans-regional framework are also available.[4] Though these works are important but most of

---

[1]   Irfan Habib, *An Atlas of the Mughal Empire: Political and Economic Maps, with Detailed Notes, Bibliography and Index*, Delhi, 1986, pp. 2-3, Sheet 1 A-B.

[2]   Irfan Habib, 'Evolution of the Afghan Tribal System', in *PIHC*, 62nd session, Bhopal, 2001, p. 300-308.

[3]   M. Athar Ali, *Mughal India: Studies in Polity, Ideas, Society, and Culture*, Delhi, 2006, pp. 316-327.

[4]   Henry George Raverty's *Notes on Afghanistan and Baluchistan*, 2 vols., Pakistan, 1982; Johannes Leon Gommans, *Horse-Traders,*

these deal with the history of Kabul within a Central Asian framework. My attempt here is to reverse the frame of reference and study Kabul within the Mughal framework, as part of the history of Mughal India.

Fortunately, there are several extant sources for the study of Kabul. We have several Persian texts (both MSS and published), letters, *akhbarat* and documents as well as the accounts of European travellers and the English Factory Records that deal with Kabul, and provide us the evidence for the reconstruction of the history of Kabul.

The Memoirs of Babur, *Baburnâma* furnishes a detailed description of the *suba* of Kabul. For consulting Babur's Memoirs, I have based myself on Beveridge English translation of the text, but have, wherever possible, collated it with the Chaghtai Turkish text (Hyderabad Codex, facsimile edited by A.S. Beveridge). I have also used Abdu-r Rahim Khan-i Khanan's most authentic Persian translation prepared under Akbar,[5] and occasionally the English translations by Leyden and W. Erskine as well as Wheeler M. Thakston.

Gulbadan Bano *Humayunnama* is also an important text, and provides evidence concerning the court culture in Kabul. The most important text undoubtedly is the *Ain-i- Akbari* of Abul Fazl. For the *Ain*, I have mainly relied on Blochmann's edition but for the statistical portion I have used two early

Mercenaries and Princes: The Formation of the Indo-Afghan Empire in the Eighteen Century, Brussels, 1993; *History of Civilization of Central Asia from 16th to the mid 19th Century,* (Vol. V) ed. Chahryar Adle and Irfan Habib, Unesco pub. 2005.

5   *Baburnâma,* Persian tr. Abdu-r Rahim Khan-i Khanan (1589) litho., Bombay, 1308/1890.

manuscripts in the British Library Add.7652 and 6552. The *'Āin's* statistical data has been of considerable use to me for analyzing the revenue statistics of the *suba*.

The statistical data in the *'Āin* are supplemented by the later works in Persian, such as *Mujalis-us-Salatin, Bayaz-i-Khushbui, Dastur-ul-'Amal-i-Alamgiri, Farhang-i-Kardani, Dastur-ul-'Amal-i-Shahjahani, Zawabit-i-'Alamgiri, Muntakhab-ut-Twarikh* (by Jagjivan Das) *Dastur-ul-'Amal-i-Navisandagi* etc. All these texts provide revenues statistics at different periods of time in the *suba* of Kabul. All these works are available in microfilms, photocopies and rotographs at the Research Library, Department of History, Aligarh Muslim University, and Maulana Azad Library.

Ni'āmatullah *Tarikh-i-Khanjahani* or *Makhzan-i-Afghani*, probably completed in 1613, provides a rich history of Afghans and other tribes.

For the political history of the *suba* during Aurangzeb's reign much information is extracted from the *Akhbarat-i-Darbar-i-Mu'alla*. The *Akhbarat* contain day to day reports of the events at the court of the Mughal Emperor, Aurangzeb, during the period from 4 to 51 regnal years. It throws light on the tenure conditions and power of the various administrative officials serving in Kabul – *Governors, Faujdars, Thanedars* and *Qiledars*, etc.

Besides the well-known Persian sources, I have also consulted the contemporary and later European traveller's accounts, which provide a lot of information on Kabul that is not found in the Persian sources. Elphinstone's Account of 'Kingdom of Caubul, 1809', is of much value in providing early modern ethnographic material. The physical geography of Kabul is based on the evidence found in contemporary and near-contemporary sources. Since the evidence in contemporary sources is scarce, I have, in my study of human geography also looked at the sources of the later period. For the information on languages and dialects of various tribes of Kabul I have relied on Grierson's *Linguistic Survey of India*.

Chapter - I

Kabul was an extremely important part of the Mughal India. Kabul had come under Babur's control in 1504 and became Babur's stepping stone on his way to the eastward conquest. It was formally incorporated in the Mughal empire in 1585. Kabul, from the time of its annexation by Akbar in 1585, remained a part of Mughal India till 1739, when it was seized by Nadir Shah. For the Mughals, control of Kabul was strategically very important. The concern stemmed not only from the prestige attached to Kabul as the only part of the original dominions of Timur still held by the Mughals, but also from a realization of its strategic importance. In a famous observation, Abul Fazl in 1595 described Kabul and Qandahar as "twin gates of Hindustan",[6] and the later historian Sujan Rai, a native of Punjab (1694), attributes the prosperity of the Punjab in the Mughal times to the safety obtained from foreign invasion through the Mughal possession of Kabul.[7] Kabul's prosperity was, indeed, a result of environmental factors, but, it is equally important not to minimise the role of the Mughal state.

---

[6]   Abul Fazl, *Ain-i-Akbari,* ed. H. Blochmann, Bib. Ind., Calcutta, 1867-77, I, p. 591.

[7]   Sujan Rai Bhandari, *Khulasatu-t Twarikh*, ed. Zafar Hasan, Delhi, 1918, pp. 66-67.

Towards the close of the sixteenth century, the *suba* of Kabul was divided into the following seven *sarkars*: Kashmir, Pakli, Bimbar, Swat, Bajaur, Qandahar and Zabulistan (Ghazni).[8] However, Mughal imperial control over Qandahar was intermittent, and while they controlled it from 1595 to 1622 and then again from 1638 to 1648, for the rest of the period it was outside Mughal control.[9] Kashmir was likewise constituted into a *sarkar* of the Kabul *suba* in 1585, but during Jahangir's reign it became a separate province.[10] Since Qandahar and Kashmir were part of the Kabul *suba* for a relatively short span, my study does not delve in any great details on both these places, and focuses instead on the *sarkars* viz. Bajaur, Bimbar, Pakli, Swat and Ghazni that remained a part of the *suba* of Kabul all through the sixteenth and seventeenth centuries.

The region of Kabul was bounded on the east by the river Indus; on the south it had Qandahar; on the west by Herat and on the north it was separated from Balkh and Badakhshan by the Hindu Kush mountains.[11] (See Map 1.1)

---

8   *Ain*, I, p. 562; *Khulasatu-t Twarikh*, p. 88. The number of *sarkar* given in *Khulasat-ut Twarikh* is eight. Although Pakli was a *sarkar* of the *suba* Kabul but later it was transferred to the *suba* of Kashmir.

9   The Mughal could never maintain their control over Qandahar. The Mughals regained Qandahar from the Safavids in 1595, they lost it to them in 1622, and after recovering the city in 1638, the Mughals lost it again and permanently to the Safavids in 1649.

10   *An Atlas of the Mughal Empire,* p. 6, sheet, 3 A.

11   *Ain*, I, p. 590.

SUBA OF KABUL 17th CENTURY

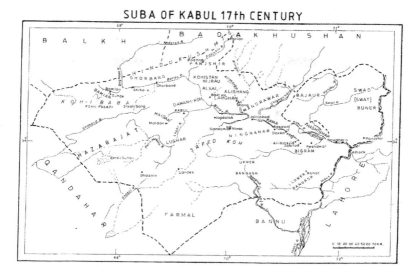

A.) Major physical features:

Kabul has a rich landscape and the effort in this chapter
is to describe its physical features together with the region's
human geography. On the basis of the evidence found in the
contemporary and near contemporary sources, I have in this
chapter discussed the mountains, routes and passes, climate,
rivers and rainfall in the *suba* of Kabul during the Mughal
period. Incidental references in the contemporary and near-
contemporary sources enable us to explore the region's human
geography. However, since the evidence in contemporary
sources is scarce, I have, in my study of human geography,
also looked at the sources of the colonial period. This is indeed
hazardous, but I have persisted with it nonetheless under the
assumption that the geographical features of a place take a long
time to change, sometimes several centuries together.

1. Mountains:

The Kabul *suba* was for the most part mountainous, although it also contained numerous fertile valleys and alluvial spaces which were interspersed amongst the mountains. Kabul was bounded on all sides by lofty mountains covered with perpetual snow. The region had an abundance of mountain tracts and valleys (*darras*) and quite modest flat lands.[12]

The *suba* of Kabul was separated in the north from Balkh and Badakhshan by the Hindu Kush mountains.[13] The lofty range of Hindu Kush mountains provided no easy access northward between Kabul and Turkistan.[14] The province, Babur writes, was "difficult for foreign enemies to penetrate". He points out snow usually made all but one of the Hindu Kush passes impassable for four to five months during the winter, and after the melt-off began in April flooded rivers in the narrow mountain valleys prevented large forces from crossing the mountains for an additional two to three months. He further says that the famous passes of Hindu Kush were so high and the wind so strong that the birds being unable to fly were obliged to creep over the top. They were often caught by the people, who killed and roasted them.[15]

---

12   Mounstuart Elphinstone, *An Account of the Kingdom of Caubul and its Dependencies in Persia, Tartary and India,* London, 1839, I, pp.126-135.

13   Babur, *Baburnama,* tr. A.S. Beveridge, London, 1921, I, p. 200; *Ain,* I, p. 590.

14   C. Wessels, *Early Jesuit Travellers in Central Asia: 1603-1721,* first published, 1924, reprinted, New Delhi, 1992, pp. 16-17. The formidable and steep mountain range of the Hindu Kush barred Benedict Goes way.

15   *Baburnama,* Persian tr. Abdu-r Rahim Khan-i Khanan,

The Hindu Kush was not a single, narrow chain of mountains but rather a series of ridges with impassable snow bound peaks and deep precipices.[16] The Hindu Kush in its south-western approach was less significant to its own spurs but it became prominent when it reached a point north-west of Kabul in the Shibar pass where it provided way to the Koh-i-Baba Range (Father of Mountain), where the highest peak reached 16,922 feet. The Hindu Kush was threaded by many passes—the most important and accessible ones were: Khawak, Bazarak, Parian, Salang, Shibar, Hajigak (Iraq Pass) and Aq Rabat.[17]

To the west of Kabul was the Koh-i-Baba, with its highest peak, Koh-i-Fuladi, rising over 16,922 feet. Many of the peaks in these ranges rose to over 15,000 feet above sea-level. It was high, rocky, generally snow-capped and impassable; only practicable at certain times and seasons, but for months these passes remained closed. It divided the Oxus and Kabul basins.[18] The Koh-i-Baba and the uplands of Hazarajat with

---

Bombay, 1308/ 1890, pp. 81-82; pp. 204-205, 224.

[16]   Ibn Battuta, *The Travels of Ibn Battuta*, tr. H.A.R. Gibb, reprinted, Delhi, 1993, III, p. 586. The term Hindu Kush appears in the writings of Ibn Battuta, who crossed them about 1333. He describes the word as meaning "Hindu Killer" due to the belief that many of the slaves brought from India die on the passage through this mountain owing to the severe cold and quantity of snow.

[17]   Arnold Fletcher, *Afghanistan: Highway of Conquest*, New York, 1965, p. 6.

[18]   Thomas Holdich, *The Gates of India Being An Historical Narrative*, London, 1910, pp. 215, 263 (*Koh-i-Babar*); *Atlas*, p. 2, Sheet 1 A-B.

an average elevation of 10,000 feet formed the natural barrier of Kabul on its west.

The Salang range traversing west and south-west to the north of Bamian bifurcated into the Pamghan range and joined the Koh-i-Baba. The Pamghan range (a noble offshoot of the Hindu Kush) projected south-westwards to separate the basin of the river Helmand from that of Arghandab, and extended into the arid southern Afghanistan. This range to the north-west of Kabul was 15,440 feet above sea level. The Pamghan Mountains as described by Babur "were a snowy range and out of these ranges issued a number of rivers like the Helmand, the Dughaba of Qunduz, the Balkhab and the Sind. On one of these ranges that most of the villages dependent on Kabul lied".[19]

The *Safed koh* (*Safed koh* is a Persian word meaning "white mountain" called *Spinghur* in Pashto) projected eastwards from the southern Hindu Kush, skirting the basin of Helmand and Arghandab, stretched near north of Ghazni with peaks 15,619 feet. It was separated from the main Hindu Kush range by the Kabul river valley. It stretched along the south of Ningnahar, dividing it from Bangash. No road crossed it. It was called *safed koh* because its snow never melted. The Sulaiman mountains, farther south reaching 11,532 feet in the Takht-i-Sulaiman, formed an important watershed between Helmand and the Indus river. To the east of Kabul, was a non-snowy mountain

---

[19]   *Baburnama*, I, p. 209 (*Safed koh*), pp. 215-16 (Pamghan mountain), where the entire sentence is erroneously rendered. Babur here refers to the complex mountain chain of the Koh-i-Baba and Sanglakh; Cf. *The Gates of India*, p. 97.

called *Siyah koh* (Black Mountain) extended between Ningnahar and Lamghan.[20]

2. Routes and Passes:

Kabul was a land-locked country and was placed at the transit of a vibrant and expanding trade; Kabul's excellent position at the confluence of major lines of trade routes made it a place of importance for all political powers in the region. Towards the close of the sixteenth century, Abul Fazl writes, it was of considerable significance for Mughals, as it was one of the two gates to Hindustan, the other being Qandahar. Kabul commanded the road to Central Asia and Qandahar proceeded up to Iran and beyond.[21]

Both Babur and Abul Fazl tell us that there were no less than seven routes frequented by the merchants between Kabul and Central Asia. Three of these routes originating from the Panjshir valley were: Khawak, the highest one, Tul, the next lower and Bazarak. Among them the Tul road was the best but was longer than the other two, as its name indicates. The road through Bazarak was the most direct. Another route passed through Parwan, which had seven minor passes known as *Haft-Bacha* (seven younglings).[22] There were other passes such

---

[20] *Baburnama*, pp. 82; I, p. 209. In Turkish called *Qara-Tagh* meaning non-snowy.

[21] *Ain*, I, p. 590.

[22] *Baburnama*, I, pp. 204-5; *Ain*, I, p. 590; George B. Cressey, Crossroads: *Land And Life in south-west Asia*, New York, 1960, pp. 547-548. At present the main pass across the Hindu Kush is the Salang Pass 12,000 feet. It directly connects the north of the country with Kabul, but snow closes the route for several months. A modern highway crosses the mountains at a height

as Purandeh, Salang, Qipchaq and Shibar; the last two were relatively easier to traverse.

There was a main route from Kabul to Bamian which ran northwards from Kabul through Qarabagh and Charikar[23] and then turned to the west along the Ghorband river and crossed two passes, namely the Unai Pass and the Iraq Pass or Hajigak.[24] From the Bamian the route went north via the Aq Rabat Pass and the *Dandan-i-Shikan* Pass (tooth-breaker). A section of the same road from Charikar went to the Tul pass after crossing these points such as Parwan, Gulbahar, Rukha and Bazarak.[25] This road crossed and recrossed Panjshir river eleven times. It is a matter of interest to observe that all the passes over the Hindu Kush converged on the important strategical position of Charikar, adjoining the junction of the Ghorband and Panjshir rivers. Humayun went to the *tuman* of Panjshir from Parian.[26] During 1398-99 Timur is said to have

---

of 3,363 meters. Constructed during 1956-1964 under the supervision of Soviet engineers, it replaced the lengthy and difficult route west of Kabul via the Shibar Pass, near the Bamian valley. In 1933 the first automobile road across the Hindu Kush was completed, leading north from just west of the Shibar Pass, along the Bamian river.

23 Sidi Ali Reis, *The Travel and Adventures of the Turkish Admiral*, Sidi Ali Reis in India, *Afghanistan, Central Asia and Persia during the years 1553-1556*, tr. A. Vambery, London, 1899, p. 65. He also went to Qarabagh from Kabul and then to Charikar and Parwan.

24 C. Wessels, pp. 16-17; Cf. *Gates of India*, p. 387. Iraq is shown in his maps as Kashka.

25 Ibn Battuta, III, p. 589. Parwan was situated at the junction of the Panjshir and Ghorband river, 45 miles north of Kabul; Lahori, II, pp. 461, 512-14.

26 Abul Fazl, *Akbarnama*, ed. Agha Ahmad Ali and Maulvi

taken his army to Parian from whence he detached a part of his force to act to the north of that place and he himself proceeded to Khawak at the head of Panjshir valley and attacked the Kafirs of Kator.[27]

The Shibar was a leading pass from the head of the Ghorband valley into Bamian. It crossed an open and rather flat watershed which connected the western ends of the Hindu Kush with the Koh-i-Baba range; it was of special importance as being open practically all the year round, thus forming almost the only communication between Kabul and the provinces of Turkistan during the winter. The district between the Shibar Pass and the Zuhak Bamian, comprising a string of narrow river-valleys, was known as Darra or Abdarra. Both Babur and Lahori describe this route as open in the winter and difficult only in the times of floods. The latter says it was the easiest route for Balkh.[28] Babur informs us that all the Hindu Kush roads but Abdarra, were closed for three or four months in winter owing to snow drift; the time to cross was during the three or four months of autumn when the snow was less and the water was low, as even during summer water rose in the valley bottom because of glacial melt.[29]

Another road from Kabul passed through the *tuman* of Maidan and joined the Abdarra route in the west of Zuhak

---

Abdu-r-Rahim, Bib. Ind., Calcutta, 1878, I, p. 283.

[27] Sharfuddin Yazdi, *Zafarnama,* ed. Maulvi Muhammad Ilahabad, Asiatic Society of Bengal, Calcutta, 1887-88, II, ff. 8-19. Since the infidels dwelt in narrow passages and precipices and there was no road to get to them owing to the deep snow, the expedition was not entirely successful.

[28] *Baburnama,* I, p. 205; II, p. 873; Abdul Hamid Lahori, *Badshahnama*, Bib. Ind., Calcutta, 1866-72, II, pp. 512, 669-70.

[29] *Baburnama,* I, pp. 204-6; *Ain,* I, p. 590.

Bamian. Lahori calls it the Maidan route. Moorcroft took this route in his journey from Kabul to Bamian.[30] The road then went to Ghalghal, a fort situated in the neighbourhood of Zuhak and then to Bajgah. It is quite clear that this Ghalghal is the same Gulgala situated in the Bamian valley, as discussed by the 19th century European explorers.[31] Again there were two important routes: one from Zuhak and the other from Ghalghal that joined in the vicinity of Bamian. They also went to the Sadbarg pass (Hajigak Pass of modern maps). An important place on this route was Siyah Sang through which Nazar Muhammad passed in 1628 on his way to Kabul.[32] In the west, a route from Bamian went to Herat through Yakh Aulang.[33]

To the south of the province of Kabul went a leading road to Qandahar via Ghazni. Ghazni lay about a hundred miles south-west of Kabul and was connected with that city by a fairly passable route, that was a section of road from Kabul to Qandahar which as a whole was celebrated for the easy

[30]   Lahori, II, p. 670; William Moorcroft and George Trebeck, *Travels in the Himalyan Provinces of Hindustan and the Panjab, in Ladakh and Kashmir, in Peshawar, Kabul, Kunduz and Bokhara….. from 1819 to 1825*, ed. H.H. Wilson, London, 1837, II, pp. 381-3.

[31]   *Ibid.*, pp. 387, 392-3; Alexander Burnes, *Travels into Bokhara, Together with a Narrative of a Voyage on the Indus [1831-33]*, London, 1834, I, p.183. The distance between Zuhak and Bajgah was 27 *kuroh.* Cf. Sidi Ali Reis, p. 65. He took one of the Parwan passes, which started from the place of the same name leading to Bajgah and from there in the valley of Andarab. This was the one followed by Babur.

[32]   Lahori, I, part, I, p. 209.

[33]   *Baburnama*, I, pp. 308-11.

passage it provided in a rugged mountainous land.[34] There was an alternative route to Qandahar which passed through Arghandeh (Arqandi) and Maidan and then joined the Ghazni route somewhere below Sujawand.[35] Humayun took this route when marching from Qandahar to Kabul.[36] There were two leading roads to south via Ghazni. One was the Tunnel-rock (Sang-i- Surkh) road, passing Barak and going to Farmal; the other was one along the Gomal, which also came out at Farmal but without touching Barak.[37]

Abul Fazl records that there were five possible routes that connected Kabul and Hindustan. The Karapa route which passed through Jalalabad was not recorded by Babur but was in use during Akbar's time.[38] We know from the *Kalimat-i-Taiyibat* that Karapa was also called *Safed Khak*. Aurangzeb renamed *Safed Khak* as Mughalabad.[39] Others were Bangash which was reached by crossing the Indus at the Dhankot ferry. Naghr and Farmal by which Indus had to be crossed at the Chauparah ferry. The most important of these was the Khyber,

---

[34]   *Gates of India*, p. 512.

[35]   Muhammad Waris, *Badshahnama,* transcript of Riza Library Rampur, MS. In the Department of History, Aligarh, No. 86, p. 91.

[36]   Bayazid Bayat, *Tazkira-i-Humayun-o-Akbar*, ed. M. Hidayat Hosain, Bib. Ind., Calcutta, 1941, pp. 128-130 he says that in the winter of 1552-53, Humayun set out from Kabul for Qandahar by way of Charkh and the Kharwar Kotal.

[37]   *Baburnama*, I, p. 235.

[38]   *Ain,* I, p. 590.

[39]   Inayatullah Khan Kashmiri, *Kalimat-i-Tayyibat,* Salar Jang, MS. ed. S. M. Azizuddin Hasan, Delhi, 1982, p. 66; Saqi Mustaid Khan, *Ma'asir-i-Alamgiri*, Bib. Ind., ed. Calcutta, 1871, p.145.

which gained much of its importance when Akbar made it fit for the wheeled conveyance.[40]

Although it is often supposed that the Khyber Pass has always been the major opening into India from Afghanistan, there is no historical evidence that it was assigned such importance earlier. When Ghazni, not Kabul, was the main centre of power under Mahmud of Ghazni (998-1030) and his successors, and under Muizzuddin of Ghor (d. 1206), the main route to India lay through the Kurram river valley. Timur in his invasion of Delhi also used the same route.[41] Babur is, in fact, the first even to use the Khyber Pass;[42] and the convenience of its use was obvious to anyone based on Kabul for it offered the shortest route into India. One must remember that the Khyber route avoided a difficult northward swing of the Kabul river by leaving that river valley at Dakka and running eastward through passage in the hills to Jamrud, where the route reached relatively level country to reach Peshawar.[43]

It was in June 1581 that Akbar marched on his Kabul campaign against his foster brother, Mirza Hakim, and he stopped at Attock or Atak Banaras on the Indus. The same year he began construction of a lofty fortress at Attock, which was placed under the charge of Khwaja Shamsuddin Khafi. Monserrate who accompanied Akbar on his journey to Kabul has also left a detailed account of these events.[44]

---

[40]   *Ain,* I, p. 590.

[41]   Ibn Battuta, III, PP. 589-590; *Zafarnama,* II, ff. 8-19.

[42]   *Baburnama,* I, pp. 206, 411-413.

[43]   *Atlas,* sheet, 1 A B, p. 3.

[44]   Fr. A. Monserrate, *Commentary on his Journey to the court of Akbar,* tr. J.S. Hoyland, annotated by S.N. Banerjee, Cuttack, 1922 pp. 155-156.

By 1587 the Khyber Pass between Attock and Kabul had been at least temporarily secured. Towards the close of sixteenth century the road was levelled, allowing wheeled carts to reach Kabul, and perhaps for the first time in Indo-Muslim history the Khyber Pass became the most important commercial route between north-western India and Kabul.[45] Akbar's main motive was to improve all the overland routes from India to Kabul which passed through Afghan and Baluchi tribal territory and to ensure "obedience of the turbulent of that border". Abul Fazl records that as a result of enforcing peace in the area "the helpless obtained a means of subsistence, the seekers of traffic obtained confidence and world traversers had security".[46] Akbar's chief engineer, Qasim Khan built the road: 'A road previously hard to negotiate even by horses and camels', states Abul Fazl in his *Akbarnama*.[47] Akbar was so pleased with Qasim Khan that he made him in due course, the *subedar* of the Kabul *suba*.[48]

ShahJahan improved this road by having bridges and caravansarais built at either end of the Pass. The bridges at Gandamak and Surkhab were built under the supervision of his well known engineer Ali Mardan Khan.[49]

The journey through the Khyber Pass began just west of Peshawar which commanded the eastern end of the Khyber

[45]   *Akbarnama*, III, p. 792.

[46]   *Ibid.*, p. 521.

[47]   *Ibid.*, p. 735.

[48]   *Ibid.*, p. 569; Abdu-l Qadir Badauni, *Muntakhabu-t Twarikh*, ed. Ali Ahmad and Lees, Bib. Ind., Calcutta, 1864-69, II, p. 372.

[49]   Moorcroft and Trebeck, II, pp. 370-371; *An Atlas of the Mughal Empire*, sheet I A-B; see also Ebba Koch, *Mughal Architecture*, Munich: Prestel, 1991, pp. 66-68.

Pass then went northwest to the Jalalabad plain a distance of
approximately 30 miles.[50] Khyber was a narrow, steep-sided
pass and is 3,500 ft. in height from the plain, it was always
blocked by snow in the winter months. Khyber though unsafe,
was gradual in ascent and relatively a short route to Kabul from
Hindustan. This must have added to its value as a commercial
route. Jahangir defines this pass as *marpich* or snake-twisted.
In April-May 1609 Jahangir went through this serpentine pass
in royal procession, from Peshawar to Jalalabad in about a week
to meet the Afghans.[51] When Nadir Shah was advancing from
Kabul towards Hindustan found the Khyber Pass closed against
him by the Afridis and Shinwaris, the Orakzai tribes led him
by a road through Tirah. Charles Masson who left Peshawar for
Kabul during his visit about 1826-1838 reports that two other
routes such as Abkhora and Karapa were far more secure for
traders than the Khyber but not so level nor so direct.[52]

South of the Khyber route from Peshawar to Kabul and
separated from it by the range of *Safed koh* was an alternative
route via the Kurram valley. The next important link between
India and Afghanistan, south of Kurram, was the Tochi valley.
It had been utilized in the past for sudden raids from Ghazni

---

[50] *Badshahnama*, p. 603; *Khulasat-ut Twarikh*, p. 85. The journey
      from the capital city of Kabul province went through these
      places—Basawal, Jalalabad plain, *Charbagh* or *Bagh-i-safa*,
      Nimla *pul* and Gandamak, Surkhab, Jagdalak, Khwurd Kabul
      and Butkhak.

[51] Jahangir, *Tuzuk-i-Jahangiri*, ed. Saiyid Ahmad, Ghazipur and
      Aligarh, 1863-64, pp 49-52; Beveridge, ed. And Rogers, trans.,
      I, pp. 101-6.

[52] Charles Masson, *Narrative of Various Journeys in Balochistan,
      Afghanistan and the Punjab: 1826-1838*, London, 1842, I, p.
      147; Cf. Moorcroft and Trebeck, II, pp. 347-48.

in spite of the difficulties imposed by nature. The Tochi route and to the south of it, Gomal, must have been regarded as highways to Ghazni. In 1510 Babur was warned not to follow the Gomal route back to Kabul because of the danger of high water in the river as well as due to the threat of Afghans.[53] (For the routes and passes see Map 1.2)

SUBA OF KABUL MAJOR ROUTES

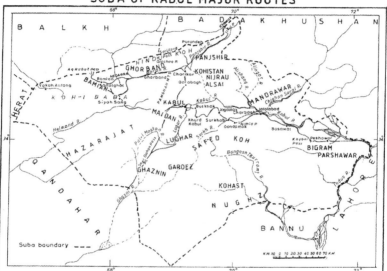

3. Rivers:

A remarkable feature of the physical geography of this region was the paucity of large rivers. None of them reached the sea or even survived beyond the limits of the country of their origins. It should be kept in mind that physical

---

53   *Baburnama*, I, p. 235.

geography of a place is not a historical constant, immutable and unchanging. From time to time, there is evidence to suggest that the rivers changed courses, and patterns of rainfall moved in unpredictable direction.

The principal rivers of Kabul were Kabul, Kunar, Helmand and Ghazni. The Kabul river (*Khatiban* R.) was an important river of Kabul,[54] which issued from the slopes of Sanglakh ranges near Unai Pass, 45 miles west of the Kabul city. The Kabul river with its tributaries drained the north eastern districts. These tributaries were the Panjshir, Alishang and Alingar, Surkhab and Kunar from the north and the Logar river (*Pul-i-Mastan*) from south, besides numerous minor streams.[55] The Kabul river rising near Unai pass ran through the Maidan district and so on to the capital. From here it ran eastward to Jalalabad, where it turned south east to Dakka. From Dakka it went north east, and then turned east and south again eventually debouching into the Peshawar valley at Michni. Having received the waters of the Panjkora, Swat and Bara rivers, it fell into the Indus at Attock after an entire course of 300 miles.[56]

---

[54] *Ain*, I, p. 592; *Khulasatu-t Twarikh*, p. 84. That the *Khatiban* is the modern Kabul river is clarified from the statement that it entered Kabul from Lalandar (a narrow valley through which the Kabul river passes).

[55] Ibn Battuta, III, p. 587. The river Panjshir was the principal tributary of the Kabul river; Le Strange, *The land of Eastern Caliphate, Mesopotamia, Persia and Central Asia from the Moslem Conquest to the time of Timur*, Cambridge university Press, 1930, p.7.

[56] L.W. Adamec, *Historical and Political Gazetteer of Afghanistan*, Graz (Austria), 1985, p. 3

The Gomal and the Kurram rivers (Babur, in fact, gives to Kurram the name of Bangash R.),[57] with its tributaries: the Kaitu and Tochi all had their sources in the Kabul. Of these the Gomal was lost in the soil before it was free from the hills from where it started; and the Kurram a stream of no magnitude, and fordable throughout its course, joined the Indus near Isa Khel.[58] The Gomal river, south of the Tochi, had been regarded in history as the highway to Ghazni.[59]

The two important tributaries of the Kabul river, the Alishang and the Alingar as well as the Chighan Sarai (Kunar river) merged into each other and joined the Baran river near the district of Mandrawar. Abul Fazl writes that the Kabul river at the junction where it merges with these rivers was known as Baran river.[60] The Chighan Sarai or Kunar river was by far the most important of the northern tributaries of the Kabul river. It issued in the Hindu Kush near Karkot pass and after passing through Chitral formed the eastern boundary of Kafiristan. It joined the Kabul river at Jalalabad. It was also called as the Chitral river.[61]

The Ghazni river was formed in a little valley some 14 miles north of Ghazni from three rivulets which having united passed through different channels fertilizing a few fields and

---

[57]   *Baburnama*, I, p. 233

[58]   H.W. Bellew, *Afghanistan: A Political Mission in 1857, with an Account of the Country and People*, First Published, London, 1920, first reprint, Lahore, 1978, p.7.

[59]   *Gates of India*, p. 136.

[60]   *Ain*, I, p. 592; Cf. *Baburnama*, I, p. 211. The Chighan Sarai river after passing through Kafiristan from the north-east, unites with the river Baran in the *buluk* of Kama and then passed onwards to the east.

[61]   *Gates of India*, p. 100; Raverty, pp. 105-110, 121.

were then lost. These streams were—Gardan-i-Masjid from
the north-east; Sar-i-Ab from the south-west; and the Shimiltu
from the north-west. Many dams were constructed there
during the time of Sultan Mahmud of Ghazni. The dam of
Band-i-Sultan in the north of Ghazni was built during his time
but was repaired during the reign of Babur.[62] Even in 1836, it
was the source of irrigation for a large tract west of Ghazni.[63]

The Bamian river which drained the valley of that name
was one of the chief affluents of Surkhab. Of all the rivers
to the west of Kabul, the Helmand (Etymander) was the
largest and the most important one. It also issued from near
the Unai pass, but on its northern side, and went southwest
through the Hazarajat. Then ran through the heart of
Qandahar and Girishk before reaching the lake of Sistan or
"Abistada-i-Hamun". Though fordable for most part of the
year throughout the whole of its course, the Helmand was still
a considerable stream.[64] During the summer months all these
streams, with the exception perhaps of the Helmand, became
almost exhausted, long before they had run their course. A
considerable volume of their water was also much reduced
by the numerous small channels that were cut off for the
purpose of irrigation, by which a large stream was sometimes
entirely drawn off before they reached any other river. It may
be observed of all the rivers of this region that their size at the
mouth was never equal to the expectations they raised when
seen drifting from the mountains.[65]

---

[62]   *Baburnama*, I, p. 219.
[63]   G. T. Vigne, *Personal Narrative of a visit to Ghazni, Kabul and
        Afghanistan*, London, 1840, pp. 138-9.
[64]   Elphinstone, I, pp. 152-3.
[65]   *Gates of India*, pp. 83-85.

4. Climate:

The climate was as diversified as its physical configuration. For the climate of Kabul Babur says, "the climate is extremely delightful, and in this respect there is no such place in the known world".[66]

The winter at Kabul was extremely cold and rigorous. From the beginning of December snow would begin falling very heavily till the beginning of March, and occasionally even till April. Kabul was the part of an arid and semi-desert belt. Dry and cold winter with much snow was a permanent feature. The summers could also be unpleasant, and during summer season, furious dust storms made life miserable. However, the summer heats at Kabul were tempered by cool breezes from the adjacent snow-clad mountains. Besides the cool breezes from the snowy ranges of Hindu Kush and Hazarajat, the summer heat at Kabul were, to a considerable extent, mitigated by the influence of the south-east monsoon, which after its long course from the sea over Hindustan, here exhausted itself in clouds and occasional showers.[67]

Owing to the greater or less elevation of the different parts of the country, the climate of this region was extremely varied. In Kabul the winter was very severe and snow remained for two or three months. Towards its west in Hazarajat it was even worse. Ghazni was also very cold;[68] In Jalalabad on the other

---

[66]   *Baburnama,* I, p. 203; See *Memoirs of Babur,* tr. John Leiden and William Erskine, annotated and revised, Sir Lucal King, I, Oxford, 1921, p. 221.

[67]   Adamec, p. 4; H..W. Bellew, p. 6.

[68]   Ibn Battuta, III, p. 590; Charles Masson, II, p. 222. The country being more elevated than Kabul, the temperature of

hand the heat of summer was quite intense and was made worse by frequent storms. The Koh-Daman (Daman-i-Koh) was considered the most favoured spot as regards the climate.[69]

The direction of the winds also influenced the climate. Some blew over ridges of the snowy mountains; others were heated in summer, and rendered cold in winter, by their passage over deserts and other arid tracts of great extent. Some districts were refreshed in summer by breezes from moist areas while others were so enclosed by hills as to be inaccessible to any wind.[70] The character of the climate generally was decidedly dry, being little subject to rain, clouds or fogs.

5. Rainfall:

In discussing the rainfall in this region, I have based myself on the accounts of the colonial period. In the north-eastern parts of Afghanistan the south-west monsoon was felt with much less violence than in India, being exhausted at no great distance from the sea.

The rainy season extended from October to April, but the annual precipitation was only thirteen inches in Kabul, and as little as two or three inches in the lowlands. Kabul received as much as two inches in twenty four hours.[71]

---

the atmosphere is generally lower, and the winter is more severe.

[69]   Adamec, p. 4.

[70]   Elphinstone, I, pp. 173-5.

[71]   George B. Cressey, p. 558. Rainfall is seven inches in Qandahar. Although winter precipitation predominates, the south occasionally receives the rain from the Indian monsoon. Thus Qandahar, which normally has a complete dry summer, experienced sharp rains for three weeks in July 1956, with a total of 1.6 inches. Such untypical conditions distort the

Many areas of the Kabul country, such as Pakli, Buner and Swat had all a share of the monsoon rains,[72] which diminished as they went west, and at Swat were reduced to a month of clouds, with occasional showers about the end of July and beginning of August. During this short period the monsoon appeared in some cloud and showers at Peshawar, and in the Bangash and the Khattak countries. The rainfall to the east of the Khyber pass was no more than fifteen inches, falling mostly during the summer monsoon, whereas to the west, the amount dropped to eight inches, occurring largely in winter.[73] It was still less felt in the valley of the Kabul river, where it did not extend beyond Lamghan; but in Bajaur and Panjkora, under the southern projection of the Hindu Kush, in parts of Kafiristan, and in Tir near the Takht-i-Sulaiman, the south-west monsoon was heavy and formed the principal rains of the year.[74] In Bannu rainfall was reported only eleven inches but the Kohat valley which lies higher than Bannu, rainfall was relatively high i.e. sixteen inches.[75]

The region, one could conclude, was free from periodical rains. The rainfall was small and except on irrigated lands, there was an absence of moisture.[76] Although there was little

---

monthly averages.

[72] *Ain*, I, p. 585.

[73] George B. Cressey, p. 547.

[74] *Ibid*; Walter Hamilton, *Geographical Statiscal and Historical Description of Hindustan and the Adjacent Countries*, Delhi, 1971, II, p. 536.

[75] O. H. K. Spate, *India And Pakistan: A General And Regional Geography*, London, 1954, pp. 426-427, 436.

[76] Mohan Lal, *Travels of Mohanlal*, London, 1846, p. 47. Mohan Lal Kashmiri (1812-77) was Alexander Burnes secretary (*munshi*) and closest adviser. He has acoompanied Burnes on

or no rainfall in the country, in the winter snow-storms were frequent and the melting of the snow provided the required amount of water for cultivation of crops.

B) Human Geography

i) Economic Aspects:*

Agriculture in this region was restricted by geographical conditions, especially by the paucity of soil and water resource and lack of precipitation that the rainfall could not sustain cultivation of the soil. Approximately, not much more than ten percent of its total area was under cultivation both irrigated and non-irrigated.

About 85 percent of the Afghans people were farmers and their economy depended on the soil and resources that lie beneath it. According to an estimate given by the Ministry of Planning of Royal Government of Afghanistan in the 19th century "Kabul is 4,720 square kilometres in area and has an agricultural population estimated at from 188,391 to 263,517". Agriculture provided an estimated 70 percent of the country's income, and agricultural and animal products were the basis of all its exports.[77]

---

his trip to Bukhara. His work is a memoir of his Central Asian travels with Burnes; Brian Robson, *A road to Kabul*, London 1928, p. 18.

*   For full discussion on economy see chapters 3 and 4.

[77]   *Afghanistan: Ancient land with modern ways*, Produced by the Ministry of Planning of Royal Government of Afghanistan, p. 125; Adamec, p. 316.

The country's crops were as varied as its climate and topography. Jalalabad basin which had a milder winter climate produced citrus fruits, sugar cane, and rice all by irrigation from the Kabul river and its tributary the Lamghan. Sugar cane and citrus fruits were also grown in the hot Helmand valleys. In Kabul fruits were almost country-wide produced and provided one of Kabul's most important harvests. Apricot, peaches and grapes etc. were grown nearly everywhere. Kabul also produced sizable harvests of apples, pears, plums and cherries. Its mulberry plantings not only yielded large fruit harvests, but were an important source of silkworm eggs for the country's fast growing sericulture industry. Helmand area produced cotton-crop which was primarily produced in Qataghan province. As far as its export was concerned, agricultural products were overwhelmingly predominant. India together with many neighbouring countries for years depended on Kabul fresh and dried fruits.[78]

Though agriculture was practiced on small plots where water was channelled or on the multi acre tracts spread across the valleys, but we cannot ignore the fact that agriculture in this region was quite difficult. Therefore, despite a relatively small population, shortage of agricultural land was a perennial problem. For centuries, the people throughout the country tried to extend cultivatable land by digging canals and constructing huge network of underground channels, the so called *karez or qanat*.[79] This explains why Babur (1483-1530),

---

[78] Donald N. Wilber, *Afghanistan: Its People, Its Society, Its Culture*, New Jersey, 1962, pp. 189-190.

[79] *Ibid.*, p. 27; Ann K.S. Lambton, *Landlords and Peasants*, London, 1953, pp. 216-217; *History of Civilization of Central Asia from 16th to the mid 19th Century*, vol., V, pp. 375-377.

coming from Farghana was quite surprised by the cultivation without irrigation in India. He noted, "it is a remarkable fact that irrigation was not needed for either the autumn or the spring crops in India".[80]

Given the relatively low area of arable land, however, Afghans depended heavily on a semi-pastoral existence. Pastoralism, which was important in the Afghan economy, was a way of life followed by the nomads as well as by sedentary agriculturists who supplemented their economy by raising cattle, sheep and goats. The pastoral economy involved nomadism, the herdsmen in mountainous area moved from lower ground in winter to higher elevation in summer in a set territorial pattern.[81]

Each spring, the nomads and semi-nomads moved their herds into the mountains of Kabul. In the autumn they returned to their villages or winter camps. The winter quarters were found in the south-west and west; in the low-lying, warm and monsoon affected districts along the North-west frontier in the east and south-east of the country. In the south-west and the west of the country the nomads were predominantly Durrani Pashtuns, although they were joined by Pashtun Ghilzais, another Pashtun tribal confederacy. The nomads and semi-nomads were generally called *kuchi* in Afghanistan, mostly kept sheep and goats. Their products (meat, dairy, hair

---

Karez is the Pashto word while *Qanat* is the Arabic name used in Iran and Western Afghanistan.

[80]   *Baburnama,* II, p. 486. In his homeland, as around Osh, there was an abundance of *aqar-sus* (canals of running water) and it was on these canals that all cultivation in Turkistan depended.

[81]   Gommans, pp. 20-21, 29-30.

and wool) was exchanged or sold in order to purchase grain, vegetable, fruits and other products of settled life.[82]

> 'The *Kuchis* were herders and traders, and in many instances quite wealthy travelling salesmen. In the town they visited during winter they bartered their herds for such manufactured necessities as tea, sugar, salt and sometimes tobacco. They packed these goods on their camels as they moved off to the highlands for summer grazing and a bit of brisk trading. In the remote mountain villages they bartered their manufactured goods for local produce, such as nuts, fruits, wool and four-legged wealth. With the start of autumn they repeated the cycle. The *Kuchis* were trusted to take produce on consignment, trade it in a distant bazaar, and returned the proceeds the following season'.[83]

In spite of the fact that the nomad's mobility threatened the cultivated lands, it appears that there was some sort of economic interdependence between sedentary agriculture and pastoralism. The market forces were often in favour of the pastoral nomads. There were many instances in which pastoralism contributed to the efficiency and mobility of the Central Asian rural economy. In this way, an extensive network of exchange developed along the routes annually followed by the nomads and semi-nomads. We must not forget the fact

---

[82] George B. Cressey, pp. 562-563. See Steingass, *Kuchi* is a Persian word meaning a wandering tribe (and robbers).

[83] Mary Bradley Watkins, *Afghanistan Land in Transition,* New York, 1963, pp. 11-13.

that the pastoral nomads in pre-modern times were not only shepherds but also traders and cavalrymen.[84]

Every year in April-May several hundred thousand of these pastoral nomads together with numerous other merchants and travellers gathered in and around the Indus and then migrated to Ghazni, Kabul, and beyond to the pastures of Qarabagh. In October – November they returned to the south following the same itinerary, leaving most of their families and flocks behind in the summer camp in the Derajat and the winter camps near Ghazni.[85] They preferred beasts of burden for such movements viz. camels (the Bactrian type two-humped and so were dromedaries), donkeys, sheep and rarely horses, the sheep being by far the most important. On the backs of these animals much of the merchandise of the country was transported.

During the winter season, these trading nomads were to be seen in most of the larger cities of India with various products of their country, such as fruits, madder, asafoetida, wool and woollen fabrics, furs, together with horses, raw silk, shawl, wool especially from Bukhara. They took back cotton piece-goods, chintzes, tea spices, metals and brocades, silk and muslin of Indian manufacture.[86]

Animal husbandry was also widely practiced. Sheep, goats and chicken were found in almost every village in the country. Pastoralism was obviously of great importance. Goats and fat-tailed sheep probably accounted for 80% of the livestock,

---

[84]   Gommans, p. 21.
[85]   *Ibid.*
[86]   *Ibid.*, Gommans, pp. 29-30.

and much of the petty local traffic was carried on camels and donkeys.

Given the porous connection between them, we cannot draw a diverse line between the agriculturists and pastoralists. The economic activity of the great mass of the population remained primitive and many added a variety of petty trading or handicraft activities to their primary pursuits.[87]

ii) Linguistic:

The Kabul country comprised of many distinct tribes, differentiated by language and dialects. The linguistic diversity in Kabul was immense, and each tribe either had a distinctive language or a dialect. When Babur captured Kabul in 1504 he found that eleven or twelve languages were spoken in Kabul such as Arabic, Persian, Turki (Mangoli), Hindi, Afghan (Pashto), Pashai, Parachi, Gabri, Birki and Lamghani. If there be any country, he states, 'with so many differing tribes and such a diversity of tongue, it is not known to me'.[88]

Kabul was, in Mughal India, a region of immense linguistic diversity. Even so, Persian and Pashto were the dominant language in Kabul, and between them, perhaps, Persian had an edge over Pashto. Persian was the language of Tajik inhabitants while Pashto which belongs to the Indo-Iranic language family was spoken by the Afghans, some of whom knew Persian colloquially.[89]

---

[87]   *India and Pakistan,* pp. 426-27, 436.

[88]   *Baburnama,* I, p. 207. Afghani was the earliest name of Pashto language, both names were used in the seventeenth century and later.

[89]   G.A. Grierson, *Linguistic Survey of India, Eranian Family,* Vol.

In Kabul there was a great admixture of races, including Tajiks, Hazaras, Qazilbashs and Kafirs, who spoke the languages of the locality of their origin. With the exception of Hazaras and Kafirs, who belonged to the more remote districts, Pashto was generally understood, and the Afghans also understood the language spoken by the Hazaras and the Kafirs.

The Hazaras living to the west and south-west of Kabul spoke "archaic" Persian, that was a mix of both Turkish and Persian. Their language was Persian, but it contained many Turkish words and some of these were specifically identifiable as Chaghtai Turkish.[90]

A much larger ethnic group, widespread in Kabul was Tajik or Parsiwan. They spoke Afghan Persian or Dari, quite similar to the Persian spoken in eastern Afghanistan. Since they spoke Persian, the Tajiks came to be known as Parsiwan, i.e., 'those who spoke Persian'. The Tajiks consisted of two principal groups. The mountain Tajiks, who spoke an archaic Iranian language, lived in high mountain valleys of north of Kabul. The other who dwelt in plains throughout several areas of country and spoke Persian.[91]

X, Delhi, First Published, 1921, Reprinted, 1990, pp. 6, 9. Pashto belongs to the Eastern group of Iranian language family and that it is derived from Zend or from a dialect closely allied to Zend.

[90]   Donald N. Wilber, p. 46.

[91]   G.P. Tate, *The Kingdom of Afghanistan: A Historical Sketch,* Bombay and Calcutta, Times of India Office, 1911, pp 196-197. *Farsiwan* is the corruption of the word *Parsi-Khwan* or Persian speaking;; H.W. Bellew, *Races of Afghanistan* New Delhi, 1980, pp. 111-112.

Persian-Tajik was generally regarded as an important cultural language, and Persian was widely known even among ethnic groups which did not have Persian as their mother tongues. It is worth noting that Pashto was rarely learnt as second language and did not serve as a *lingua franca* in the country. In oral traditions of the period Pashto was described as rattling a stone in a pot.[92] Elphinstone states, Pashto though rough, is a manly language, and not unpleasing to an ear accustomed to oriental tongues.[93]

Pashto was spoken by the majority in south and east of the country. It was also the dominant language in the district of Kohat, Bannu and in the Yusufzai's area, which included the areas of Swat, Bajaur and Buner.[94] But in the large cities like Jalalabad and Ghazni, Persian was generally the common language of communication.

The dialect of Pashto can be divided into two groups. The Afghans of the north-east pronounced the letter 'kh' and the letter 'g' while those of the south-west pronounced them 'sh' and 'zh' respectively. The name Pakhto (hard i.e. 'kh' 'g') and Pashto (soft i.e. 'sh' 'zh') reflect the two main

---

[92]   Grierson, p. 9. According to a well known proverb Arabic is science *ilm*; Turkish, accomplishment, *hunar;* Persian, sugar; and Hindustani, Salt; but Pashto is the braying of ass! In spite of these unfavourable remarks, though harsh sounding, it is a strong, virile language, which is capable of expressing idea with neatness and accuracy.

[93]   Elphinstone, I, p. 253.

[94]   Donald N. Wilber, p. 58; Grierson, X, p. 5. Originally the language of Yusufzai's country was not Pashto but Kohistani, and Indo-Aryan form of speech, which still survives in a few localities, but has been superseded by Pashto.

dialect of the Pashto language.[95] The hard dialect Pakhto was employed by the Ghilzai and the Afridis while Pashto the soft dialect was spoken by the Waziris and Khattaks. The two dialects, to certain extent, overlapped and gradually became indistinguishable from each other as the tribes intermarried, and intermixed with one another. In and around the city of Ghazni where Persian was spoken; the Afghan dialect was the north eastern Pakhto.[96]

The Great Ghilzai tribe, which extended from the proximity of Qandahar to near Jalalabad, spoke the same dialect. The Afridis inhabiting the Khaibar region also used the north – eastern Pakhto.[97] It was spoken by Bangashi and in the north centre district of Kohat. Over the great part of the district the dialect was the north-eastern; only in the east and south, amongst the Khattaks was the south western dialect spoken.[98]

There were two main branches of the Khattaks – the eastern or Akora Khattak and the western or Teri Khattaks. The Akora Khattaks inhabited the Khattak country of Peshawar and the north-east corner of the Kohat along the west bank of the Indus. The western, or Teri, Khattaks occupied the south and centre of the Kohat district. About Lachi, in that district they met the Bangashi, who occupied the north-west and north-centre. Other speakers of the south-western dialect

95   Elphinstone, I, p. 253; *History of Civilization of Central Asia,* V, pp. 722-724.
96   Grierson, p. 6-7.
97   Grierson, pp. 24, 31, 35, 46.
98   Grierson, pp. 24, 56. The number of north-eastern dialect Bangashi – 107,492.The number of south-western Khattaks – 85,891. The total number of Pashto speakers – 193,383.

were the remaining Pathan tribes of Bannu among whom the principal were the Marwats, the Niyazis, the Bannuchis and the Waziris. In the Bannu district two local dialects were spoken: the Bannuchi dialect was spoken by the educated Pathans and the Marwat dialect which is spoken by the tribes of same name who inhabit the south of the Bannu district.[99]

Waziri Pashto was an important dialect and was spoken in Waziristan and part of the Bannu district. The Waziris were divided into two main divisions: Mahsuds (10,000) and Darwesh Khel (24,500).[100]

The Darwesh Khel again was divided into Ahmadzais (12,000) and Utmanzai (12,500). The Utmanzais lived in the Tochi and the hills adjoining it on both sides and extend on the north almost into the Kohat district. The Ahmadzais lived around Wana and in the western part of the Bannu district along the border. The Mahsud inhabited the heart of Waziristan and were completely surrounded by the other Waziri tribes and by the Bittanis. The dialect spoken by these tribes did not vary greatly from one another, but considerably in vocabulary and even in idiom, from the dialect spoken by the Pathans of the Kohat and Peshawar frontier. When a northern Pathan and Waziri meet for the first time they were scarcely intelligible to each other and certainly misunderstood one another when conversation turned complex. Grierson did not find a single northern Pathan who could speak Waziri Pashto.[101]

---

[99]   *Ibid.*, pp. 66, 69.

[100]   *Ibid.*, pp. 91, 96. The figure in bracket represents the estimated fighting strength of each tribe, and don't include women and children.

[101]   *Ibid.*, pp. 96-97.

The tribe, Baraki, who were known to their neighbours as Ormur spoke the Ormuri language. They were not Afghans, but were included among the people, termed Tajiks and lived around Kanigoram in Waziristan and about Barak in the province of Logar, and Butakhak on the road between Jalalabad and Kabul, south of the river of that name. They were a wandering tribe and often wandered to various places for trading purpose. We find a village belonging to them in the Peshawar district. Here they gave up their language and spoke Pashto. In the Loghar valley the Ormur spoke Persian while those of the villages of Barak retained their own form of speech and also in Kanigoram.[102]

Besides these tribes, there were several other minor ethnic groups that settled in Kabul such as Mongols, Arabs, Lamghani (mostly Tajiks or Farsiwan), Dehgani and Kafirs. There were also other groups that originated in the Indian sub-continent, or at least ethnically closely related to the people of India and Pakistan. The oldest of these were probably the speakers of Dardic (Indo-Aryan) languages including Pashai.[103]

Pashai which was also called Lamghani because it was spoken in the tract known as Lamghan opposite Jalalabad and Dehgani or *Kohistani* because most of the speakers belonged to the Dehgan tribe or that for the most part located in the highlands of Kabul. The Pashai speakers inhabited an area

---

[102]   *Ibid.*, pp. 123-124. Though spoken in the localities (Logar valley and in the heart of Waziristan) surrounded by a Pashto-speaking population, and yet bears only the most distant relationship to that language. Pashto is an East Iranian language while Ormuri is a West Iranian language.

[103]   *The Indo-Aryan Language,* ed. Gordan and Dhamesh Jain, London, 2003, p. 826.

that stretched from the Salang pass in the north of Kabul, and south and eastward along the fringes of the mountains of Nuristan, to the banks of the Kunar river north of Jalalabad, but the riverain villages on the left bank of the Kabul river spoke Pashto not Pashai.[104]

Marco Polo in 1270s refers to the Pashai country in the following ways, "you must know that ten days journey to the south of Badashan there is a province called Pashai, the people of which have a peculiar language and are idolaters".[105] The number of people speaking Pashai has been estimated 100,000.[106]

Another ethnic group in Kabul was that of Nuristanis. They lived in the secluded mountains north-east of Kabul and south of Hindu-Kush. Before its conquest by Amir Abdul Rahman Khan in the winter of 1895/96 it was known as Kafiristan (Land of Infidels). Regarding the language of Nuristanis, it was till lately assumed that because the Nur consisted of two main groups: the black coat (*siyah-posh*) and white coat (*safed-posh*), there were, therefore, two languages spoken, corresponding to these two groups. But according to Grierson there are four different languages spoken by

---

[104]   Grierson, p. 89.

[105]   Marco Polo, *The Book of Ser Marco Polo*, tr. and ed. Henry Yule and Henri Cordier, First edition, 1871, First Indian edition, New Delhi, 1993, I, pp.170-172.

[106]   Grierson, p. 89. Another Dardic (Indo-Aryan) language, now almost extinct, is Tirahi, which used to be spoken in some villages south of Jalalabad by people who apparently had been pushed out of Tirah (further south, on the other side of the *Safed koh*) by Afridis.

them such as Kati (Bashgali), Wai, Presun or Wasi-veri and Ashkund.[107]

It appears that the *Siyah-posh* Kafir, who roughly speaking, peopled the northern half and the east of Kafiristan, spoke various dialects of a language, apparently resembling Bashgali (the speech of the people inhabiting the valley of the Bashgal river). It was called Kati. The *Safed-posh* Kafirs inhabited the centre and the south-east of the country and consisted of three tribes: the Wai, the Presun and the Ashkund. The Wai and the Presun tribes spoke different languages which were mutually unintelligible, and both of which were unintelligible to the *Siyah-posh* Kafirs. These tribes were unable to converse without the help of interpreters. Regarding the dialect of the Ashkund Sir George Robertson says, "It is most difficult to get any information of them, they are probably allied to the Wai".[108]

In the 19th century, according to one estimate the total population of Kabul and its immediate environs was about 9,000 families or 50,000 to 60,000 souls. Among these approximately 4,500 families were Qizalbashs, who along with the Hazaras were set apart from the Kabulis by their Shia beliefs.[109] The Qizalbash or redheads, so named because of their red caps was allied to the Tajiks, both being of Persian

---

[107]   G.A. Grierson, *Linguistic Survey of India, Indo-Aryan Family North-Western Group,* first published, 1919, reprinted, 1990, VIII, Part, II, pp. 29-31, 68.

[108]   Sir George Robertson, *Kafirs of Hindu Kush,* London, 1896, pp. 74-78.

[109]   Burnes, II, p. 335; Vigne, p. 165; Elphinstone, I, p.417. He estimated the Qizalbash population of Kabul at ten to twelve thousand souls.

origin and speaking the same language or dialect. The Qizalbash formed the single most literate group in Kabul and were exclusively found in urban settlements.[110]

There were several other small tribes like the Hindkis and Jats, who spoke Hindi or rather a dialect of that tongue. There were also some Kashmiris and Armenians settled at Kabul, but there number was insignificant. (See Table-1.1 for the linguistic diversity of various ethnic groups).

To conclude, the human geography of Kabul was marked by considerable heterogeneity, and the human landscape was divided into numerous tribes and ethnic groups. Holding these tribes together was a formidable job for any political authority, and most powers failed in the effort. The Mughals were, indeed, an exception. It is to the credit of the Mughals that they were successfully able to develop administrative structures and rituals of legitimacy that held the warring tribes together under their dispensation.

---

[110]   Masson, II, p. 297; Christine Noelle, *State and Tribe in the nineteenth century,* 1997, pp. 25-26.

Table-1.1

Ethnic Groups	Language & Group
Afghans or Pashtuns Ghilzai (Southeast) Durrani (Southwest)	Pashto (Iranian)
Tajiks	Pashto (Iranian)
Hazaras (Central Mountains) (Western Mountains)	Archaic Persian(Iranian)
Turko Mongol Turkmen Uzbek Kirghiz Qizalbash	Turkmen (Turkic) Uzbek (Turkic) Kirghiz (Turkic) Persian
Nuristani or Kafiri	Dardic (Sanskrit)
Baluchi	Baluchi (Iranian)
Brahui	Dravidian
Hindus	Lahanda
Jews	Hebrew
Arabs	Arab
Kurds	Kurdish

(Courtesy Donald N. Wilber)

Chapter - II

Political and Military History

Kabul came under the control of Mughals when in 1504 Babur captured it from Muqim Khan, a descendant of Ilkhans of Persia. Muqim Khan had taken Kabul in 1501 after the death of Timurid ruler Ulugh Beg, Babur's uncle, son of Abu Said.[111]

In spite of some sort of geographical protection against external danger, owing to its location, Babur's position was not very secure during the early years of his rule in Kabul. He had few reliable troops at his disposal including his untrustworthy brothers and relatives. At the same time there were certain fundamental problems in ruling Kabul. The province was inhabited by Afghan tribes and many other ethnic groups, most of whom were either autonomous or completely independent. The Afghans were accustomed to a life of turbulence and

---

[111]   *Baburnama*, I, pp. 195-196. Cf. Gulbadan Bano Begam, *Humayun Nama*, MS (Or. 166), ed. Annette S. Beveridge, reprinted, Delhi, 2006, p. 5. Zanun Beg Arghun, a descendant of Ilkhans of Persia, ruled over Ghur, Sistan, Zamindawar and Garmshir. He made Qandahar his capital. His son Muqim's capture of Kabul raised their reputation temporarily; See also William Erskine, *History of India Under Baber*, New Delhi, 1994, pp. 215-16; Cf. Mohibbul Hasan, *Babur Founder of the Mughal Empire in India,* Delhi, 1985, p. 148.

feud, could neither reconcile themselves to the loss of their sovereighnty nor submit easily as a peaceful population.[112] These conditions rendered administration in Kabul quite difficult. Yet despite all these difficulties, Babur gradually started consolidating his position in Kabul.

In 1504 the Kabul province consisted of fourteen *tumans*. Babur reports that he shared his dominion with his brothers (Jahangir Mirza and Nasir Mirza), Andijanis or old servants and *Mehman-i-Beglar* or 'guest begs', turkish tribe considered itself the guest of Uzbek Khans not as their subjects.[113] Babur allotted nothing at all from the Kabul *vilayat* to any one else. He kept all the Kabul *vilayat* for himself including the fort and all land constituting the Kabul *tuman*.[114]

Kabul was a small country, its bare mountains and narrow valleys around it could not support the large number of families of the tribes who had come with him from Samarqand, Hisar and Qunduz.[115] Mirza Haydar Dughlat informs us that the impossibility of supporting an army on the limited resource of the Kabul strengthened Babur's decision of making raids upon the Indian provinces.[116] By 1525 Babur felt that his position

---

[112]   *Baburnama*, pp. 83, 92-95; I, pp. 207, 230-32.

[113]   *Ibid.*, pp, 83, 92; pp. 207, 227. Jahangir Mirza received Ghazni while Nasir Mirza got Ningnahar, Mandrawar, Nur valley, Kunar and Chighan Sarai; all these territories were included in the Lamghanat proper. Other *begs* were assigned villages as fief.

[114]   *Ibid.*; Gulbadan Begam, p. 49. Gulbadan Begam whose information is based on her father's autobiography also confirms this.

[115]   *Baburnama*, I, p. 228.

[116]   Mirza Haydar Dughlat, *The Tarikh-i-Rashidi*, ed. N. Elias, tr. E. Denison Ross, Patna, 1873, p. 201. Kabul scant resource could not support Khusrau Shahi "2000 men" who had joined

in Kabul was well-secured. Kabul became a staging ground and it was from here that he set out his march to conquer north-India.

Babur was succeeded by his son Humayun, who divided his father's territorial possession among his brothers. Kabul was under the jurisdiction of Mirza Kamran.[117] After Humayun's defeat at the hands of Sher Shah, he was barred by his brother to enter Kabul. In 1545 Humayun with the support of Safavid army recovered Kabul from Kamran having earlier occupied Qandahar. Humayun with unwise generosity forgave the traitor, who again advanced on Kabul and reoccupied it. Finally in 1549 Humayun occupied Kabul from Kamran. On the death of Humayun in 1556, the two years old Mirza Hakim, the foster brother of Akbar received the possession of Kabul. Though Akbar had built a strong fort at Attock on his side of the Indus, he had allowed Hakim to rule independently in Kabul until 1585.[118] After the death of Mirza Hakim in 1585, Kabul became for all practical purposes a province of the Mughal empire.[119]

Babur earlier.

[117] Gulbadan Begam, p. 49. See tr. pp. 29, 33.

[118] Monserrate, pp. 140-142. In 1581 he accompanied Akbar on his march to Kabul; Cf. Munis D. Faruqui, 'The Forgotten Prince: Mirza Hakim and the Formation of the Mughal Empire in India', in *Journal of the Economic and Social History of the Orient*, vol., xxxxviii, 4/2005, pp. 487-523,

[119] Nizamuddin Ahmad, *Tabaqat-i-Akbari*, ed. Nawal Kishor, Lucknow, 1875, vol., II, pp. 367-68; *Akbarnama*, III, pp. 467-468, 473.

1. Administrative Divisions:

With the incorporation of Kabul in the Mughal Empire, the Mughal ruler established a centralized bureaucratic administrative system in the *suba*. Imperial control over the *suba* was stringent, and even though Kabul was distant from the imperial control,[120] the Mughal court exercised considerable control over the rule structure. The Mughals had successfully established a centralised administrative system, quite akin to the system in other parts of the imperial domain. The administrative structure was marked by a near-absolute control of the Mughal court in the management of the affairs in the *suba*. The centralised administrative structure was supported by the administrative division of the *suba*, into compact and manageable centres of local authority.

For the sake of administrative convenience the *suba* of Kabul was subdivided into seven *sarkars*: Kashmir, Pakli, Bimbar, Swat, Bajaur, Qandahar and Zabulistan. Despite the fact that Kashmir was made a separate province during the reign of Jahangir, it was occasionally entrusted to the *subedar* of Kabul by the successive Mughal rulers. In such situations, the *subedar* of Kabul governed Kashmir through a deputy appointed by him with the approval of the Emperor. In 1634, Ali Mardan Khan, the Persian commandant of the fort of Qandahar was made *subedar* of both Lahore and Kashmir and occupied these positions till 1640.[121]

---

[120] Terry, *Early Travels in India (1616-19)*, ed. W. Foster, London, 1927, p. 291; Joannes De Laet, *The Empire of the great Mogul*, tr. J.S. Hoyland and annotated S.N. Banerjee, Bombay, 1928, p. 5.

[121] Shah Nawaz Khan, *Ma'asir-ul-Umara*, ed. Abdu-r Rahim and

The *sarkars* of Kabul were further subdivided in a number of districts or *tumans*. Babur informs that at the beginning of the sixteenth century, these *tumans* were fourteen in number.[122] In 1595, according to Abul Fazl the number of these *tumans* increased to twenty.[123]

In Kabul, as was the case with Samarqand and Bukhara, a *tuman* was a political unit consisting of several towns and villages.[124] *Tuman* was a Mongol term for 10,000 fighting men, but during the late Timurid period it was used to refer to a subdivision of a *Vilayat*. It is interesting to note that in his description of the Kabul *suba*, for which he used the term *vilayat,*[125] he equates Lamghanat on the east with Qunduz to the north. He seems to mean that Lamghanat, like Qunduz, was not included in the Kabul *vilayat*, but was situated on its boundary. Initially he identifies Lamghanat as a *vilayat* and

Ashraf Ali, Bib. Ind., II, p. 798.

[122] *Baburnama*, I, p. 207.

[123] *Ain*, I, p. 592. While the number given by Abul Fazl is nineteen, in which he had not included the *tuman* of Kabul; *Khulasat-ut Twarikh*, p. 88, these *tumans* were thirty six in number; Raverty, p. 682. According to him, Kabul *suba* was divided into twenty two *muhallas* or *tumans*

[124] *Ibid.,* In Andijan and Kashghar the Turkic term *Orchin* was used, whereas in India districts were called *Pargana*.

[125] Babur, *Baburnama*, Chaghtai Turki text: Hyderabad Codex, Facsimile ed. A.S. Beveridge, London, 1905, reprinted, 1971, f. 128 a, 144 b; tr. I, pp. 199-200, 204; Lamghanat, ff. 131 b, 133 b; pp. 207, 210; Farmal, f. 139 b; p. 220, 227.

not as a *tuman*.[126] Similar was the case of Ghazni which he sometimes identifies as *vilayat* and sometimes as a *tuman*.[127]

It may be pointed out that the chroniclers of thirteenth and fourteenth centuries have used the term *vilayat*, which certainly meant the largest administrative unit and no doubt synonymous of the modern province. By the time of Lodis, the *vilayat, sarkar, iqtas* had taken a definite shape. When Sher Shah came to power he reorganized the administrative units with necessary modifications and changes. Indeed, he found the *sarkar* an ideal administrative unit so he designated many a *vilayat* as *sarkar*.[128]

Babur also uses the Turkic term *buluk* for the subdivision of Kabul, which was a territorial unit smaller than a *tuman*, but not a *tuman* necessarily in all cases.[129]

---

[126] *Ibid.*, p. 200. He says on the east it has Lamghanat, Peshawar, Hashtnagar and some countries of Hindustan, while on page 207, for the sub-division of Kabul country, he explains Lamghanat has five *tumans* and two *buluks*. ff. 137 b-138 a; p. 217. Ghazni as a *vilayat* belonged to the third climate, as Kabul belonged to fourth climate. He also included it in the list of fourteen *tumans*.

[127] *Ibid.*, p. 217. Ghazni as a *vilayat* belonged to the third climate, as Kabul belonged to fourth climate. He also included it in the list of fourteen *tumans*.

[128] For an excellent discussion on *vilayat* see Iqtidar Husain Siddiqui, *Evolution of the Vilayat, the Shiq and the Sarkar in Northern India (1210-1255)*, in *Medieval India Quarterly*, ed, K. A. Nizami, Aligarh, 1963, V, pp. 10-35; I. H. Siddiqui, *Sher Shah Sur and His Dynasty*, Jaipur, 1995, pp.131-172. That is why the *vilayat* of Bengal, Malwa and Multan were well-organized into *sarkars* during the reign of Emperor Akbar.

[129] *Baburnama*, I, p. 207. See footnote, the two *buluk* of Nur valley and Chighan Sarai were in Lamghanat *tuman*. Kama was the *buluk* of Ningnahar which was a *tuman* of Lamghanat proper;

Babur informs that during the sixteenth century Bajaur, Swat and Peshawar were under independent Afghan chiefs, but earlier these were the dependencies of Kabul.[130]

The Lamghanat (Laghman) had five *tumans* and two *buluks*. The largest of these was Ningnahar (Nagarhar). During Babur's time the headquarters of Ningnahar was at Adinapur, but during Akbar's time it was transferred to Jalalabad. Abul Fazl, who is clearly most reliable in matters connected with the geography and revenues, calls it Nek Nihal, adding that it contained nine rivers.[131] According to Raverty, Ningnahar is the corruption of Nekanhar, *Nek* signifying in Persian "good" and also "many" and *anhar* is the plural of *nahar* "a stream or rivulet".[132] It was in former times also called *Jui Shahi*. Bayazid Bayat informs us that Humayun in 1552 built a fort at *Jui-Shahi*, where later on another fort was constructed called Jalalabad after the name of Jalaluddin Muhammad Akbar.[133]

Kama was the *buluk* of *tuman* Ningnahar. Alishang, Alingar and Mandrawar were the three main *tumans* of Lamghanat. Kunair with Nurgal was another *tuman*, which was situated on the border of Bajaur.[134] The two *buluks* of Lamghanat were Nur valley (*darra-i-Nur* or the valley of Light) and Chighan-Sarai. The *tuman* of Najrao was situated northeast of Kabul in the *Kohistan* (hill country).[135] Towards the east of Najrao was situated Alasai, which according to Babur,

---

Ain, I, p. 592.

[130]   *Baburnama*, I, p. 207.

[131]   *Ain*, I, p. 592.

[132]   Raverty, p. 51.

[133]   Bayazid Bayat, p. 161.

[134]   *Baburnama*, I, p. 211; *Ain*, I, p. 595.

[135]   *Ibid.*, p. 213; *Ain*, I, p. 593.

was placed between warm and cold belts. Babur identifies it as a *buluk* of Kabul while Abul Fazl describes it as *tuman*.[136] Similarly Badrao (Tag-au) inhabited by Kafirs, Afghans and the Hazaras was one of the *buluks* of Kabul, but was referred to as *tuman* by Abul Fazl.[137] Badrao, Nur Valley, Chighan-Sarai, Kama and Alasai were few of the *buluks* of Kabul.

The *tuman* of Panjshir also called Panjhir was the northern most *tuman* of the Kabul *Suba*, lying at in immediate vicinity of Kafiristan. The *tuman* of Najrao to the north-east of Kabul adjoined Panjshir in the direction of north-west.[138] The two eastern most *tumans* were Hashtnagar and Porshor or Parshawar (later Bigram). Hashtnagar is mentioned by Babur,[139] but is not mentioned in *Ain-i-Akbari*. The *tuman* of Porshor is called Bigram by Akbar's time, but had also begun to be popularly called Peshawar. The route from Attock to the Khyber Pass went through this city.[140]

Tuman of Bangash was a mountainous district, which lay to the south-east of Kabul. This *tuman* was divided into two parts: the upper or *bala* and the lower or *pain* Bangash. This division led to the use of the name Bangashat for the entire territory.[141] The upper Bangash included the territory of Kurram and the fertile Parachinar plain while the lower

[136]   *Ibid.*, p. 220; *Ain*, I, p. 593.
[137]   *Ibid.*, p. 221.
[138]   *Ibid.*, p. 214; *Akbarnama,* I, pp. 283-288; Lahori, II, p. 461.
[139]   *Baburnama,* I, pp. 200, 410-411; *Akbarnama*, III, pp. 525-526. He spells Ashtnagar.
[140]   *Ibid.*, 1971, f. 131b. Beveridge has not recorded this *tuman; Ain*, I, p. 592; *Akbarnama*, III, p. 599.
[141]   *Khulasatu-t-Twarikh,* p. 86. He writes it Nekshab which according to Irfan Habib is a misprint. Compare, *Atlas*, p. 3, Sheet, 1 A-B.

Bangash included the territory of Kohat. Babur identifies lower Bangash with the territory of Kohat. Lahori informs us that Kohat (to the west of Bangashat) served as the headquarters of the commandant (*thanedar*) of both upper and lower Bangash.[142]

The *tuman* of Gardez was also called Zurmat and was situated few miles south of Kabul and to south-east of Ghazni. It consisted of eight 'mauzas' (villages or townships). Gardez was the seat of authority where the *darogha* or the superintendent of the *tuman* resided.[143] *Tuman* of Logar was situated a few miles to the south of the Kabul city. It was enclosed from all sides by the mountains of greater or less elevation. Though mountainous throughout, this *tuman* rendered grassy and excellent pastures on which account it was visited by *kuchis* or nomads of certain clans of Ghilzais.[144] Ghazni and Maidan were other *tumans* in this direction.

The *tuman* of Ghorband was to the north-west of Kabul. It had many villages but yielded little revenue.[145] Koh Daman extended towards north from Kabul to beyond Qarabagh. In its total revenue this *tuman* was only second to the city of Kabul. *Tuman* of Zuhak Bamian was famous for its fort. Lahori says that the fort of Zuhak was the headquarters of this *tuman*.[146] Naghz, Bannu and Farmal were the southern *tumans* of the Kabul *suba*.[147]

---

[142]   *Baburnama*, I, p. 382; Lahori, II, pp. 158, 486.

[143]   *Ain*, I, p. 593; Raverty, pp. 685-686.

[144]   *Ibid.*

[145]   *Baburnama*, I, p. 214; *Ain*, I, p. 594.

[146]   Lahori, I, pp. 260-261.

[147]   *Baburnama*, I, pp. 206, 233; *Ain*, I, p. 590.

The chief district officer of *tuman* was called *Irman*. The *Irman* had to pay a fixed amount of revenue to the treasury of Kabul.[148]

To conclude, one of the essential features of Mughal administrative system in Kabul was the division of the *suba* into smaller administrative-cum-territorial units, called *tuman*. Each tuman was administratively controlled by a petty official, called *Irman*. In addition, Kabul was also divided into *buluk*. While the relationship between *tuman* and *buluk* is not clear but from the sources *buluk* was a smaller territorial unit than the *tuman*. Mughal centralism was crucially dependent on the administrative division of the *suba* into smaller territorial units.

2. Governors and Other High Officials:

Within a year of Kabul's annexation to the Mughal empire, Akbar divided the entire Mughal empire into a number of *subas* or provinces in 1586, headed by a *subedar*, described variously as *nazim, sahib-i-suba, faujdar-i-suba* etc.[149] During Akbar's reign he was initially designated as *sipahsalar*, since the office was technically a military one, but later came to be known as the *subedar*.[150] Kabul was placed under the charge

---

[148] *Kaifiyat-i-Subajat-i-mumalik-i-mahrusah-i-Hindustan,* B. M. Or. 1779, f. 232 a. cited in Ishtiaq Husain Qureshi, *The Administration of the Mughal Empire,* Patna, 1994, p. 237.

[149] *Akbarnama,* III, pp. 282-283. When Ahmadnagar, Berar and Khandesh were conquered the number was raised to fifteen; Lahori, II, pp. 710-711. During Shahjahan's reign the number increased to twenty two; *The Apparatus of Empire,* p. xxvi.

[150] *Ain,* I, pp. 280-282. Under the Caliphate the head of the province was called *Wali*. During the Sultanate period as well as under Surs he was called *Hakim* or sometimes *Nazim*. In

of Raja Man Singh. The sources of this period suggest that after the annexation of a province, Akbar entrusted its over all administration to the *subedar*.[151]

The post of provincial governor occupied an important position in the Mughal bureaucracy. He was the vice regent of the sovereign and was responsible for the general administration, welfare and prosperity of his *suba*.[152]

The governor of a province was directly appointed by the imperial order known as *farman-i-sabati*.[153] The provincial governor was usually a noble of extraordinary military abilities and organizational skills.[154] Loyalty was, of course, an extremely important criterion in selection, but considerations of ability and merit were never ignored, either. In 31st regnal year, Akbar appointed an assistant *(naib)* governor for each *suba*, to assist the governor, and to take his place in his absence or when indisposed. Abul Fazl gives the list of appointments of the *subedar* and *naib subedar* for each *suba*. Kabul as mentioned above was under the charge of Raja Man Singh and Zain Khan Koka, with the former designated as the *subedar*, and the latter, the *naib subedar*.[155] The *subedar* of the sub-province such as Kashmir and Qandahar were appointed usually on the recommendation of the *subedar* of the Kabul province to

---

south he was known as *Tarafdar*.

[151] *Akbarnama*, III, p. 511.

[152] *Ibid.*

[153] *Ibid.*, p. 194; P. Saran, *The provincial government of the Mughals: 1526-1658*, Allahabad, 1941, p. 176.

[154] J. Sarkar, *Mughal Administration*, fifth edn., Calcutta, 1963, pp. 48-53; Saran, pp. 183-188; M. Athar Ali, 'Provincial Governor Under Aurangzeb An Analysis', in *Medieval India A Miscellany*, vol., I, Delhi, 1969, pp. 96-133.

[155] *Akbarnama*, III, pp. 511-512.

which they were attached. Sometimes the *subedar* himself held the office of *subedari* of these sub-provinces. In the 14th R.Y. of Shahjahan's reign, Ali Mardan Khan occupied both these offices together.[156]

There were certain fundamental problems in ruling Kabul. Kabul was inhabited by the Afghan tribes and other ethnic groups, most of whom were either autonomous or completely independent. These conditions rendered administration in Kabul quite difficult. Usually, high ranking nobles were appointed as the governor of Kabul. After its annexation, the first Mughal governor was Man Singh (1585-88), Akbar's favourite Rajput commander.[157] Man Singh's selection for the task of administrating Kabul during this time reflected the implicit confidence of Akbar in him. The high position of Man Singh in the Mughal bureaucracy is evident from his *mansabs* of 5,000, which later increased to 7,000/7,000 *zat* and *sawar*. Akbar also honoured him with the title of Raja.[158] After Man Singh, it seems, Rajputs were excluded from the office, and the charge of Kabul was placed exclusively under the command of a high noble of either Turkish or Persian racial background, except when it was entrusted to a Prince.[159] As for the group from which the *subedars* came, it seems that both Turkish and Persian were favoured for the office under Akbar. During Jahangir's reign, who is generally supposed to have followed a pro-Persian policy chose from both these groups for the post of *subedar* of Kabul. However, the sharp rise of Persian is evident in Shahjahan's reign. Out of his eight *subedars* of the province,

[156]   Lahori, II, p. 222.
[157]   *Akbarnama*, III, p. 511.
[158]   *Ibid.*p. 570; The *Apparatus of Empire*, pp. 11, 12.
[159]   *Ibid.*, 569; *Muntakhab-ut Twarikh*, II, p. 372.

five were Persian. And under Aurangzeb almost all the *subedars* appointed were Persian. As for the other groups (Afghan and Indian Muslim) none was ever appointed *subedar* of Kabul. (For the racial background of the *subedars* see Appendix-A in the end of this chapter). However, Akbar had other plans for the Rajputs.[160] He wanted them to play a more active role in the affairs of north-west frontier. Bhagwan Das was appointed *sipahsalar* of Lahore jointly with Said Khan and Man Singh was sent as the commander of the Indus region.[161] We find that many Rajput rulers were given important posts in the province. The Ambar records now preserved in the Rajasthan State Archives contain considerable information on their activities in those capacities.[162]

The young Prince Sulaiman Shikoh, son of Dara Shikoh was the *subedar* of Kabul in the 26th year of Shahjahan's reign.[163] When the charge was under the Prince, a capable and experienced person was appointed as *Ataliq* (guide or preceptor) to the young prince. In this case, Dara Shikoh was the *Ataliq* of Sulaiman Shikoh.[164] During the last years of Aurangzeb's

---

[160]   Satish Chandra, "Mughal Relation with the Rajput States of Rajasthan", in *Essays on the Medieval Indian History*, Delhi, 1987, p. 387. Akbar had the *tuyul* of the Rajputs transferred to the Punjab from Kabul.

[161]   *Akbarnama*, III, pp. 262, 336-37, 344-53, 397; *Tabaqat-i-Akbari*, II, pp. 545-52; Badauni, II, pp. 294-95.

[162]   These *Arzdashts* are in both Persian and Rajasthani languages. They are cited by Sumbul Halim Khan, '*Rajputs in Afghanistan-The Amber Rulers services in suba Kabul (1676-88)*', *Proceedings of the Indian History Congress*, 56th session, 1995, pp. 209-212.

[163]   Waris, p. 142 a

[164]   Saran, pp. 172-173. The *Ataliq* was also supposed to act as the deputy governor and it was his responsibility to look after the proper functioning of the administration.

life, Kabul was under the charge of his son, Muazzam (later came to be known as Bahadur Shah (1707-12).[165]

Akbar did not tolerate incompetence or maladministration in provincial government and never hesitated in removing even his favourite officers from their charge if their conduct was found to be unsatisfactory or complaints against them reached the court. In 1587 Akbar appointed Zain Khan Koka as the *subedar* of Kabul and sent Man Singh to chastise the *Tarikis*. Abul Fazl records that Man Singh was recalled from Kabul because he disliked the cold climate of Kabul and failed in dispensing justice to the people of Kabul.[166] This suggests that the imperial administration was receptive to the grievances of the people, and was not even averse to remove the *subedar* of a province, on the complaints of the people. Sometimes they were transferred or removed within the same year of appointment.[167]

The office of *subedar* was never left vacant. When the *subedar* was transferred to a distant *suba,* for the pending period, some able officer was dispatched to hold charge in the meantime. When Said Khan Bahadur Zafar Jung (*subedar* of Patna) was appointed *subedar* in 1650, Lahrasp Khan,

---

[165]   *Ma'asir-i-Alamgiri*, pp. 394-395.

[166]   *Akbarnama*, III, pp. 517-518. Rajput clan behaved with injustice to the people of Kabul and Man Singh ignored that matter. He did not look closely into the case of the oppressed consequently Akbar removed him from that position; *Badshahnama*, II, pp. 282-283, 420. We find that during the reign of Shahjahan, Tarbiyat Khan was removed from the governorship of Kashmir because people complained against him. On the other hand Zafar Khan was given the charge because people liked him.

[167]   *Ma'asir-i-Alamgiri*, p.140. In the 18th R.Y. of Aurangzeb Diler Khan was appointed and dismissed the same year.

the *mir bakhshi*, was ordered to proceed and take charge of governorship till Said Khan reached Kabul.[168]

The *subedar* occasionally was the *faujdar* of adjacent *sarkar* as well.[169] In 1609-10 Taj Khan, the acting *subedar* of Kabul was also the *faujdar* of Multan.[170] During Shahjahan's reign in 1631-32 Said Khan Chaghtai the *subedar* of Kabul was also the *faujdar* of Bangash.[171] This suggests that one person could hold two or more offices, and even in the case of *subedar,* there was no attempt to restrict him to one office, that of the governor.

There is a *Farman* in *Mirat-i-Ahmadi* containing necessary commands on the duties and powers of governor.[172] The *subedar's* military force came from three sources. The first call was made on troops assigned to each province by the imperial court. The second source of troops for the *subedar* came from the contingents raised by the *mansabdars* posted in the province, against their *sawar* obligations. These troops were paid and maintained by the *mansabdars* from their assignments or *jagirs,* in accordance with their *sawar* ranks. The third source was the contingents provided by the 'loyal' *Zamindar*s who maintained their own military force. According to the *Ain-i-Akbari* the total number of troops in the service of the governor of Kabul—

---

[168]   Waris, pp. 109 b, 113 a, 118 a.

[169]   Saran, pp. 225-226.

[170]   *Tuzuk-i-Jahangiri*, p. 80; Mutamad Khan, *Iqbalnama-i-Jahangiri*, ed. Abd al Haiy and Ahmad Ali, Bib. Ind., Calcutta, 1865, p. 44

[171]   *Ibid.; Iqbalnama-i-Jahangiri*, p. 44; *Lahori,* I, p. 400.

[172]   Ali Muhammad khan, *Mirat-i-Ahmadi*, Calcutta, 1928, I, pp. 163-169; tr. M. F. Lokhandwala, Baroda, 1965, p. 140.

Cavalry = 28,187

Infantry = 212,700 [173]

It is not clear from the *Ain*, if these figures include the soldiers provided by the *zamindars,* but from the modest size of the contingent, it would seem that this is not the case. Conscious of the strategic significance of the *suba,* the Mughal rulers maintained a strong contingent in Kabul. Lahori states that those *mansabdars* who had *jagirs* in any of the *subas* of India and were posted in the same *suba* were required to maintain one-third of their *sawar* rank. But if posted outside the *suba* of their *jagir,* they were to maintain only one-fourth, and if in Balkh, Badakhshan and in Kabul, one fifth.[174] In order to encourage the nobles to serve in Kabul, they introduced the rule of 1/5th whereby their military obligations were reduced to one-fifth, without a corresponding reduction in *mansab.* According to the rule of one-fifth a *mansabdar* holding 5,000 *sawar* rank was to bring to muster 1,000 men and 2,200 horses, a *sawar* rank of 5,000 all *du-aspa sih-aspa* would require 2,000 men and 4,400 horses. The rule of one-fifth was introduced by Shahjahan, and applied only for distant states, in particular, Kabul. [175] In the 25th year of Shahjahan reign, Raja Jai Singh was ordered to march with Aurangzeb on the Qandahar expedition. Jai Singh was asked to bring his contingent according to the rule of 1/4th and if not feasible than according to 1/5th rule.[176]

---

[173]   *Ain*, I, pp. 594-595.

[174]   Lahori, II, pp. 505-507; *Mirat,* I, p. 228. (Shahjahan's *farman* of 27th R.Y.).

[175]   *Ibid.*; M. Athar Ali, *The Mughal nobility under Aurangzeb,* 2nd edn. Delhi, 1997, pp. 54-55.

[176]   *Jaipur Document* No. 79, p. 145, cited in *The Mughal nobility*

In order to retain firm control over provincial administration, the imperial court regularly transferred or recalled the *subedar*. The tenure of the provincial governor depended upon the will of the emperor. The term of his office was not fixed but usually varied from three to four years.[177] There were exceptions, and a few governors with extraordinary abilities were allowed to stay in office for a much longer duration. We find the duration of the tenure of the *subedar* of Kabul (as also that of Bengal and Gujarat) was longer than elsewhere. The average period of their term during the time of Akbar was 2 years and 10 months; in Jahangir's time 3 $\frac{1}{2}$ years and 3 years and 2 $\frac{1}{2}$ months in Shahjahan's period. The term of governor was longer under Shahjahan e.g. Said Khan served as the governor of Kabul for nine years.[178] During the long reign of Aurangzeb, Amir Khan the governor of Kabul held the post for 21 years with conspicuous ability and success. [179] He received a robe of honour, a special sword and had a rank of 5,000 with 5,000 *sawar*, of which 1,000 were two-horse and three-horse. Amir Khan, with his practical skill and military strength succeeded in maintaining peace and order in Kabul.

---

under Aurangzeb, p. 55.

[177] Manrique, *Travel, 1629-43,* tr. C.E. Luard assisted by H. Hosten, Hakluyt Society, London, 1927, I, p. 53. Says that the tenure was short; Francois Bernier, *Travels in the Mughal Empire: 1665-68,* tr. A. Constable, 2nd, edn. revised by V.A. Smith, London, 1916, p. 231. He reports that the tenure of governor was longer in India than in turkey; W.H. Moreland, *India at the death of Akbar,* London, 1920, p. 31. He divides the tenure into two divisions—*kachha* and *pakka.*

[178] Manrique, I, p. 53. According to him the tenure was short; *The Apparatus of Empire,* p. xxiii.

[179] *Ma'asir-i-Alamgiri,* pp. 82, 113, 157

He tactfully employed the hillmen by enlisting them in the imperial army. All this enabled him to pay regular subsidies to the clansmen living along the north western passes.[180]

At the same time the Mughals took no time in removing the *subedars* from their position when they were found wanting. We come across many occasions when the *subedars* were transferred or dismissed and their *mansabs* reduced when they failed in maintaining peace and order or suppressing rebellion and disturbances in their provinces.[181] Lahori states that during the 1st year of Shahjahan's reign, Muzaffar Khan was the *subedar* of the Kabul *suba* but the same year, he was removed from that position and Lashkar Khan was appointed.[182] In the 18th R.Y. of Aurangzeb Diler Khan was appointed and dismissed the same year. [183]

After Amir Khan's death, de-stabilization set in once again, but order was restored by Prince Muazzam. The Prince took charge in 1699, retained the position till Aurangzeb's

---

[180] *Kalimat-i-Tayyibat,* p. 66. Aurangzeb appreciates Amir Khan's administrative skills.

[181] *Akbarnama,* III, pp. 517-518. Man Singh was recalled from Kabul when he failed in dispensing justice to the people of Kabul.

[182] *Lahori,* I, p. 213, II, pp. 190-191, Shahjahan discovered that Muzaffar Khan was strongly advised by the most experienced person not to proceed to Kabul but he did not pay heed to them. The Afghan tribes who were ever ready to plunder and molest, occupied the road in his front and began to plunder the baggage of his force. As he left no experienced officer to guide his rear, a deal of property was carried of and he did nothing to remedy this disaster and did not turn back to aid them. On this account Lashkar Khan was sent as the new *subedar* with a force of 15,000.

[183] *Ma'asir-i-Alamgiri.*p. 140.

death in 1707. He re-established peace and order in the *suba* by winning over the recalcitrant Afghans.[184] The Afghan tribes were egalitarian and independent and they had accepted Mughal overlordship on their own terms. Money could bring about co-operation, but rarely ensured loyalty. The Mughal emperors never tried to tax the Afghan tribes; instead they gave them massive subsidies annually in order to keep open the communication. During Aurangzeb's reign an amount of 600,000 rupees a year was paid from Royal exchequer to Afghan chiefs to secure their allegiance (the Afridi tribe alone received Rs. 125,000). Even then Mughal control of Kabul was intermittent. Shah Alam had a large and efficient army at his disposal, but for restoring peace in the *suba*, he relied on the policy of conciliation with the hillmen and martial tribesmen. Although the Mughal government faced major financial problems during the decade following the death of Aurangzeb, the disbursement to soldiers and the salaries to petty functionaries were never interrupted. The troops posted at Kabul received salaries and pensions for performing the important duties of protecting the passes and checking subversion in that region. As a result of this the Central government had not experienced for a long time either foreign invasion or revolt by the hillmen.[185]

In 1709 Nasir Khan, formerly the *faujdar* of Jamrud was appointed *subedar* of Kabul and held the post till his death

---

[184]   *Ibid.*, pp.394-395; Ghulam Husain Khan Tabatabai, *Siyar-ul Mutakhirin*, Nawal Kishor, Lucknow, II, part, III, p. 376.

[185]   Muhammad Bakhsh Ashub, *Tarikh-i- Shahadat-I Farrukh Siyar- wa Julus-I Muhammad Shah*, B.M. MS. Or. 1832, f. 99, cited in Zahir Uddin Malik, *The Reign of Muhammad Shah: 1719-1748*, Delhi, 1977, p. 161.

in 1719. After his death his son also entitled Nasir Khan was
appointed to that post whose appointment was later confirmed
by the Emperor Muhammad Shah in 1720. His Mother was
of Afghan race so he was expected to succeed easily in ruling
the province and keeping the passes open.[186]

During the reign of Muhammad Shah a sum of Rs 12,
00,000 was sent annually to Kabul to meet the requirement of
the *suba*.[187] *However, owing to factional conflicts at the court,*[188]
the supply of funds to the suba was severely disrupted. Nasir
Khan, the governor, could not meet the expenditure of the
State, nor was he able to pay regular salaries to his troops,
thereby compromising the law and order situation in the
province.[189] This was the condition when, in 1738 Nadir Shah
at the head of 80,000 horses advanced to Kabul, it easily fell to
him. The Persian invader paid a heavy amount to the Afghan
chiefs for providing him with safe passage through the Khyber,
in both directions.[190]

---

[186] *Ma'asir-ul- Umara*, III, p. 833. William Irvine, *Later Mughal*,
       Delhi, 1971, pp. 404-5. During the reign of Farrukhsiyar,
       Sarbuland Khan was governor, when the king was deposed,
       the latter returned to the court. Later on when his appointment
       was confirmed he left for Kabul in 1719.

[187] *Seir Mustaqherin*, tr., I, p. 300.

[188] The eighteenth century was marked by intense, faction ridden
       conflicts at the Mughal court. The role of these factional
       conflicts in the decline of the Mughal Empire has been studied
       in impressive detail by Satish Chandra, *Parties and Politics at
       the Mughal court: 1707-1740,* Delhi, 1979.

[189] *Seir Mustaqherin*, tr., I, p. 300.

[190] Christine Noelle, *State and Tribe in the nineteenth century
       Afghanistan: The reign of Amir Dost Muhammad Khan (1826-
       1863),* 1997, pp. 164-5.

The eighteenth century in Kabul, was indeed, like the rest of Mughal India, a period of destability and disorder. Irfan Habib describes the eighteenth century in India as a period of reckless rapine, anarchy and disorder.[191] This is indeed, quite an appropriate characterization in so far as Kabul in the eighteenth century is concerned.

3. *Diwan*

In the provincial administration, *diwan* was next to the *subedar* in official rank but in no way subordinate to him. In fact, both these officers shared the responsibility of the over all administration of the *suba*. The *diwan* was appointed directly by the Emperor, on the recommendation of imperial *diwan*, under a *hasb-ul-hukm* and the *sanad* appointing him bore the seal of the *wazir-ul-Mulk* or *diwan-i-ala* (imperial *diwan*).[192] In 1595, Akbar issued an order that all the provincial *diwan* should report their proceedings to the Emperor in accordance with the suggestion of the imperial *diwan*, Khwaja Shamsuddin.[193] From then onwards, there was a clear cut distinction between the function of the *subedar* and *diwan*. Whereas earlier, the provincial *diwan* was subordinate to the *subedar*, after 1595,

---

[191]   Irfan Habib, *The Agrarian system of Mughal India: 1556-1707*, Delhi, 1963, p. 351

[192]   Ali Muhammad khan, *Mirat-i-Ahmadi, Supplement*, ed. Syed Nawab Ali, Calcutta, 1930, p. 173. Before 1596 he was chosen by the governor and hence subordinate to him. The letter appointing governor was called '*farman*' while those of other appointments were called '*sanad*'.

[193]   *Akbarnama*, III, p. 670. Henceforth he emerged as the independent in charge of provincial revenue and became rival of the governor.

the *diwan* was appointed, promoted and removed directly by the emperor on the recommendation of the imperial *diwan*.

The *diwan* was the head of the department of the finance in the province. His main duty was to look after the revenue administration and to keep a proper account of the expenditure in the *suba*. The *diwan* was responsible for the revenue administration. The collection and disbursement of revenue was undertaken by his office. He was also involved in the dispensation of justice in the civil disputes. He supervised the functioning of the *sadr* department, as well. He was supposed to keep his counterpart at the centre well-informed about all developments at the province through regular reports.[194]

Akbar appointed experienced and efficient persons to the office of *diwan*. In the 31st R.Y. Akbar appointed Nizam-ul Mulk as the *diwan* of Kabul.[195] During 1594-95 this charge was under Khwaja Ghias Beg.[196] During Jahangir's time in 1610-11 Muiz-ul Mulk was appointed to this post. His rank was 1,000 *zat* and 225 *sawar*, which later on was increased to 2000 *zat* and 275 *sawar*.[197] Lahori and Waris inform us that every year the charge of this office was given to different persons. During 1638-39 Mir Yahya Kabuli was appointed *diwan* of Kabul, replacing Sheikh Abdul Karim.[198] In 1643-44 Mir Samsamudaullah was given the charge and Ghazi Beg in 1647-48.[199] The following year Ghazi Beg was again

---

[194]   *Mughal Administration*, p. 53-54.
[195]   *Ibid.*, p. 511.
[196]   *Ibid.*, p. 670.
[197]   *Tuzuk-i-Jahangiri*, p. 83.
[198]   Lahori, II, pp. 129-130.
[199]   *Ibid.*, p. 348; Waris, p. 10 b.

appointed to the same office.[200] In 1651 an Iranian noble Shaikh Musa Gilani was appointed to the office of *diwan*.[201] Under Shahjahan the provincial *diwan* held many posts at the same time. In the 21ˢᵗ R.Y. of Shahjahan, Musa Gilani was *diwan, amin* and *faujdar* of Multan.[202]

During Aurangzeb's time in 1695 we have an instance of combined charge when Arshad Khan was both *diwan* and deputy *subedar* of Kabul.[203] During Prince Muazzam's governorship of Kabul, Munim Khan was promoted to the *diwani* of Kabul and subsequently due to his excellent services to the court to the *naib-subedari* of Lahore.[204] In 1704, Munim Khan was given the rank of 1500 *zat* and 1,000 *sawar*.[205] His rank by 1707 advanced to 5,000 with 5,000 horses.[206] Munim Khan administered the *jagir mahal* of Muazzam (Shah Alam) with considerable efficiency. Once the expenditure exceeded the revenue from the *jagir*, the *diwan* reduced the size of Prince's army and dismissed unworthy favourites who surrounded him.[207]

The position of *diwan* in the *suba* of Kabul was an important one, for he was the man responsible for enforcing fiscal discipline, so crucial for the stability of Mughal control.

---

[200]   Waris, p. 107.

[201]   *Ibid.*, pp. 111 b, 114 b.

[202]   *Ibid.* In 1651-52. He again held many offices at the same time such as *Diwan, Bakhshi* and *Waqia-navis* of Multan.

[203]   J.N. Sarkar, *Mughal Polity*, Delhi, 1984, p. 147.

[204]   *Ma'asir-i-Alamgiri*, p. 153. Prince Muazzam held the charge of Kabul and Lahore till the death of Aurangzeb.

[205]   *Kalimat-i-Taiyibat*, p. 26

[206]   Khafi Khan, *Muntakhab-al Lubab*, ed. K. D. Ahmad and Haig, Bib. Nd. Calcutta, 1860-74, II, p. 573.

[207]   *Ma'asir-ul-umara*, III, pp. 667-677.

It is for this reason that, as we saw, persons of exceptional talent, acumen and honesty were appointed to the office.

4. *Bakhshi*

In order to strengthen the administration of the *suba* Akbar appointed rightly-acting clerks to the lofty office of *bakhshi*. In 1586 Akbar sent a *bakhshi* to every *suba*.[208] *The provincial bakhshi* was appointed by the emperor and was placed directly under the *Mir Bakhshi*. He usually held the office of provincial *waqianavis* (diary-writer), as well.[209] The military establishment of the *suba* was under his charge. He was responsible for the recruitment, equipment and proper maintenance and periodical muster of *dagh-o-chehra*. He was the paymaster of the *mansabdars* and the army posted in the *suba*. In case of the death of a *mansabdar*, he resumed the *jagir* and settled the dues of the deceased with his family. The provincial *bakhshi* was in direct contact with the central government and acted independently of the *subedar*, and, on occasions, even served as a check on the authority of the latter.

The first *bakhshi* of the Kabul *suba* appointed immediately after its annexation in 1585 was Khwaja Shamsuddin.[210] In 1603-1604 Khwaja Rahmatullah was appointed *bakhshi* of

---

[208] *Akbarnama*, III, p. 511. In *Ain*, Abul Fazl does not describe the function of the provincial *Bakhshi*. But from references in other contemporary and subsequent authorities we find that the *bakhshi* in the provinces performed the same duties as the *Mir Bakhshi* at the Centre.

[209] *Mirat Supplement*, p. 175; William Irvine, *The Army of the Indian Mughals*, Delhi, Reprint, 2004, p. 40.

[210] *Akbarnama,* III, p. 511.

Kabul.[211] During the time of Jahangir Mahabat Khan was given the charge of this office in 1613-1614 and in 1622-1623 Mirak Khan.[212]

When we look at the reign of Shahjahan, we find that the office circulated among a select group of persons alone. Ishaq Beg Yazdi was, for example, the *bakhshi* of Kabul *suba* in 1639-40, 1644-45 and then again in 1646-47.[213] Next year 1647-48 Qazi Nizama was given this post.[214]

The provincial *bakhshi,* who was also the *waqianavis* (news-reporter) in his *suba*, kept the central government informed of all the important events of the province such as: revenue collection, military campaigns, law and order situation and also the activities of all local officers.[215] Therefore, the governor and the *diwan* had to be watchful of the *bakhshi*. Later on, besides the *waqia-navis*, a *swanih-navis* or *swanih-nigar* was also posted at some places to send intelligence reports. The latter was to act as a spy or a check on the former. The *swanih-navis* who was also styled as *khufia-navis* was to reside secretly in the *suba* and report news to the centre. The local officers under such situation were bound to act as a check on one another.[216]

---

[211] *Ibid.*, p. 826.

[212] *Tuzuk-i-Jahangiri*, p. 116, 373; Kamgar Husaini, *Ma'asir-i-jahangiri*, Or. 171; ed. Azra Alavi, Bombay, 1978, p.73 b.

[213] Lahori, II, pp. 156, 401, 534.

[214] Waris, p. 16 b.

[215] Jean de Thevenot, '*Relation de Hindostan, 1666-67'*. A. Lovell's tr. of 1687, reprinted with correction by S. N. Sen in *The Indian Travels of Thevenot and Careri*, New Delhi, 1949, III, pp, 19-20.

[216] *Mughal Administration*, pp. 61-64.

In addition to these, another official called *amin* was occasionally appointed in some provinces. In 1586 Akbar had appointed Mir Sharif Amuli as *amin* and *sadr* of Kabul.[217]

5. Local Administration:

At the local level, administrative responsibility was shared by various officials amongst them following officials: *faujdar, thanedar, qiledar* are given here.[218]

i) *Faujdar*:

The *sarkar* was under the charge of *faujdar*.[219] Within the Kabul *suba* there were seven *sarkars* viz. Kashmir, Pakli, Bimbar, Swat, Bajaur, Qandahar and Zabulistan. The *faujdars* in the *suba* Kabul had many difficult tasks to perform. Since Kabul was a frontier province of Mughal empire, the *faujdar* here had to keep watch over the frontiers and suppress the turbulent tribes settled in and around the area under his jurisdiction. He had to control rebellious chiefs as well as aggression from beyond.

From 1585 onwards Akbar found himself involved in prolonged tribal war involving the Yusufzai and the Mandar tribes as well as the Raushanai movement in the north-west.

---

[217]   *Akbarnama*, III, p. 477; *Ma'asir-ul-Umara*, III, p. 285. Jahangir promoted him to the rank of 2,500. *Amin* was a term applied to a great variety of officers. During the 17th century he was a revenue assessor under the provincial *diwan* and in the 18th century the *sadr amin* was a judge.

[218]   *Mirat Supplement*, pp.169-185.

[219]   *Dastur-ul Amal*, Br. Mus. MS. Or. 2026, f. 34 a.

Therefore in order to quell these disturbances he appointed
his most able officers as the *faujdar* of this region. In 1586
the *faujdar* of Bigram (Peshawar) Sayyid Hamid was killed
by the Raushanais (Tarikis).[220] Mutlab Khan was sent to the
Bangash area. In 1611 Muiz-ul Mulk the *faujdar* of Kabul
boldly resisted and killed many of the followers of Tarikis in
the absence of the *subedar* Khan Dauran.[221] The latter was
assigned the whole of the *sarkars* of Kabul, Tirah, Bangash,
Swat and Bajaur with the task of suppressing the rebellious
Afghans in those regions.[222] In 1617 Raja Kalyan, son of Raja
Todar Mal was made *faujdar* of Bangash. A year after the
death of Jahangir, Said Khan was the *faujdar* of Bangash
who saved and ransomed Buzurg Khanum, wife of Muzaffar
Khan the *subedar* of Kabul.[223] During the reign of Shahjahan,
Saadullah Khan, the Wazir, introduced some changes in the
local administration. He created the administrative unit of
the *chakla* which comprised a few *parganas* and each *chakla*
was placed under a *faujdar*.[224] *While this was not implemented
in all the subas* of the Mughal Empire, with same uniformity,

---

[220]   *Tabaqat-i-Akbari*, II, pp. 368-371; *Akbarnama*, III, pp. 509,
513-14. They called themselves the Raushanai but the Mughal
chroniclers bitterly referred to them as the Tarikis. (See chapter
6 for their tussle with the Mughals. Abul Fazl gives a detailed
account of this movement and the Mughal operation against
them.

[221]   *Masir-ul Umara*, II, pp. 642-645; *Tuzuk-i-Jahangiri,* pp. 325-
26. In 1607-08 Shah Beg entitled Khan Dauran was made the
subedar of Kabul.

[222]   *Ibid.*, pp. 61, 96-97.

[223]   Lahori, I, p. 125, 213; II, pp. 190-191.

[224]   *Khulasat-us Siyaq*, Aligarh Muslim University, MS. ff. 25 b,
26 a-b.

the effort signified the pre-eminent position of the *faujdar* in local administration. In 1638-9, Raja Jagat Singh was *faujdar* of Bangash.[225] Khushhal Beg Qaqshal and Ishaq Beg were the *faujdar* of Bangash in 1650. Sher Khan Tarin was the *faujdar* of Ghazni.[226]

According to the *Ain* the *faujdar* was the most important officer among the lower rung of administration. Though he was subordinate to the provincial governor, he could have direct communication with the imperial government.[227] He was appointed through the *farman-i-sabati*, by orders of the imperial court, in just the same manner in which other high appointments were made.[228]

Abul Fazl states that the *faujdar* had to look after three branches of administration—revenue, police and army.[229] On the revenue side his part was only indirect and he was only expected to assist the *amalguzars* (revenue collectors) in the realization of revenue from the peasants.

As the very word, '*faujdar*' indicates, he was first and foremost a military commander. Manucci uses the term 'lord of army' for him.[230] He regularly inspected the local militia

---

225 Lahori, II, p. 144.

226 Waris, pp. 100 b, 120 a.

227 *Ain,* I, p. 282. *Ain* gives a sort of instruction given to every *faujdar* by the government at the time of their appointments; also see *Mirat*, I, pp. 257-258.

228 Munshi Nand Ram Kayasth Srivastava, *Siyaqnama*, Litho, Nawal Kishor, Lucknow, 1879, p.67; *Ma'asir-ul-Umara*, I, p. 594.

229 *Ain,* I, p. 282. The function and duties ascribe to him indicate that he combined in himself the office of an executive officer and that of a military commander.

230 Niccolao Manucci, *Storia do Mogor or Mogul India: 1656-1712,*

and kept it well-equipped. The *faujdar* was entrusted with the task of suppressing refractory elements and policing the *sarkar*. He had to control the armed force of the *sarkar* and guard the frontiers.[231] The *faujdar* supervised the roads for the safety of the merchants and travellers passing through his *sarkar*. He was held responsible for all thefts and dacoities committed in the area under his jurisdiction.[232] He provided safety to the *banjaras* (grain- carriers) and other merchants, carrying commodities from one place to another. The *faujdar* was held accountable for any robbery or incident of theft that occurred in his domain. There are instances when they were transferred or dismissed if they failed to nab the culprit.[233] The *faujdar* realized tribute from the tribal chiefs, who had acknowledged imperial suzerainty.[234] The *faujdars* posted at the borders were sometimes appointed to defend the forts and military stations which were constructed on the borders.[235]

In 1667 Kamil Khan was the *faujdar* of Attock who fought bravely against the rebellious Yusufzais.[236] During the time of Aurangzeb it was observed that there was no coordination between the *faujdar* and the *diwan*, they quarrelled with each other. Aurangzeb took decision to assign these two posts to one

tr. W. Irvine, Indian Text Series-1, Royal Asiatic Society, Calcutta, 1966, II, pp. 450-51.

[231]   *Mirat*, I, pp. 257-258.

[232]   *Siyaqnama*, 67; Finch (1608-11), *Early travels in India: (1583-1619)*, p. 157; Thevenot, p. 50.

[233]   Manucci, II, p.450. When merchants or travellers were robbed in day light, they were obliged to pay compensation.

[234]   Saran, p. 288.

[235]   *Akbarnama*, III, pp. 491, 492, 517-18; *Ma'asir-ul Umara*, II, 160-170, 123-129.

[236]   *Alamgirnama*, pp. 1042-44.

person.[237] In 1738 Baqi Khan was the *faujdar* of Ghazni when Nadir Shah attacked Kabul.

The *faujdar* supervised the work of petty officials involved in revenue collection, such as, *amin, amil, karori, qanungo* and *chaudhary.* He also looked after the functioning of the petty officials, dealing with executive matters, in particular, *kotwal, thanedar, waqianavis, swanihnavis* and *harkaras.*[238]

He kept in touch with the local news-reporter and secret agents like *sawanihnavis* and *khufianavis,* and informed them about the activities to be reported to the imperial court. Sometimes these *faujdars* undertook excessive acts of oppression and bribed the *waqianavis* and the *Khufianavis* so that news of their oppression might never reach the imperial court.[239]

ii) *Thanedar:*

Akbar established a network of *thanas* throughout his empire. In a *faujdari* there were a number of *thanas* or military outposts. *Thanas* were an enclosed quarter or fort where cavalry, infantry, musketeer and gunner were posted for the maintenance of law and order.[240] In a city these *thanas* were established everywhere in disturbed areas at a distance of one or two *kos* from each other and at each of these a number of *sawars* were stationed.[241]

---

[237] *Kalimat-i-Taiyibat*, f. 3 b, p. 27

[238] *Nigarnama-i-Munshi*, ff. 122-123 b, 133 a-b, 260 a-b.

[239] Manucci, II, pp. 450-51

[240] *Mirat Supplement*, p. 170; For a general view of the position of *thanedar* see M.P. Singh, *Town, Market, Mint and Port in the Mughal Empire: 1556-1707*, Delhi, 1985, pp. 79-82.

[241] *Ibid.*, p. 170. We see that in Ahmadabad city these *thanas* were

The appointment of a *thanedar*, the head of the *thana* was made by the imperial government by virtue of royal orders, directly, or on the recommendation of the *nazim* or the *diwan* of the *suba*.[242]

There were many important *thanas* throughout the Kabul region, such as the *thana* of Jamrud, guarding the Khyber pass, Dakka, Sarai Ali Masjid, Khairabad, Lamghan, Barikab, Jagdalak, Surkhab and Gandamak. The *thana* of Zuhak near Ghorband was strategically located at the main routes leading to Balkh from Kabul. Kohat was also an important *thana* from where the *thanedar* checked the activities of the rebels in Tirah. Babur informs us that Adinapur was the headquarters of the *tuman* Ningnahar which during Akbar's time shifted to Jalalabad.[243]

The importance attached to the services rendered by these *thanedars* in the Kabul *suba* may be judged from their high *mansabs*. Maharaja Jaswant Singh held the *thanedari* of Jamrud in the 14th year of Aurangzeb's reign. His rank at this time was 7000/7000 (50,000 *do aspa sih aspa*). The hereditary title of Mirza Raja was also conferred upon him in the same year.[244] The importance of Jamrud was obvious to any government based at Kabul as the Jamrud fort was situated at the mouth of the Khyber Pass.[245] Similarly Fateh Khan Alamgir Shahi, the *thanedar* of Logar in Kabul *suba* held a rank of 3000/1200.[246]

---

established at a distance of one or two *kos*.

[242]   *Ibid.,* pp. 6, 189.

[243]   *Baburnama*, I, p.207; *Ain*, I, p.592; *Khulasat-ut Twarikh*, p. 85.

[244]   *Ma;asir-i-Alamgiri*, p. 109; *Alamgirnama*, pp. 331-32; *Ma'asir-ul-Umara*, III, pp. 599-604.

[245]   Burnes, I, pp. 116-117; *The Imperial Gazetteer of India*, Haryana, 1908, XIV, p. 52.

[246]   *Ma'asir-ul-Umara*, III, pp. 46-47.

It seems that these *thanedars* were to a considerable degree independent officers who could receive orders directly from the imperial government.

Their mansabs varied in accordance with the importance of the *thana*. Some of the *thanedars* enjoyed considerably high ranks and were given the charge of the *thanas* which were of great strategic importance. Though the *thanedar* was not concerned with the internal administration of the town, sometimes he acted as an important local officer and held other posts as well. During 1642-45, Khalil Beg was the *thanedar* of Ghorband and Zuhak.[247] Lahori states that he was also the *qiledar* of Zuhak.[248]

During 1631-32, after Islam Beg Shamsher Khan, Urdsher was the *thanedar* of Bangash *bala* and Abdul Baqa brother of Said Khan was *thanedar* of Bangash *payan*.[249] Lahori describes Kohat as the headquarters of the *thanedar* (commandant) of upper and lowered Bangash.[250] Said Khan who was the *thanedar* of Peshawar very well defended the town when it was attacked by evil doers.[251] During the reign of Shahjahan, in 1634-37, we find that Raja Jagat Singh was given the charge of the *thana* of Bangash,[252] who later became its *faujdar*.[253] Shahjahan, in 1637

---

[247] Lahori. II, pp. 332, 401, 406.

[248] *Ibid.*, p. 301.

[249] *Ibid.*, I, p. 417, 486. There was a distinction between the upper (*bala*) and lower (*payan*) Bangash. The upper Bangash meant the territory for Kurram, which also include the fertile Parachinar plain. While lower Bangash included the territory of Kohat.

[250] Lahori, II, p. 158.

[251] *Ibid.*, I, Part I, pp. 313-314.

[252] *Ibid.*, I, Part II, pp. 64, 242.

[253] *Ibid.*, II, p.144.

appointed Pira Purdi Khan as the *thanedar* of Bangash after Raja Jagat Singh.[254] During Aurangzeb's reign, Aghar Khan was the *thanedar* of Gandamak. In 1675 when the emboldened Afghans attacked Fidai Khan the *subedar* of Kabul on his return from Kabul to Peshawar, Aghar Khan came to his rescue, in the same year he was appointed as the *thanedar* of Jalalabad. The other capable officers such as Hazbar Khan went Jagdalak and Abdullah to Surkhab and Barangab.[255] The *thanas* of Lamghan, Gharib Khana, Danki and Bangashat were also given in command of efficient officers.[256]

Ali Muhammad Khan informs us that a *faujdari* constituted a number of *thanas* attached to the office. [257] While some of the *faujdari* comprised the *thanas* described as *huzuri* or *huzur-i-mashruti,* others included the one known as *zamima* and *painam*. The difference between the two—in *huzuri* or *huzur-i-mashruti*: the number of *sawar* attached and stationed at each *thana* was separately specified. These *thanedars* were quite independent and could have direct communication with the central government.[258] In *zamima* or *Painam*; the *sawar* rank attached to each *faujdar* was specified but the number of *sawar* and *payada* stationed at each *thana* was left to the direction of the *faujdar*.[259]

The main duties of the *thanedar* were to maintain law and order and to communicate news to the centre.[260] They

---

[254]   *Ibid.*, I, Part, II, p. 242.

[255]   *Ma'asir-i-Alamgiri,* pp. 145-146

[256]   *Ibid.*

[257]   *Mirat Supplement*, pp. 194, 196, 199, 200, 203.

[258]   *Mirat*, I, pp. 274-75.

[259]   *Mirat* Supplement, pp. 194, 196, 199, 200-203.

[260]   *Muntakhab-ul-Lubab*, II, p. 495.

had to check theft and robbery and guard roads for the merchants and travellers. These *thanedars* guarded the areas against the recalcitrant Afghan clans and provided safety to the imperial servants and their families and escorted them to their destination. It was his responsibility to provide protection to *banjaras*.[261] They helped in supplying food grains and other commodities for the royal army on campaign.[262] These *thanas* were quite significant for the defence of the city.

iii) *Qiledar:*

The North West frontier of India was a source of great insecurity for the Mughals. The Mughal emperors safeguarded the frontier by building military bases to secure the empire against aggression from beyond as well as from internal disturbances. They built a chain of strong forts and outposts strongly garrisoned and well-equipped all along the frontier area at strategic points and entrusted these forts to their most able and trusted warriors.

The military officer stationed at these forts was known as *qiledar*. He was appointed directly by the imperial court.[263] The commandant of the fort was independent of the *subedar* and the *faujdar* and also of the authority controlling the adjoining local areas. The *qiledar* reported directly to the imperial court, and was in direct contact of the central administration. The *subedar* and the *faujdar* were to assist the *qiledar* in situation of threat to security. We find certain references in the sources

---

261   *Mirat* Supplement, p. 172; *Mirat,* I, pp 143-44, 314.

262   Lahori, I, Part, I, p. 505; II, p. 35.

263   *The Army of the Indian,* pp. 268-269.

that suggest that the *qiledar* took up the charge of offices like *subedari, faujdari, thanedari and kotwali* in the absence of these officials.[264] When a *faujdar* was transferred or removed, until the time that the new incumbent took charge, the *qiledar* was required to look after the entire general administration of the town and assume the charge temporarily.[265]

Akbar built a number of new forts in the north-west frontier of his empire. The most massive fortress of Rohtas near Balnath,[266] on the Indus and the Lahore fort[267] were constructed to defend the north-west against the hostile elements. The fort of Jamrud near the entrance of Khyber pass was also one of them.[268] The most important fort towards the north-west was that of Attock on the Indus. Its foundation was laid by the Emperor's own hands when he was returning from Kabul in 1581[269]. At that time Mirza Yusuf Khan was the *qiledar* of this important fortress. In 1581 when Mirza Hakim invaded from Kabul, Yusuf Khan efficiently dispersed the invaders. Despite his success, he was considered unfit for the policing of the frontiers, and was replaced by Raja Man Singh.[270] Owing to its strategic importance, the fort of Attock was always placed under the charge of a high ranking noble.

---

[264]   *Iqbalnama-i-Jahangiri*, p. 192; Lahori, I, Part, I, p. 369; *Ma'asir-i-Alamgiri*, p. 132.

[265]   *The English Factories in India, 1618-21*, ed. W. Foster, Oxford, 1906-27, p, 101.

[266]   *Ibid.*, pp. 195-196.

[267]   Badauni, I, pp. 386-387.

[268]   *Ibid.*; Jahangir, *Tuzuk-i-Jahangiri*, pp. 48-49.

[269]   *Akbarnama*, III, p. 355. It was one of the great fortresses of the Mughals and they did not permit any stranger to enter it if he did not hold a passport from the Emperor; Tavernier, I, p.76.

[270]   *Ibid.*, pp. 336-337.

During Jahangir's reign, the fort of Attock was transferred to Zafar Khan, son of Zain Khan Koka from Ahmad Beg.[271] Zain Khan Koka built a fort near Jalalabad, when he was appointed to subjugate Yusufzai Afghans and called Naushehr (new-castle). Jahangir spent Rs. 50,000 upon it.[272]

Forts in this area served as watch station against hostile elements of the area.[273] Kabul and Qandahar were to be held at all costs, it was perhaps for this reason that these forts along with other forts in this region were made strong-holds, and provided with all possible means of defence. The fortress of Kabul was known for its strength. During Shahjahan's reign, Shiv Ram Gaur a Rajput was the *qiledar* of Kabul and after him its charge was given to Shad Khan.[274] In 1649 Khalilullah Khan was made *qiledar*.[275] Fazil Beg was removed from this post in 1650 and Nasir Beg Sildoz took the charge same year.[276] The following year Asadullah son of Sher Khwaja took his charge.[277] During 1651-52 Fathullah Khan son of Said Khan was *qiledar* of Kabul after whom Mir Abdul Maali was made *qiledar*.[278] In 1656-7 Shuja'at Khan was made the *qiledar* of Kabul fort.[279]

271 *Tuzuk-i-Jahangiri*, p. 48.
272 *Ibid.*, pp. 49-50.
273 *Akbarnama*, III, p.355; *Mazhar-i-Shahjahani*, pp. 232-33; *Alamgirnama,* p. 237.
274 Waris, p.11 a.
275 *Ibid.*, p. 67 b.
276 *Ibid.*, p. 103 b.
277 *Ibid.*, p. 135 a.
278 *Ibid.*, p. 144 a.
279 Muhammad Salih Kambu, *Amal-I Salih*, ed. G. Yazdani, Bib. Ind., Calcutta, 1923-46, III, p. 263.

We find a large number of fortresses in this region. Babur describes the fort of Adinapur to the east of Kabul and to the north of the Surkh Rud River. It served as the headquarters for the commandant of Ningnahar *tuman*.[280] Similarly Zuhak was the main fort and headquarters of the *tuman* Zuhak Bamian.[281] The fort of Ghalghal was situated in the neighbourhood of Zuhak. It is quite clear that this Ghalghal is the same Gulgala situated in the Bamian valley, as discussed by the 19th century European explorers.[282] The *tuman* of Gardez had the fortress which served as a headquarter for the commandant of Zurmat *tuman*.[283] The fort of Pesh Bulaq was situated between Dakka and Jalalabad. Jahangir spent 20,000 rupees for its repair.[284] During the reign of Shahjahan in 1643-44 the fort of Ghorband was under the charge of Khalil Beg.[285]

The other important forts were of Bishud (erected by Humayun to fight against the Afghans), Jalalabad and Peshawar.[286] The fort of Peshawar was kept under the charge of *faujdars*. Saiyid Hamid the *faujdar* of Peshawar was killed by the Raushanais towards the close of the year 1586.[287]

Aurangzeb did not rely on the Afghans because of their habits of loot and plunder. Since the charge of the fort was a

---

[280]   *Baburnama*, pp. 207-208, 209.

[281]   *Ain*, I, p. 594; Lahori, I, pp. 260-61; Cf. *Atlas*, p. 2, sheet 1 A-B.

[282]   Moorcroft and Trebeck, II, pp. 387, 392-3; Burnes, I, p.183. The distance between Zuhak and Bajgah was 27 *kuroh*.

[283]   *Ibid.*, p. 593; *Atlas*, p. 3, sheet, 1 A-B.

[284]   *Akbarnama*, III, p. 512; *Tuzuk-i-Jahangiri*, pp. 49-51.

[285]   Mobad, *Dabistan-i-Mazahib*, Ibrahim b. Muhammad's ed., Bombay, 1875, pp. 178-193; *Sikh History from Persian Sources*, ed., J.S. Grewal and Irfan Habib, Delhi, 2001, p. 75.

[286]   Bayazid Bayat, pp. 217, 218; Raverty, p. 55.

[287]   *Tabaqat-i-Akbari*, II, p. 371; *Akbarnama*, III, pp. 510-11.

responsible post, he did not assign the post of *qiledari* to the Afghans.[288] The fort in this area was necessary for retaining hold over the country. The *qiledar* was required to keep his garrison well-equipped and in a state of readiness.[289] He was to store sufficient provision to thwart a possible siege operation by the adversaries. The commandants of these forts usually communicated the local news to the imperial headquarters, these forts served as official postal offices as well. The *qiledar* appointed many news reporters in various streets and *bazars* of the area in order to retain touch with the popular views and opinion.[290]

The three local officials—*faujdar, thanedar* and *qiledar* were the bulwarks of local administration. The significance that the imperial court assigned to these officials is evident from the fact that they were all appointed by imperial orders, directly by the court. Since they were appointed by the court, they were accountable to the court alone, and were largely independent of the authority of the governor and any other official of the *suba*.

It is evident from our study of the administration in Kabul that the administrative system there followed the prevailing Mughal procedure and norms. The rule structure in Kabul was identical to the one we find in other *subas* of Mughal India. As far as the administration is concerned, Kabul could not lay claims to any distinctiveness, and was no different from other Mughal provinces.

---

[288]   *Kalimat-i-Taiyibat*, ff. 34 a, 87 a, pp. 36, 45.
[289]   *Mazhar-i-Shahjahani*, pp. 232-33.
[290]   *Dastur-i-Jahankushan*, ff. 54-55 a.

Appendix-A

Following Tables A, B, C, & D present the list of the *subedars* posted at Kabul under Akbar, Jahangir, Shahjahan and Aurangzeb in a chronological order.

Table- 2. 1

Akbar

R.Y.	Date	*Subedar*	Racial Background	Source
30 – 32	1586 – 88	Man Singh	Rajput	AN, III, 511 – 12,
32	1588 – 89	Zain Khan Koka	Iranian	,, 518.
33 – 38	1589 – 93	Qasim Khan	Turkish	Badauni, II, 372; AN, III, 569
39 – 40	1594 – 96	Qulij Khan	Turkish	AN, III, 654, 702.
41 – 45	1596 – 1601	Zain Khan Koka	Iranian	,, 721; M.U, II, 362 – 370
46	1601 – 02	Shah Quli Khan Mahram	Iranian	AN, III, 799; Zakh. Kh 34 a.
47	1602 – 03	Hasan Beg Shaikh Umari	Turkish	AN, III, 820.

Farah Abidin

Table- 2. 2

Jahangir

R.Y.	Date	*Subedar*	Racial Background	Source
1	-	-		-
2 – 4	1606 – 09	Shah Beg Khan-i-Dauran	Turkish	*Tuzuk*, 61, 96.
5	1609 – 10	Taj Khan Kabuli	Turkish	,, 80, *Iqbalnama-i-Jahangiri*, 44; Zakh.Kh, II, 361.
6 – 7	1610 – 12	Qulij Khan	Turkish	*Tuzuk*, 96
8 – 11	1612 – 17	Shah Beg Khan-i-Dauran	Turkish	,, 96, 100
12 – 18	1617 – 22	Mahabat Khan	Iranian	,, 196, 353, 391.
19 – 22	1623 – 27	Khwaja Abul Hasan	Iranian	,, 393; Qazwini, 131 b. *Iqbalnama-i-Jahangiri*, 238.

Table- 2. 3

Shahjahan

R.Y.	Date	*Subedar*	Racial Background	Source
At the time of Jahangir's death	1627	Khwaja Abul Hasan	Iranian	Lahori, I, 125; Qazwini, 131 b.
1 – 4	1627 – 31	Lashkar Khan	Iranian	Lahori, I, 125, 400; Qazwini, 159 b.
4 – 13	1631 – 40	Said Khan Chaghtai	Turkish	Lahori, II, 222; MU, II, 429 – 437.
14 – 23	1640 – 49	Ali Mardan Khan	Iranian	,,
23 – 24	1649 – 51	Qulij Khan Said Khan Murad Bakhsh (Prince)	Turkish Turkish	Waris, 86 b, 113 a, 91 b.
24 – 29	1651 – 55	Mahabat Khan Dara Shikoh (Prince) Sulaiman Shikoh (Prince) (Dy. Subedar)	Iranian	,, 125 a; *Amal-i-Salih*, III, 135. Waris, 142 a.
30	1655 – 56	Baqi Beg Ghairat Khan Bahadur Beg		Waris, 244 b.
31 – 32	1656 – 57	Mahabat Khan	Iranian	*Amal-i-Salih*, III, 261.

Table- 2. 4

Aurangzeb

R.Y.	Date	*Subedar*	Racial Background	Source
1 – 4	1658 – 62	Mahabat Khan	Iranian	*Alamgirnama,* 129, 194, 219, 229, 302; M.A, 38, 71.
4 - 10	1662 – 67	Amin Khan	Iranian	*Alamgirnama,* 661, 741, 761, 842, 847, 1042-44; M.A, 38, 57, 61.
11 – 13	1668 – 70	Mahabat Khan Muhammad Amin Khan	Iranian	M.A, 71, 84, 104.
13 – 14	1670 – 71	Muhammad Amin Khan	Iranian	M.A, 136; M.U, III, 593.
15 – 16	1672 – 73	Mahabat Khan	Iranian	M.A, 136; M.U, III, 593.
17 – 20	1674 – 77	Fidai Khan Azam Khan	Iranian	M.A, 136, 157.
20 – 41	1678 – 99	Amir Khan	Iranian	,, 153, 157, 170, 270, 82, 113, 146, 394.
42 – 51	1699 – 1707	Muazzam (Prince) Nasir Khan (Dy. In 44th R.Y.1701) Sher Zaman (Dy. 45th R.Y.1703)		M.A, 394-95, 492, 497; *Siyar-ul-Mutakherin,* II, part, III, 376.

After Aurangzeb's death

1709 – 1719	Nasir Khan	Iranian	M. U. I, 591-593.
1720 – 1739	Nasir Khan (s/o former Governor)	Iranian	M.U, III, 833.

Chapter – III

Agrarian Economy

Even as the Kabul *suba* was largely mountainous; it contained, in the Mughal period, significant areas of *arable land*, as well. The arable land existed along the base of the hills, and was quite productive.[291] Apart from the nomadic tribe fold, a large number of the population of this region was supported by agriculture. In the *suba,* agriculture was practiced in narrow strips along river valleys.[292]

Along with food grain production, Kabul was rich in the production of a wide variety of fruits. Strategically placed on the trade route connecting northern India with Central and West Asia, the agrarian surplus generated by Kabul sustained a thriving export trade. At the same time, the agrarian surplus created considerable differentiation in village communities and led to the persistence of an intermediate agrarian class between the producer and the state. As in other parts of Mughal India, the bulk of agrarian surplus was appropriated by the state, leaving the peasantry with the minimum necessary subsistence. [293]

---

[291]   Burnes, II, pp. 399-330, 334.

[292]   Elphinstone, II, p. 5.

[293]   Irfan Habib, *Agrarian System of Mughal India: 1556-1707,* second revised edition, 1999, pp. 230-236.

1. Agriculture:

Even as the province of Kabul was known for the production of a wide variety of fruits, it also produced a variety of food grains, as well. Babur in his memoirs gives a detailed account of agricultural production in Kabul. He informs us that grain production in Kabul was modest, and a four or five fold return was reckoned as a good yield.[294] Extensive cultivation, however, was reported to the south of Kabul river basin and its tributaries.[295] Around Kabul, food grain cultivation was practiced in the plains between the mountains and the valley. Agriculture was also practiced in the flat valley bottoms as well. On the slopes, however, nothing but only the grass (*buta-kah*) could be found, which was very suitable for feeding horses. The mountain to the west of Kabul had extensive flat tops, where the crops were grown.[296]

Wheat and barley were the staple crops and were grown all over the region in large quantity.[297] The cultivation of rice and other pulses was also undertaken. The eastern and southern parts of *suba* Kabul produced a larger agrarian variety,

---

[294] *Baburnama*, I, p. 203; Cf. *Tuzuk-i-Jahangiri*, pp. 45-46. Jahangir in the account of second regnal year mentions that when the royal standard reached Attock on the way to Kabul, he asked the *Bakhshis* of that region to allow only important officers to cross the Indus as the Kabul *suba* could not support a large army.

[295] Vigne, pp. 163, 174. The Whole of the northern part of the plain of Kabul is well irrigated by rivers.

[296] *Baburnama*, I, pp. 221-222.

[297] Percy Sykes, *A History of Afghanistan*, London, 1940, I, p. 12; Adamec, p. 316.

compared to the rest of the *suba*. Around Lamghan, to the
east of Kabul, extensive cultivation was reported.[298]

The Hindu Kush mountains were covered with perpetual
snow but on the sides of the valleys,[299] wheat and barley
were cultivated, depending on the seasonal rains. The valley
bottoms well-irrigated from the streams produced all sort of
crops such as wheat, rice, barley, pulse, sugarcane and Indian
corn. Agricultural production, however, was not uniform,
but quite uneven, with some places producing far in excess
to the others.[300] Jalalabad, watered by the Kabul river, was
extremely fertile, produced abundant crops especially rice and
sugarcane. Wheat and Indian corn were also cultivated around
Jalalabad.[301]

Rice was widely cultivated in Kabul. Elphinstone noticed
that rice was grown in most parts of Kabul, but in very unequal
quantity and quality: 'it was most abundant in Swat and best
about Peshawar'.[302]

Babur informs us that Ningnahar which had ample
irrigation produced good quality of rice along with corn.[303]
In Lamghan rice was cultivated on steep top. There were
rice fields at the bottom of the hills around Alishang watered

---

[298]   *Baburnama,* I, pp. 207-208.

[299]   *Ibid.,* p. 214. Babur speaks of the villages on the skirts of the
        Hindukush mountains. In the footnote Beveridge mentions
        that they include places "rich with parallel" in agricultural
        products and level land.

[300]   Elphinstone, I, p. 394.

[301]   *Ain,* I, p. 586; *Khulasat-ut-Twarikh,* p. 86.

[302]   Elphinstone, I, pp. 393-394.

[303]   *Baburnama,* I, p. 207-8, 342, 373-374. Rice fields were all at
        the bottom of the hills. From there, Babur's soldiers collected a
        mass of rice; *Ain,* I, pp. 588-9.

by the Alishang river, from where Babur's soldiers collected huge quantities of rice. In Alingar also, all sorts of grain were produced.[304] Another major rice producing tract was the upper Bangash.[305]

The productivity of rice in Bajaur was perhaps, moderate since in 1519, when 4,000 *Kharwar* (ass loads) of rice were demanded from the cultivators, they were unable to meet the demand and were ruined.[306]

Ghazni did not enjoy an abundance of cultivable land. The River Ghazni watered four or five villages and three or four others were cultivated from under-ground water-course (*Karez*). Agriculture in Ghazni was quite cumbersome because of the quality of soil; the soil had to be top-dressed every year. But the seed yield ratio in Ghazni was higher than in Kabul. The crops produced in Kabul were exported to India and yielded high profit.[307] Jalalabad had sizeable amounts of irrigated land. Sugarcane was extensively cultivated there. The other crops produced in Jalalabad were rice, wheat and barley. All these were exported to India.[308] In the well irrigated Bigram, a high quality rice called *sukhdas* was grown. The area in and around Bigram and Peshawar was well-irrigated from

---

[304] *Baburnama,* I, pp. 210, 342. Alishang and Alingar were two *buluks* of Lamghan proper which lies to the east of Kabul; Elphinstone, I, p.132.

[305] *Khulsat-ut-Twarikh,* p. 86; Cf. *Central Asian Civilization,* pp. 400-3.

[306] *Baburnama,* I, p. 374; A. Burnes, I, p. 334. Emperor Babur, after the capture of Kabul, imposed a tax of 30,000 *Kharwar* of grain on Kabul and Ghazni, but next year when became well acquainted with the country found that the levy was exorbitant.

[307] *Baburnama,* p. 218

[308] *Ibid.,* p. 208; *Khulasat-ut-Twarikh,* p. 86; Vigne, pp. 230-31.

the Kabul river, the Indus, the Bara and some other streams of lesser importance.[309] The valley of Peshawar was intensively cultivated and produced the finest quality of rice. It was called Bara rice, because it was grown on ground irrigated by the Bara river.[310]

One of the chief articles produced was asafoetida, which was found in the hills in many parts of this region. According to Elphinstone, "it requires no attention, but that which is necessary for extracting the gum. It is a low bush, with long leaves, which are generally cut off near the bottom of the stem: milk exudes from the plant cut, and generally hardens like opium. It is spoiled by exposure to the sun. The Afghans, therefore took care to shelter it, by placing two flat stones over it, in such a manner that they support each other".[311] Lucerne which was called *reeshka* in Persian and *spusta* in Pashto was also produced there; madder and tobacco among them the latter was considered to be of a highly fine quality.[312]

A large quantity of wheat was produced at Bajaur whereas Swat produced a surplus of rice. In the district of Bannu owing to the irrigation facilities in the district, a huge quantity of grain was produced. The main crops produced in Bannu were rice, wheat, sugarcane and melon. In the north of the district date was grown as well. In the district of Butakhak land

---

[309]   *Baburnama*, I, p. 230; *Khulasat-ut-Twarikh*, pp. 85-86; Cf. sheet 1 A-B, p.3.

[310]   *Ibid.*; William T. Couch, *Collier's Encyclopedia*, XV, New York, 1957, p. 598.

[311]   Elphinstone, I, p. 395; *Atlas*, p. 3 – also see the map of *Southern Afghanistan Political and Economic*, p. 2 A-B, he locates, in his *Atlas,* the mart for asafoetida in Qandahar.

[312]   Elphinstone, I, p. 395.

was well cultivated.[313] In their elevated valleys the Hazaras cultivated wheat, barley and rice. They grew a special variety of wheat called *dundan-i-shutur* or camel's tooth because of its shape. It was nearly double the size of the ordinary grain.[314]

Wheat and barley were the chief agricultural products of Kabul.[315] But the production of these grains was not always sufficient to meet the demands of the province, and thus an inter-provincial export trade existed. Cereals were imported from Ghazni and rice from upper Bangash, Jalalabad, Lughman and even Kunar. There were two harvests per year in most parts of the province of Kabul. The first season began during the autumn and ended in summer. During this season wheat, barley, peas and some beans were produced. The second season began in spring and ended in autumn, when rice, gram, millet and *mung* were produced. The first harvest season, which was called *bahari* (from the Persian word *bahar;* in India it is called *rabi)* or spring harvest was by far the most important in the region west of Sulaiman range. In the east the harvest was called *pauiz*[316] or *tirmaee* may be the most considerable on the whole. In Bajaur, Panjkora and towards the Indus the most important harvest was that which was reaped in summer. In all these areas wheat was the chief grain. In Peshawar, Bangash and Daman Koh the harvests were nearly equal. The Hazara country and in general all the coldest part of the province

---

[313]   Angus Hamilton, *Afghanistan Description and Travel*, London, 1906, p. 243.

[314]   Vigne, pp. 169-70.

[315]   Elphinstone, I, p. 399.

[316]   *Pauiz* means the fall of leaf or autumn and called *Kharif* in India.

sowed their only harvest in spring, and reaped it in the end of autumn.[317]

The land which was irrigated naturally and depended on seasoned rainfall and snow was known as *Lalmi*. The *lalmi* land was also known as *Khushkaba* (without water land).[318] On the other hand the land irrigated artificially from rivers and canals were called *rudi*.[319]

2. Fruits:

The province of Kabul was well-known for the variety and abundance of fruits. Babur tells us that fruits were produced in Kabul during both the summer and the winter seasons. According to Babur, during the winters, Kabul produced great quantities of grapes, pomegranate, apricot, apples, quinches, pears, peaches, plums, almonds and walnuts. During the summers, on the other hand, Kabul produced oranges, citron, amluk (diospyrus lotus), sugarcane, watermelon and muskmelon. The climate in Lamghan was particularly suitable for the production of oranges, citron, amluk and other fruits. [320] The valley grew plenty of grapes, and was well-known for two varieties: - the *ara-tashi* and the *suhan-tashi*. The former

---

[317] Elphinstone, I, pp. 392-394.

[318] *Ibid.*, p. 399.

[319] Raverty, p. 425.

[320] *Baburnama*, I, pp. 202-203. Kabul was known for its temperate fruits viz. the grapes, pomegranate, apricot, apple, pear, peach, plum and walnut. In the hotter valleys, even sugarcane, orange and citron were cultivated; Sykes, I, p. 12.

was yellowish, and the latter was red in colour. The wine prepared from the grapes in Kabul was great in demand.[321]

There were many fruit growing villages in the foothills of the Hindu Kush.[322] Grapes were so plentiful that in certain places grape-wine was consumed in place of water. In and around the city of Kabul an excellent grape known as water grape was grown together with rhubarb and *badrang*.[323] Jahangir tells us that all sorts of fruits were grown in Kabul. He informs us that there were many good varieties of grapes, but the *Sahibi* and *Kishmishi* in particular, were exceptionally tasty. *Shah alu* (Cherry) and *Zard alu* (Khubani) were found everywhere in Kabul.[324] In the village of Gulbahar (north of Kabul) cherries were grown in abundance. Jahangir once ate nearly hundred of them.[325] He tells us that the sweet cherry was not found in Kashmir before its annexation by Akbar. It was brought from Kabul by his official Ali Quli Afshar and propagated by means of grafting. By the same method he increased the cultivation of apricot.[326] The Mughal emperors were greatly influenced by the Persian and Central Asian horticulture and brought these new methods to India. Therefore we find that during seventeenth century there was

---

[321] *Baburnama*, I, pp. 210-211.

[322] *Ibid.*, pp. 214-215.

[323] *Ibid.*, p. 203. Rhubarbs were also called rewash the green leaf-stalks, Burnes, II, p.169, I, p.154 and *badrang* was a large sort of cucumber.

[324] *Tuzuk-i-Jahangiri*, p. 55; *Badshahnama*, II, pp. 582-3; Steingass describes *Zard alu* as plum.

[325] *Tuzuk-I-Jahangiri*, p. 50.

[326] *Tuzuk-i-Jahangiri*, pp. 299. *Shah alu* in the Persian text ought to be rendered sweet cherry and not simply cherry; Lahori, vol. I, part II, p. 30. He tells that *shah alu* was called *gilas* in Kashmir.

extensive application of grafting which improved the quantity as well as quantity of certain fruits.[327]

The region to the north of Kabul produced many varieties of fruits. The district of Najrao produced fruits in abundance and excellent type of grapes as Babur records in his memoirs.[328] Grapes and pomegranates were also grown in Alsai, though the pomegranates were of a slightly inferior quality and were locally consumed but few of them were sent to Hindustan.[329] The grapes of Kabul were considered inferior to that of Qandahar, but they were produced in large quantities and were of different kinds. These grapes were wrapped in cotton and were then packed in wooden boxes for export to India.[330]

Muskmelon and water melon were grown in abundance in Kabul. They were not of a very good quality when compared to Khurasan and Qandahar.[331] Abul Fazl reiterates Babur's observation that the Kabul melons were not of good quality.[332] Jahangir has mentioned that melons of Badakhshan were inferior to Kariz melons.[333]

---

[327] *Kitab Shujaratum Nihal or Risala-i Mazruat*, Lindesiana, No. 484, British Museum, Add. 1771, ff. 157 b- 259 a; *Shahjahan nama,* British Museum, Or. 174, f. 102 a. Sadiq Khan tells that during Shahjahan's reign the practice of grafting became widespread. And as result of this application, the quality of *santra, kaunla* and *narangi,* which were earlier mere varieties of lemons, was now greatly improved.

[328] *Baburnama,* I, p. 213; *Ain,* I, p. 593.

[329] *Baburnama,* I, p. 221.

[330] Vigne, p. 174.

[331] *Baburnama,* I, p. 203.

[332] *Ibid.,* p. 218; *Ain,* I, pp. 67, 71; Francisco Pelsaert, 'Remonstrantie', *c. 1826,* tr. W. H. Moreland and P. Geyl, *Jahangir's India,* Delhi, 1972, pp. 31, 48.

[333] *Tuzuk-i-Jahangiri,* p. 132.

In the Kabul *Suba* pomegranates were grown in abundance. Among pomegranates, especially of the seedless variety grown in Ningnahar had such a reputation that it was sent to distant places as gifts.[334] The seed-less variety of pomegranates were also produced in and around Jalalabad and were exported to India.[335] Paghman to the north west of Kabul and Lamghan to the north-east were rich in a variety of fruits. Peaches, pears, orange, citrons together with other fruits of hot climate were grown in abundance. A few date trees were also found at these places. The well irrigated area for fruit production was Ningnahar, where Babur laid out four gardens. At Ningnahar, he also introduced bananas in 1508-9, which as he claims grew well.[336]

In the valley of Kohistan (Koh Daman), Istalif alone was known to have six thousand orchards. In the valley of Kohistan there were plenty of mulberry trees. The plain of Kohistan was naturally well irrigated by the Ghorband and Panjshir rivers.[337]

Alubalu, a kind of plum or sour cherry of Kabul was of a good quality. Babur informs us that he introduced and planted them in Kabul.[338] There were date trees in Kabul, but they were found towards the east and west of Kabul.[339]

Apart from the fresh fruits, a great variety of dried fruits were also produced in the province of Kabul. Walnut, almond

---

[334]   *Ibid.,* I, pp. 207-208; Raverty, p. 50.

[335]   *Khulasat-ut-Twarikh,* p. 85.

[336]   *Baburnama,* I, pp. 210-11. (Lamghanat), 216 (Paghman), 208 (Ningnahar); *Ain,* I, p. 585; *Khulasat-ut-Twarikh,* p. 86.

[337]   Lahori, II, p. 582; Vigne, p. 217.

[338]   *Baburnama,* I, p. 203. Steingass explains *alubalu* as sour-cherry.

[339]   Burnes, I, p. 154.

*   M.S. Randhawa, *Paintings of Baburnama*, National Museum, New Delhi, 1983.

and neosia (chilghoza) were important dry fruits. Neosia and a small variety of walnut (*badamchas*) grew in plenty in the wild on the slope of the mountains in Lamghan and Bajaur. Chilghoza wood was burnt to get fire or light. Walnut woods were used for heating. Honey was collected from the hill-tracts in Kabul, except toward Ghazni one could find bee hives throughout the Kabul district.[340]

3. Horticulture:

During Mughal times, in Kabul, we find quite a large number of gardens. Babur greatly admires Kabul, in his memoirs, and says that its gardens and flowers render Kabul in spring a heaven. Gulbadan Bano in the *Humayun Nama* and Jahangir in his memoirs also refer to the beauty and charm of the gardens in Kabul.[341]

The Principal charm of Kabul lay in the surrounding gardens, groves, orchards watered by sparkling streams and canals with delightful embankment.[342] Babur laid out several gardens in Kabul such as *Bagh-i-Shahr Ara, Bagh-i-Kalan, Bagh-i-Banafshan, Bagh-i-Padshahi* and *Bagh-i-Chinar.* The *charbagh* which was the largest of all city gardens is said to have been originally the work of Babur. The *Shahr-Ara* garden (Pride of the city) was made by Shahr Bano Begum, daughter of Mirza Abu Said, Babur's own aunt.[343] The garden had all

---

[340] *Baburnama,* I, pp. 203, 213, 223; *Ain,* I, pp. 592.

[341] Gulbadan Begam, pp. 78-79, 216; *Tuzuk-i-Jahangiri,* pp. 323, 327, 338.

[342] Vigne, pp. 161-162.

[343] *Baburnama,* I, p. 268; Gulbadan Begam, pp. 78-79; *Tuzuk-i-Jahangiri,* pp. 51-55. Another Shahr Bano was Babur's sister.

sort of fruits and grapes and for sweetness it had no match. Jahangir in his memoirs praises both these gardens. At the time of Jahangir's sojourn here during an expedition in the Bangash territory these gardens were improved and renewed.[344]

Babur tells us that in 1508-9 he laid out four gardens known as the *Bagh-i-Wafa* (Garden of fidelity), on a raising ground near Adinapur and had Surkh-rud between it. Fruits like oranges, citron and pomegranate grew in abundance in these gardens. He informs that "the garden lies high, has high running-water close at hand, and a mild winter climate. In the middle of it, a one-mill stream flows constantly past the little hill on which are the four garden-plots. In the south-west part of it there is a reservoir, 10 by 10, round which are orange-trees and a few pomegranates, the whole encircled by a trefoil-meadow. This is the best part of the garden, a most beautiful sight when the oranges take colour. Truly that garden is admirably situated".[345]

Babur brought bananas and planted there, and according to him, they grew well. The year before, Babur had sugarcane planted there, which again did well.[346]

Even after Babur had established his rule in India, he found time to write to his governor in Kabul, Khwaja Kalan, with instructions that the gardens he had planted there should be kept well watered and properly maintained with flowers.[347] In

---

[344] *Ibid;* Beni Prasad, *History of Jahangir*, Allahabad, 1962, p. 150.

[345] *Baburnama*, I pp. 208-209.

[346] *Ibid.*, I, pp. 207-208. Some of the Bananas were sent to Bukhara and Badakhshan. Both these territories were under Babur's rule. Humayun at that time was the governor in Badakhshan.

[347] Sylvia Crowe and Sheila Haywood, *The Gardens of Mughal*

one the paintings of *Baburnama,* Babur is shown, supervising
the construction of a reservoir on the spring of *Khwaja Sih-
yaran* (Three friends), in Kabul.[348]

In his memoirs Jahangir when enumerating the gardens
of Kabul, mentions not less than seven gardens such as the
Shahr-Ara garden, the *Mahtab* (moonlight) garden, Bika
Begam[349] garden, the *Urta-bagh* (middle garden), the garden
made by Jahangir's own grandmother Mariam Makani, the
Surat Khana garden, and then the *Charbagh.*[350]

Other gardens were *bagh-i-Khilwat,*[351] *Nazar-gah* garden,
Avenue garden, New garden, Town garden, Zubaida garden
and *bagh-i-Jahan-ara.*[352]

These beautiful gardens were used for many purposes.
They served as pleasure ground for emperors and royal ladies,
places of rest and holidaying. Feasts were organized there.
Babur celebrated the birth of Humayun in the *Charbagh* when
Humayun was just six days old.[353]

India, Delhi, 1973, pp. 56-62.

[348] *Baburnama*, I, p. 216; Hamid Suleiman, *Miniatures of Baburnama,* Tashkent, 1970, p. 25; Gavin Hambly, *Cities of Mughal India,* second impression, Victoria and Albert Museum London, 1977, p. 44.

[349] It was made by Babur's widow, the one who had carried Babur's bone to Kabul.

[350] *Tuzuk-i-Jahangiri*, pp. 51-52.

[351] *Baburnama*, I, p. 397.

[352] *Ibid.,* pp. 305-6.

[353] *Ibid.,* p. 344; *Miniatures of Baburnama*, p. 45.

A grand feast was organized there and all *begs* small and great brought gift.[354] Gulbadan Begam tells us that in Audience Hall garden, the royal ladies celebrated the feast of the circumcision of Akbar in Kabul, when Akbar was five years old.[355] Jahangir in his memoirs writes of the royal feasts given by Nur Jahan Begam in *Nur Afshan garden* on the occasion of Jahangir's visit there and the grand feast given by Nur Jahan in *Nur Sanai* garden.[356] When Jahangir was in Kabul he organized several entertainments in the *Shahr-Ara* garden with his courtiers and intimates as well as with the ladies of the *harem*.[357]

Throughout the Mughal period, the garden tomb became the archetypal mausoleum which continued from the time of Babur to Shahjahan. Babur in the account of 1505-6 informs that after the death of his mother Qutluq Nigar Khanum he buried her in New Year's Garden of Koh Daman.[358] The tomb of Emperor Babur stands in the middle of the *charbagh* garden. Babur directed that his grave should be "open to the sky, with no building over it, no need of a door keeper".[359] To preserve the tomb however, an open structure has now been constructed over it. It is marked by two erect slabs of white marble. In front of the grave, there is a small but chaste white marble mosque;

---

[354] *Ibid.*

[355] *Humayun Nama,* pp. 77-78. This was the garden where royal ladies rejoiced after the victory at Panipat.

[356] *Tuzuk-i-Jahangiri*, pp. 323, 327, 338.

[357] *Ibid.*, p. 51-52; Cf. *Akbarnama*, I, p. 255. Humayun has been described as holding a cooking festival in Badakhshan.

[358] *Baburnama*, I, ff. 157, 136 b; p. 246

[359] *Ibid.*, p. II, p. 709; *Humayun Nama*, p. 42. By 1539 Babur's body had not been taken to Kabul.

an inscription upon it shows that it was built in the year 1640 A.D. by the order of the emperor Shahjahan.[360]

4. Mineral Products:

It is mentioned in contemporary and near–contemporary sources that silver, copper, iron, lead, antimony lapis lazuli and asbestos were found in different parts of Kabul.

There were iron mines in the mountains north of Kabul. The author of *Ajaibu-l Tabaqat* informs us that there were iron mines in the mountains of Kabul, which was actually mined near Ghorband.[361] It is reported by both Babur and Abul Fazl that on the mountains of Ghorband were mines of iron, silver and lapis lazuli.[362] According to Ricci, 'iron was found in abundance in Charikar',[363] which was situated to the north of Kabul, at the mouth of Daman- Koh. Iron ore was brought in great quantities to the market of Kabul from Charikar, after being processed there. [364]

Babur tells us that there were silver and lapis lazuli mines in the mountains around the *tuman* of Ghorband.[365] Another celebrated silver mine was in the Panjshir valley. In 1548-49,

---

[360] Alexander Burnes, I, p. 142 Alexander Burnes visited and admirably described the garden and the tomb. Mohan Lal who visited Kabul in the first half of the 19th century, also appreciated the Beauties of the spot.

[361] Muhammad Tarin bin Abil Qasim, *Ajaibu-l Tabaqat,* and MS. R. A. S., 179, p. 248.

[362] *Baburnama*, I, p. 214; *Ain*, I, p. 594.

[363] See Ricci *Commentary,* 1610, p. 532. Cited in *Early Jesuit Travellers in Central Asia*, p. 17.

[364] *Ibid.*

[365] *Baburnama,* I, p. 214; *Ain,* I, p. 594; *Khulasat-ut Twarikh*, p. 85.

when Humayun visited it, he found it in a bad condition.[366] Large quantities of precious metals were also obtained from the *tuman* of Panjshir.[367] Elphinstone reports that silver was found in small quantity, whereas gold was not found in Kabul.[368] There were mines of lead and antimony mixed in the Kabul province mostly in the areas of Afridis and Hazaras. In upper Bangash only lead was found.[369] There were iron and salt mines in Bangash (Kurram Valley), salt was mined in Kohat also.[370]

5. Means of Irrigation: Watermill

The major part of Kabul received low rainfall. The precipitation was so low that rainfall could not sustain the cultivation of the soil. In Kabul there were only few areas in which agriculture could be undertaken without artificial irrigation.[371]

Babur, a native of Farghana, surprisingly observed that irrigation was not necessary for cultivation of either the autumn or the spring crop in Hindustan. In Hindustan autumn crops depended on rainfall alone and spring crops grew even without rainfall.[372] Babur goes on to say that unlike Central Asia there was no need to dig water-courses or construct dams.

---

[366] Bayazid Bayat, p. 105; *Akbarnama*, I, p. 283; Cf. G. Le Strange, *The Land of the Eastern Caliphate*, Great Britain, reprinted, 1930, p. 350.

[367] *Ibid.*

[368] Elphinstone, I, p. 194.

[369] *Ibid.*; Vigne, pp. 208-9.

[370] *Khulasat-ut Twarikh*, p. 86; *Baburnama*, I, p. 231.

[371] See Irfan Habib in *Central Asian Civilization*, V, p. 467.

[372] *Baburnama*, II, pp. 486-488.

He missed those "channels of running water" *(aqar-sus),* an artificial technique of irrigation. In his homeland, Farghana, in the territory of Osh there was an abundance of *aqar-sus.* All the cultivation in Turkistan depended on such irrigation channels.[373]

A remarkable feature in the physical geography of this portion of Central Asia was the paucity of rivers; there were few rivers from which long surface canals could be drawn. The most common mode of irrigation was from streams. The water of streams was sometimes merely turned upon the fields but often was carried to them by small canals. It was diverted into the canals by small dams, across the bed of rivers and streams. They were swept away when the water level rose. In bigger rivers, a partial embankment was made on one side, which extended for a certain distance into the current. Although it did not entirely interrupt the streams but forced a part of it into the canal. From these canals smaller water courses were drawn off to the field, which were bounded by little banks raised on purpose to retain the water.[374]

The other method of irrigation was by the means of manmade underground channels. It was called *qanat* in Persia and *kariz* or *karez* in Afghanistan. A fourteenth century lexicographer describes the *karez* as "a stream, with its head concealed which they excavate in a line of wells".[375]

---

[373]   *Ibid.,* I, p. 4. Also see footnote; II, p. 488. Osh was in the South-eastern Farghana valley.

[374]   Elphinstone, I, pp. 396-8; Vigne, p. 163.

[375]   F. M. Qawwas, *Farhang-i-Qawwas* [c. 1342-3], ed. N. Ahmad, Tehran, 1974, p. 25; See Chardinn's description based on his travels in Iran down to 1677 in Sir John Chardin, *Sir John Chardin's Travels in Persia,* tr. E.M.D. Lloyd, London, 1720,

This remarkable system of underground channels was more a common feature of irrigation in the entire west of Afghanistan, particularly in Iran. K.S. Lambton describes the *qanat* or *karez* as "these *qanats* are underground conducts which, by using fewer slopes than that of the soil surface, bring water to the surface. The *qanat* starts in a water bringing layer....... In the upper section, the *qanat* collects through one or more galleries; in the lower section, it conducts the water through dry layer to the spot where it reaches the surface. From this point it continues as an open channel".[376]

In this type of artificial irrigation (*karez*) wells were dug at particular distances, these wells were then connected by underground channels, sloping downwards ultimately to emerge in the open on the lower ground, where the water was used for irrigation.[377] Babur reports that this sort of irrigation was undertaken in Ghazni.[378]

Another important device was the Persian wheel or the *Saqiya*. This was a wooden machine and represented a notable example of pin-drum gearing. It was enthusiastically described by Babur, who had apparently never seen it in Central Asia and Afghanistan by the 16th century. It was the principal means to water-lift in the Indus and trans-Januma regions. Babur first saw the device at Bhera, Western Panjab in 1519.[379] In his memoirs he gives a scientific description of it and states that it

ed. Percy Sykes, London, 1927, 2 vols.

[376] Ann K.S. Lambton, *Landlords and Peasants in Persia,* London, 1953, pp. 216-217, L.W. Adamec, p.316.

[377] See Irfan Habib, '*Science and Technology*', in *Central Asian Civilization,* p.468; Elphinstone, I, pp.397-8.

[378] *Baburnama*, I, p. 218.

[379] *Ibid.*, p. 388.

was in use in Lahore, Dipalpur and parts of western Punjab.[380] Mughal miniatures of Akbar's reign vividly depict this device. They show that the right-angled gearing was obtained by means of pin-drum gearing and that the gear-wheels and shaft were of wood. Three very clear depiction of Persian wheel are shown in the miniatures contained in the volume of Nizami's *Khamsa* that Akbar commissioned, A.D. 1592-95.[381]

At Peshawar and the area to the east of the Indus, the Persian wheel was in use for obtaining water. In few other places water was drawn from wells but at Peshawar from rivers, on the bank of the river the device was erected.[382] The use of Persian wheel or *Saqiya* was of considerable significance for irrigation in the more arid tracts where water had to be lifted from extreme depth. Therefore, this device had immensely contributed to the extension of cultivation.[383]

The device consisted of wood, rope and clay pots, and combined the drew-bar for circular horizontal drive from animal power, pin drum-gearing for converting it into vertical drive. The pots were borne on a belt i.e. 'potgar land' that provided continuous water flow and a braking lever.[384] Babur failed to see it anywhere in Central Asia.

[380] *Ibid.*, II, 486-7; W.H. Moreland, *India at the Death of Akbar,* London, 1983, pp. 1-.
[381] S.P. Verma, *Art and Material Culture in the paintings of Akbar's Court,* Delhi, 1978, p.103; Irfan Habib, 'Technology and Economy of Mughal India', *The Indian Economic and Social History Review,* vol., xvii, No. 1, Jan-March 1980, pp. 1-6.
[382] Elphinstone, I, p. 399.
[383] Irfan Habib, 'Changes in Technology in Medieval India', *Studies in History,* vol. II, No. 1, 1980, pp. 15-20.
[384] *Central Asian Civilization,* p. 469.

Water-mill (*Asya*) was more a common feature of Central Asia than that of India. The use of water as a source of power was quite a common element in Central Asia. The water-mill of Central Asia was of the ungeared type with a horizontal water-wheel (i.e. with a vertical water shaft, the so-called 'Norse mill'). The device is not apparently described by the sources of our period. The watermills of Afghanistan are well defined by Elphinstone in the early 19th century. "The wheel is horizontal, and the feathers are disposed obliquely, so as to resemble the wheel of a smoke-jack. It is within the mill, and immediately below the mill-stone, which turns on the same spindle with the wheel. The water is introduced into the mill by a trough, so as to fall on the wheel. The wheel itself is not more than four feet in diameter. This sort of mill is used all over Afghanistan, Persia and Turkistan".[385] Although water mills were not used in India but it was found at few places in Kashmir.

There were few tracts of land which were moist enough for cultivation. These lands were called *Lalmi* or *Kushkabah* which in Pashtu means 'grown without irrigation'. *Lalmi* crops depended entirely on the rainfall.[386] For the cultivation of wheat which was the chief grain of the province, the land had to be watered before it was ploughed. It was ploughed deeper than was usual in India and with a heavier plough. But a pair of oxen was quite sufficient for the job.[387]

---

[385] Elphinstone, I, p. 401.
[386] *Baburnama*, II, p. 488.
[387] Elphinstone, I, p. 399.

6. Taxation:

Babur mentions that agriculture in the Kabul principality was not very productive and many villages lying at the foot-hill of Hindu Kush mountains or those situated in the remote areas paid no taxes.[388] He further states that, the total income of Kabul, from the cultivated lands, the nomads and the trade (*Vilayat, Sehara-nashin and Tamgha*) was eight lakhs of *Shahrukhis*.[389]

The principal source of rural taxes was the land revenue, which was assessed on the produce according to the fixed proportions, which varied with the nature of the land, and was different in different parts of the principality. As has already been mentioned that there were two types of lands: *rudi* and *lalmi*. The *rudi* land was irrigated artificially from rivers or canals while the *lalmi* depended on rain for irrigation. On the *rudi* lands the land revenue was one fourth of the produce and on the *lalmi* lands it was one tenth.[390] Some Afghan tribes, were not subjected to this mode of assessment, but paid a fixed sum annually.[391] Every tribes of the Afghan race dwelling in Kabul had to furnish a contingent of troops to the royal army.

---

[388] *Baburnama*, I, pp. 214-215. There were many fruit producing villages. Although few of them paid taxes but not all of them were taxed.

[389] *Ibid.*, p. 221. A *shahrukhis* was a silver coin worth two fifth of the later Mughal rupee. One rupee was equal to 2.5 *shahrukhis; Cf.* Mohibbul Hasan, p. 158. The silver coins followed the Central Asian *dirham* in weight and form and were called *shahrukhis* after Shah Rukh, the son of Timur.

[390] Raverty, p. 425.

[391] Elphinstone, II, pp. 258-59.

In the Kabul principality, the tribal population did not permit the enforcement of the elaborate process of revenue assessment and collection. The principality had *nasaq* system of revenue realization. It was essentially a method of assessment based on previous records showing the revenue demand for the last ten or twelve years. It can also be inferred that it did not involve measurement. It was only in Peshawar and the plain around the city that the system of *malguzari* or *ryatgiri* was applied.[392] The Emperor Babur, after the conquest of Kabul in 1504, imposed a tax of 30,000 ass-loads or *kharwar* of grain on Kabul but later on, when better acquainted with the country, he found that the levy was exorbitant. He tells us that Kabul was a small country and agriculture was not very productive.[393] In 1519, an impost of 4000 ass- loads of grain of rice for the use of his army was imposed on the people of Kahraj valley in eastern Afghanistan. He reports that in consequence these "rustic mountain folk were ruined."[394] Manucci also reports that Kabul yielded little revenue.[395]

In and around the region south and south-east of Kabul, the Afghan tribes were the principal tax payers. In most of these areas and in Qalat-Tarnauk to the north Qandahar the large amount of tax was paid in the form of sheep. The total annual collection of sheep from these localities amounted to 26,421 heads.[396] Babur describes that he collected a large tribute in the form of sheep and horses from the Sultan Masudi

---

[392] *Khulastat-ut Twarikh*, pp. 85-86.

[393] *Ibid.*, pp. 203, 228. The impost was excessive and the province was devastated by this collection.

[394] *Ibid.*, pp. 313-74.

[395] Manucci, II, p. 426.

[396] *Ain*, I, pp. 588-89.

Hazaras. He reports that the Hazaras, who had been raiding the roads near Ghazni and Gardez, were always reluctant to pay tribute.[397]

As is mentioned above the taxes were obtained from agriculture, domesticated animals and trade. Agricultural taxes were of two kinds: *ushr* and *kharaj*. The ushr was levied principally on fruit production and *kharaj* was levied on the production of grains. The source also refers to a tax known as *savaim* (literally meaning flocks), which was levied on animals, including horses and camels as well as sheep, goats and cattle. This tax was collected in kind, e.g. one sheep in flocks of 40 to 120; two in flocks of 120 to 200, etc.[398] Babur informs us that he collected as many as four to five hundred sheep and from twenty to twenty five horses from the Hazaras.[399]

To conclude, the agrarian economy in Kabul was known for the production of food grains and fruits. Substantial tribal communities were pastoralists, and survived through cattle rearing. The *suba* provided a lot of revenues to the Mughal State, and while the state levied several taxes, the bulk of its resources came from the land revenue. (See Appendix-B for the revenue statistics)

[397] *Baburnama*, I, p. 228.
[398] Stephen F. Dale, *The Garden of the Eight Paradises: Babur and the culture of Empire in Central Asia, Afghanistan, and India (1483-1530)*, Leiden, 2004, pp. 193-194.
[399] *Baburnama*, I, pp. 252-253.

Appendix-B

Revenue Statistics of the Kabul *Suba*:

Emperor Babur in his memoirs set down the revenue of Kabul whether obtained from the cultivated land, from the inhabitants of open country and from *tamgha*[400]* impost (inland toll) – *vilayat, sehra nashin* and *tamgha* around eight lakhs of *Shahrukhis.*[401] As the *Akbarshahi* rupee was equivalent to 2.5 *Shahrukhis,* according to *Ain* the amount comes to three lakhs and twenty thousand rupees.[402]

$$1 \text{ Rupee} = 2.5 \; Shahrukhis$$
$$1 \quad ,, \quad = 40 \; Dams$$

At the close of the sixteenth century, Abul Fazl who is believed to have the best information on matters concerned with revenues, estimated the amount at 6,73,06,983 *dams* (1,682,674.9 Rs.). The increase he attributes to the improved state of cultivation and the efficiency of the officers serving Akbar. It is also worth noting that the revenues of Peshawar

---

[400] *Tamgha* means customs duties. *Tamgha* was the main revenue source of the *Suba* Kabul. A large proportion of the total revenue extraction from Kabul probably came from commerce. Agriculture in this *Suba* was not very productive.

[401] *Baburnama,* 1971, f. 140 a; p. 221.

[402] *Ain,* I, p. 594.

and Hashtnagar (a *tahsil* of it) were not included in the previous account.[403]

For fiscal purposes the Kabul *suba,* in the same manner as other *subas,* was divided into fiscal units called *mahals.* The *mahal* was a purely fiscal division.[404] It was done to ease the task of revenue collection under different head at different places in the city. The Kabul *sarkar* contained twenty two *mahals.* The total revenue from these *mahals* amounted to 80,507,465 *dams.* The city of Kabul constituted into seven *mahals.* Abul Fazl informs us that the assessed revenue of the city of Kabul amounted to 12, 75,841 *dams.*[405]

Irfan Habib in the *Agrarian System of Mughal India* has given in detail the revenue statistics of various *subas* of the Mughal India but the statistics for the province of Kabul, Qandahar, Balkh and Badakhshan are not tabulated. I have tried to collect the revenue statistics of the Mughal *suba* of Kabul and have compiled its revenue from the same sources initially utilized and listed by him. The works like *Majalis-us-Salatin* and *Bayaz-i-Khushbui* mention the revenue of the *suba* in *dam* but these figures are to be treated carefully as they include Kashmir within the *suba* of Kabul as well.

The following table presents the statistics for the *suba* of Kabul serially in chronological order. These figures have been collected from the 16th and 17th centuries sources.

---

[403]   *Ain,* I, p. 94; also see *Ain* tr. II, p.413, footnote.

[404]   H.H. Wilson, Glossary *of Judicial and Revenue Terms... of British India,* London, 1875, pp. 318-319. *Mahal* is called an estate. Any parcel of land which may be separately assessed with the public revenue is termed as *mahal.* It is a division of district yielding revenue according to assessment.

[405]   *Ain,* I, p. 594.

Table –3.I

(Assessed in *Dam* over different period, *Ain's* figure as base)

S. No.	Year	*Jama dam*	Index	Source
1	1595-96	8,09,07,465	100.00	*Ain-i-Akbari*, MS. British Museum, Add. 6552, R. No. 298, p. 258 b.
2	Pre 1627	25,00,00,000	309.00	*Majalisu-s-Salatin*, Or. 1903, R. No. 19, ff. 114 a-115 a.
3	1628-36	27,37,97,856	338.41	*Bayaz-i-Khwushbui*, MS. I.O. 828, R. No. 194, ff.180-181 a.
4	1634-35	15,00,00,000	185.40	*Amal-i-Salih* or *Shahjahan nama* II, p.427.
5	1633-38	11,36,98,362	140.53	*Farhang-i-Kardani* Abdus Salam Farsiya, 85/315, ff. 19 a – 20 b.
6	1646-47	16,00,00,000	197.76	*Badshah nama*, II, pp. 809-11
7	1638-56	13,09,00,000	161.79	*Siyaqnama*, p. 102.
8	1638-56	32,72,500	4.05	Francois Bernier, p. 457.
9	1638-56	4 or 5 million a year		Jean de Thevenot, *The Travels of Thevenat and Careri*, p. 81.
10	1646-56	10,01,00,000	123.73	*Dasturu-l-Amal-i-Navisandagi*, c. 1646-48, Add. 6641, f. 168 b
11	c.1667	15,76,25,680	194.83	*Miratu-l-Alam*, MSS. No. 314/85, p. 216.

12	1687-c.1691	16,10,49,954	199.05	*Zawabit-i-Alamgiri*, Or. 1641, British Museum, Add. 6598 R. No. 62, CAS, Aligarh, f. 12 a.
13	1695	2,65,20,000	33.76	*Khulasatu-t-Twarikh*, p. 88.
14	1701-02	20,21,61,642	249.87	*Dasturu-l-Amal-i-Shahjahani*, Add. 6588, R. No. 56, MS. Sir Sulaiman, Aligarh, ff. 19 a-23 a.
15	1707	32,07,250	40.63	Nicolao Manucci, II, p. 414.
16	1654-5	9,70,78,000	119.99	*Daturu-l-Asr-i-Alamgiri*, Aurangzeb's 3rd R. Y. R. No. 53, CAS, Aligarh, f. 116 a.
17	C1709	11,10,39,954	137.25	Jagjivan das, *Muntakhabu-t-Twarikh*, Add. 26, 253, ff. 51 a-54 a.
18	1700-11	9,70,78,000	119.99	*Dasturu-l-Amal-i-Alamgiri*, British Museum, Add. 6598, ff. 115 a-116 a.

Table – 3.2

The following table presents the Revenue returns of the *Suba* Kabul at various periods in Rupees. These figures are taken from Edward Thomas, *Revenue Resource of the Mughal Empire*. (Kashmir and Qandahar are not included).[406]

1594 Akbar	1648 ShahJahan	1654 Aurangzeb	1663-66 Bernier's Return	Date Uncertain Official Return	1697 Aurangzeb	1707 Aurangzeb
80,71,024	40,00,000	40,26,950	32,72,500	40,25,983	32,07,250	40,25,983

Table-3.3 presents the revenue of all the *tumans* of the Kabul *suba*. These figures have been collected from the *Ain* MS. Add. 7652.[407]

Table-3.3

S.No.	Name of *Tuman*	Revenue in *dam*
1	Bigram	96,92,410
2	Ningnahar	1,18,94,003
3	Mandrawar	26,84,880
4	Alishang	37,01,150
5	Alingar	15,44,670
6	Loghar	31,93,214
7	Badrao	4,13,885
8	Alasai	6,00,000
9	Panjshir	4,21,940
10	Bangash	4,21,940

---

[406]   Edward Thomas, *Revenue Resource of the Mughal Empire: 1593-1707,* London, 1871, p. 52. Also see Thomas Edward, 'The Revenue of the Mughal Empire in India', *JASB,* 1881, II, pp. 147-150.

[407]   *Ain,* MSS, Add. 7652, CAS, Deptt of History, Aligarh, R..N. 297, I, f. 292 a.

11	Kohat	7,01,620
12	Naghr/Naghz	8,54,000
13	Gardez	20,30,002
14	Maidan	16,06,799
15	Ghazni	37,68,642
16	Farmal	3,25,716
17	Daman-i-Koh	1,64,785
18	Ghorband	15,74,720
19	Zuhak Bamian	8,61,750

The various *Dastur-ul-Amals* or administrative manuals give a list of the *mahals* of Kabul at different periods, which do not always tally with one another. These figures mentioned in some of the Persian works are given below in Table-3.4

Table-3.4

S.No.	Year	No. of *Mahals*	Source
1	c.1595	22 *mahals*	*Ain-i-Akbari,* Br. Mus. Add 6552 R.No. 298, p.259b
2	1633-38	65 *mahals*	*Farhang-i-Kardani,* Aligarh MS, Abdus Samad Farsiya, 315/85 f.20a
3	c.1667	40 *mahals*	*Miratu-l-Alam,* Aligarh MS, 315/85 f.216
4	1687-c.1691	48 *mahals*	*Zawabit-i-Alamgiri,* Add, 6598, or 1641, R.No.62, f.56
5	1701-1702	48 *mahals*	*Dastur-ul-Amal-i-Shahjahani,* British Library Add.6588, R.No. 56, f.23a
6	c.1709	48 *mahals*	*Muntakhab-ut-Twarikh,* Add.26253 Jag Jivan Das R.No. 21, f.53a
7	1700-11	28 *mahals*	*Dasturu-l-Amal-i-Alamgiri,* R.No.53, f.116a

The *jama* of the revenue statistics is the amount against which *jagirs* were assigned; these were in a sense unreal in contradistinction to *hasil* which are figures of actual collection. The fact that according to Mughal regulations of the Rule of one fifth applied in the Kabul *suba* implied that *jagirdar's* expenditure was at a higher level here than in other *subas*.[408]

Lahori clearly states that *mansabdars* posted in Balkh, Badakhshan and Kabul were required to muster their contingents according to the rule of one-fifth. This is clearly stated in a *Farman* or *Dastur-al Amal* issued in 27th year of Shahjahan's reign.[409]

For these reasons the *jama* of Kabul is unlikely to have varied with production and prices. This may explain the enormous variations in its *jama* compared to the adjacent *subas* like Lahore, Thatta and Multan as shown in the *Agrarian System of the Mughal Empire*.[410] Early in the 18th century there might have been a reduction in *jama* simply to ease the condition of the *jagirdars*, who by this means could get a larger area in *jagir* against their sanctioned pay.

---

[408] *Mirat* Supplement, I, p. 228. (Shahjahan's *Farman* 27th R. Y.)
[409] Lahori, II, pp. 505-7; *Mirat,* I, p. 228.
[410] *Agrarian System of Mughal India*, pp. 458-459.

Chapter - IV

Trade And Commerce

1. Foreign Trade:

Strategically placed at the point of interaction between a thriving overland trade between South and Central (or and West) Asia, Kabul derived considerable resources from trade and commerce. It was a major emporium of overland trade, and prospered by taxing the flow of merchandise between northern India and Central Asia. Several recent studies have shown that India's overland trade to the Central Asia and Persia, through Kabul constituted the life line of several Asian countries, and the sheer volume of this trade sustained several communities and petty kingdoms in the region.[411] Communities of merchants, artisans and even petty producers found their sustenance through this trade, centered on Kabul. The crucial position of Kabul in the intra-Asian overland trade made it the home of a wide variety of merchant and artisan

---

[411] Stephen Fredrick Dale, *Indian Merchant and Eurasian Trade: 1600-1750*, New Delhi, 1994; Satish Chandra, 'Commercial activities of the Mughal Emperors during the 17th century', in *Essays on the Medieval Indian History*, Delhi, 1987, pp. 163-69.

communities, and gave the place considerable diversity and a truly cosmopolitan character.[412]

In his memoir Babur mentions that Kabul was an excellent trade mart and the entrepot of a great trade. He gives a vivid account of the trade and commerce which passed through Kabul. The country, he records was a profitable market for commodities. From Hindustan, 10, 15 or 20,000 loads of merchandise reached Kabul annually.[413]

The principal foreign trade of Kabul was with Hindustan, Persia and Turkistan.[414] Thevenot states that "the Province lies so conveniently for traffic that what is wanting in it is brought from all parts".[415] But the trade with Hindustan was by far the most considerable, though it declined later on in the period. The trade with Hindustan was more divided. Kabul's trade with the Punjab and Northern India was centered on Peshawar, while the trade with Rajputana and the places still further south, was based in Shikarpur, Bhawalpur and Multan. The exports to Hindustan were principally horses, furs, shawls, Multani chintz, madder, almond, pistachio nuts, walnuts and a variety of fruits. In Kabul there was such a surplus of fruit production that the fruits were exported, and India received a great variety of fruits from Kabul.[416]

---

[412] Monserrate, p. 150; Fray Sebastian Manrique, *Travels, 1629-43*, tr. Luard assisted by H. Hosten, II, pp. 221-22.

[413] *Baburnama*, I, p. 202.

[414] Thevenot, p. 80. The country of Uzbeks alone exported yearly above 'threescore' thousand horses there.

[415] *Ibid.*

[416] *Tuzuk-i-Jahangiri*, p. 55; Pelsaert, p. 35. He also confirms that even during the time of Jahangir all these varieties of fruits were imported to Agra.

The fruits were generally dried but a large quantity was also fresh.[417] The fruits exported in this manner were apple, pears, and pomegranate.[418] During the winters in Kabul grapes, pomegranate, apricot, apple, almonds, quinches, pear, peach, plum, sinjid were produced in abundance. During summers the region supplied oranges, citron, amluk (diospyrus lotus) and sugar-cane.[419] According to Bernier, every year many of camels loaded with fresh fruits reached imperial centre from Kabul, because in India fruits were insufficient and inferior in quality.[420] Kabul was especially famous for grapes—*sahibi* and *kishmishi*.[421] Another important type of grapes was known as *husaini*. It was seedless and long in shape. It was exported in round, flat wooden box.[422] From September to October till April grapes were brought in India with cherries which were termed as *shahalu* by Akbar.[423] Abul Fazl states that musk melons in plenty were brought from Kabul to Lahore. He also repeats Babur's observation that Kabul melons were not as good in taste as that of Persia, Balkh and Bukhara. Babur confirms this fact and adds that the melons raised from seed brought from Khurasan were tolerable. He also praises those of

---

[417] Elphinstone, I, p. 383.

[418] *Khulasat-ut Twarikh,* p. 86. The seedless variety of pomegranate produced in Jalalabad was exported to India.

[419] *Ibid.; Baburnama*, I, pp. 202-3, 210-11.

[420] Francois Bernier, *Travels in the Mogul Empire: 1656-1668*, First Indian edn., New Delhi, 1983, pp. 118-119, 397; Samuel Purchas, *Purchas his Pilgrims*, London, 1625, Glasgow, 1905, IV, p. 57; Manucci, II, p. 186;

[421] *Tuzuk-i-Jahangiri*, p. 55

[422] Vigne, p. 172. *Husaini* grapes were as good as those of the south Europe.

[423] *Ain*, I, p. 67; *Tuzuk-i-Jahangiri*, p. 55.

Bukhara, but those of Akhsi, a district north of Jaxartes, were beyond comparison.[424] According to Vigne the red melon of Kabul was not better than those grew in India and though the white one was sweet and delicious but was inferior to Bukhara melons.[425] Among the dry fruits sent to India, according to Bernier, were almonds, pistachios, walnuts, raisins, prunes and apricot.[426]

One of the chief articles of commerce of Kabul was asafoetida, of which about two hundred mounds gathered annually from plants.[427] Vast quantities of asafoetida were exported to India, where it was a favourite ingredient in the cookery.[428]

The caravans heading towards Kabul used to carry from Hindustan slaves (*barda*), white cloth, sugar candy, refined sugar, sandal wood, aromatic roots, cotton textiles, muslin, brocade, other fine manufactures and all kind of calicoes,.[429] Cotton was one of the significant Mughal imports to Kabul, which was in great demand in both Safavid Iran and Uzbek Turan. Though cotton was cultivated in all three territories, but northern India's extensive tracts of arable land had a large productive capacity than of those arid neighbouring regions. Cotton cultivation was confined to the hot climates and most of the cloth of that material used in that part, was imported

---

[424] *Ibid.*, p. 590. Also see tr. II, p. 405.

[425] Vigne, p. 172.

[426] Bernier, p. 249.

[427] Pelsaert, *Jahangir's India*, pp. 31, 48; Moorcroft and Trebeck, II, p. 395; George Watt, *Dictionary of the Economic Products of India,* Delhi, Second Reprint, 1972, III, p. 329.

[428] Elphinstone, I, p. 395.

[429] *Baburnama*, I, p. 202; Manrique, p. 180; *E F I, 1622-23*, pp. 216-33.

ready woven from India.[430] Agra was famous for calico and chintz. All these varieties of cotton were brought to Agra from regional markets and then were sent to Kabul through land-route.[431] Among Indian commodities together with sugar, indigo formed one of the principal export items. Indigo was purchased at Agra by merchants who carried them to Kabul.[432] It was probably the demand and its potential importance as a cash crop for Iran that the Safavid ruler shah Abbas attempted to introduce the cultivation of this widely used textile dye in his Mazandaran province, along the Caspian shore, where the humid climate was suitable for its cultivation. His efforts were apparently unsuccessful in curtailing the flow of Indian indigo into his country.[433]

Babur does not mention spices among the items exported to Kabul from Hindustan. Perhaps it was carried to Persia and the areas beyond via Qandahar, which was also an important route. But during the first half of eighteenth century, Burnes estimates that spices about a thousand camel-loads were consumed yearly in Kabul.[434] The spices were carried over-sea from the Malabar Coast and Bombay to Karachi and then were

---

[430] Elphinston, I, pp. 384, 394; Dale, pp. 21, 23. Cotton textiles one of India's premier exports since Roman times.

[431] Purchas, III, p. 84; Thevenot, pp. 55-56; *E F I, 1637-41*, p. 134.

[432] Mundy, II, p. 234; Manucci, II, 418.

[433] Pelsaert, pp. 30-31; Dale, p. 22. Sugar and Indigo are both listed as Indian exports to Iran in R. W. Ferrier, "An English View of Persian Trade in 1618", *Journal of the Economic and Social History of the Orient XIX/2* (1976), pp. 182-214.

[434] Burnes, II, pp. 414, 416. "*Reports and Papers, Political, Geographical and Commercial*", Calcutta, 1839, p. 56. He gives one of the first detailed reports of Indian Indigo exports to Bukhara.

sent through land-route to Kabul. Some of the best varieties of spices from India were exported to Samarqand.[435]

One of the most favoured and chief exports from India to this region were Indian slaves, both Hindus and Muslims, then these slaves were sent to the bazaars of Central Asia in a number of ways. Some of them were taken as prisoners of wars, some in exchange for Central Asian horses while others were captured during the raids on trading caravans.[436] The manuscript *Rauzat-ur Rizwan va hadikat al- gilman,* written by Badaruddin Kashmiri during the reign of Abdullah Khan Uzbek informs us that the skilled slaves were much sought after Indian commodity. Timur after his invasion of Delhi had taken many skilled slaves and stone-masons to Samarqand to work on the royal building, some of them were employed in the construction of his mosque in Samarqand.[437] Abdul Abbas Muhammad Talib, the author of *Matlab at-Talib* also speaks of Indian slaves in this region. During the eighteenth century, the slave trade entered a new phase of expansion, and India ceased to be an important source of supply, and the trade drifted to

---

[435]   Surendra Gopal, Cited in Surendra Gopal, *"Indians in Central Asia 16th and 17th Centuries",* Presidencial Address, Medieval India Section of the Indian History Congress, 52nd Session, New Delhi, 1992, p. 12.

[436]   Muzaffar Alam, *"Trade, State Policy And Regional Change: Aspects of Mughal-Uzbek Commercial Relations, C. 1550-1750",* Journal of the Economic and Social History of the Orient, Vol. XXXVII, Part I, 1994, p. 207.

[437]   R. G. Mukhninova, *Sotsialnaya Differentsiatsia Naseleniya Gorodov Uzbekistana,* Tashkent, 1985, p. 120. Cited in S. Gopal, *"Indians in Central Asia,* pp. 225-226; Trade, State Policy And Regional Change, p. 207.

the markets of Bukhara, Khiva and Kashghar and other parts of Central Asia.[438]

As far as the Central Asian trade is concerned Babur informs us that every year 7 to 10,000 caravans came to Kabul from Turkistan, Kashghar,[439] Farghana, Samarqand, Hisar, Balkh, Bukhara and Badakhshan. The merchants remained unhappy even if they made a profit of 300 to 400 percent.[440] The work *Sharaf-nama-i-Shahi* mentions that a large number of Indian merchants from north India and Bengal were involved in the trading enterprises of this region.[441] A wide range of textiles as far as from Bengal, Gujarat and Khambayat such as chints of different types, plain coarse calico (*fota*) and fine cloth of Thanesar, silk brocade (*jamawar*) and fine calico (*solagazi*) etc. were brought by the Indian merchants to the Uzbek territory.[442] The principal imports from Central Asia were silk, semi-silk textiles, crimson velvet, carpet bronze and copper utensils, knife, armour, Bukharan bow etc.[443] Other items of import besides horses, were beavers (castors), skin, musk, cochineal, cutlery, rubies, gold and silver together with *urmuk*, a fine cloth made of camel's wool as well as lamb's skin were imported from Bukhara.[444] Indian merchants bought

[438] Gommans, p. 28.
[439] Finch, Foster, pp. 168-69. The caravans from Kashghar took two to three months to reach Kabul.
[440] *Baburnama*, I, p. 202.
[441] Hafiz Tanish bin Mir Muhammad Bukhari, *Sharaf-nama-i-Shahi*, Institute of Oriental Studies, St. Petersburg Ms. No. D88, f. 451, cited in Muzaffar Alam, *Trade State Policy And Regional Change,* JESHO, Vol. XXXVII, Part, I, p. 205.
[442] *Ibid.*
[443] Bernier, p. 203.
[444] Elphinstone, I, pp. 384-385. Few of the two-hundred camels

these Central Asian goods to Kabul in order to take them to Indian markets.[445]

A variety of fresh fruits such as apples melons, quinches, grapes etc., and dried fruits such as almond, pistachio, raisin etc. were also brought from Farghana, Bukhara and Badakhshan to Kabul and were then sent to India. For almonds Babur says that Kand-i-badam (Village of the Almond) a dependency of Khujand[446] produced excellent almonds. All were sent to Hindustan and Hormuz.[447]

Bernier has stated that a large supply of dry fruits from Balkh, Bukhara and Samarqand reached India.[448] A new dimension was added during the reign of Jahangir and even fresh fruits from the region started to be sent to India, since he loved them.[449] The imports of fruits to India were more during Jahangir's reign than his father. Jahangir writes in his memoirs that though his father Akbar was fond of melons, pomegranates and grapes, yet "during his time the Kariz melons, which are the best of Khurasan, and pomegranates from Yazd and Samarqand grapes which are celebrated throughout the world, had never been brought to Hindustan".[450] Though melons from

---

were also imported from Qazak country to Kabul.

[445] Manucci, II, p. 426.

[446] *Baburnama*, I, pp. 8-9. Khujand was situated to the west of Andijan and in east of Samarqand. Kand-i-badam was five or six *yighach* (18 m.) east of Khujand. The former was not a *qasba* or township.

[447] *Ibid.*.

[448] Bernier, p. 203; *Ain*, I, p. 67.

[449] *Tuzuk-i-Jahangiri*, p. 132. These were so many that all the servants of the court had them.

[450] *Ibid.* In the beginning of the month of day [October 1615] merchants came from Persia and brought pomegranates of Yazd

Badakhshan and pomegranates from Kabul were sent to India but they bore no comparison with the Yazd pomegranates and Kariz melons. During his time the markets of Delhi and Lahore were full of different varieties of fruits sent there from the Central Asia cities via Kabul. They arrived very fresh and ripe.[451] Bernier also noted that fresh grapes, black and white, wrapped in cotton were brought from Balkh, Bukhara and Samarqand. Fruits like pears, apples, melons were imported in large quantity throughout the year. He goes on to say that large quantities of fresh fruits from the Central Asian cities (Balkh, Bukhara and Samarqand) were supplied to Delhi, which was eaten all the winter.[452]

During the seventeenth century the number of Indian merchants trading in Central Asia increased further. Towards the close of the sixteenth century political stability was established in Central Asia. Akbar had cordial relations with Abdullah Khan Uzbek as is evident from the exchange of envoys between them. Indian enjoyed easier access to Central Asia.[453] The Mughal control over Kabul gave impetus to the overland trade. Furthermore, the war in seas around India diminished the maritime Indo-Persian trade and thus facilitated the caravan trade on the northwest frontier of India passing through Kabul to the Central Asia. Anthony Jenkinson reporting on the trade of the region noted, "There

---

and melon from Kariz, which are the best of the Khurasan melons....as my revered father had a great liking for fruit I was very grieved that such fruits had not come to Hindustan in his victorious time.

[451]   *Tuzuk-i-Jahangiri*. p. 3; Manucci, II, p. 391.

[452]   Bernier, pp. 118, 249.

[453]   Badauni, II, pp. 278, 362, 365-66.

is yearly great resort of merchants to this cities of Boghar, which travel in great caravans from the countries there about adjoining as India, Persia, Balgh, Russia with diverse others... the chief commodities that are brought thither out of these aforesaid countries, are the following:

> "The Indian doe bring fine whites, which the Tartars doe all about their heads, and all the kinds of whites, which serve for apparel made of cotton wool and crasca, but gold, silver, precious stones and spices they bring none. The Indian carry from Boghar against wrought silkes, red hides, slaves and horses, with such like... I offered to barter with merchants of those countries, which came from the farthest part of India, even from the counties of Bengala, and the river Ganges, to give them Kersies for their commodities but they would not barter for such commodities as cloath".[454]

All the nineteenth century travellers agree however that the Kabul trade with Central Asia as a whole was lucrative, though it declined to some extent when compared to the previous century.[455]

---

[454] Jenkinson Anthony, *Early Voyages and Travel to Russia and Persia*, ed. By Delmar Morgan and C. H. Coot, Hakluyt Society, 1886, London, II, p. 88; Purchas, XII, p. 24.

[455] Burnes, III, pp. 315-65; Elphinstone, I, pp. 232, 383; Raverty, pp. 659-60; Mohan Lal, p. 102; Vigne, pp. 425-41.

The export to china were almost the same as those to Bukhara, while the imports were woollens of a particular kind, Chinese silk and satin, porcelain, raw silk and gold dust etc.[456]

Throughout most of the sixteenth, seventeenth and eighteenth centuries India had a vibrant trade network with West and Central Asia. By the second half of the sixteenth century Mughal emperor Akbar (1556-1605) and Safavid Shah Abbas (1587-1629) had jointly created conducive conditions for commerce in the Indo-Persian region.[457] A European traveler Sir John Chardin, who had stayed in Iran between 1666 and 1677, mentioned that Iran was a dry, barren and mountainous region. He goes on to add that there was a consistent demand for Mughal India's products in Safavid Iran because of the scarce resources and poor productivity of agriculture.[458] The exports from India primarily consisted of food and non-food crops, sugar, indigo and cotton textiles. According to an estimate in 1661 the value of cotton textiles exported overseas to Iran from the port of Surat was one million rupees, it is expected that the same amount was sent overland via Qandahar in the same year.[459] Chardin observed that "The Persian do not understand to make cloth [although] they make very fine and very light Felt Tufts. They make also calico cloth very reasonable; but they make none fine, because they have it cheaper out of the Indies than they can make it.....they understand also the painting of linen, but not so well as the

---

[456]   *Ibid.*, II, p. 315; Elphinstone, I, pp. 385-386.

[457]   K. N. Chaudhari, *The Trading World of Asia and the English East India Company, 1660-1760,* Cambridge, 1978. Cited in Dale, p. 4.

[458]   Sir John Chardin, *Travels in Persia 1673-1677,* Reprinted, N.Y., 1988, P. 128; Dale, p. 16.

[459]   Chaudhari, *The Trading World of Asia,* pp. 196-97.

Indians, because they buy in the Indies the finest painted linen so cheap, that they would get nothing by improving themselves in that manufacture".[460]

Another significant export item to Iran was tobacco, which began to be cultivated in India during Mughal Period. The bulk of these supply was shipped either overseas from the Surat port to Bandar Abbas or overland via Qandahar.[461]

While the chief articles of export from Iran were specialty crops which included the widely used food flavouring, medicinal herbs, asafoetida that was grown in the eastern parts of Iran and the luxury manufactures such as silken stuffs, a kind of cotton manufactures of various colours called *kudduk* and silken handkerchiefs which were mostly used by the Mughal elites.[462]

In Kabul both the caravans from India and those from Central Asia arrived simultaneously during June and July. Without much loss of time the merchants again left Kabul for the Indian market in October or for northern Afghanistan and Turan in mid-April and mid-November because during most of the winter the Hindu Kush passes were blocked by snow, the merchants were forced to stay north of Amu Darya.[463] In the meantime they dealt with other Central Asian merchants from Khiva, and Kokand. At the beginning of spring the merchants chose going northward to Orenburg and coming southward to Kabul.[464] During the early years of 17th century the caravans for Central Asia started from Kabul, which usually consisted

---

[460] Chardin, *Travels in Persia*, pp. 278-79. Cited in Dale, p. 23.

[461] Tavernier, I, pp. 4-5; *English Factories*, 1642-1645, p. 85.

[462] Elphinstone, p. 385; Dale, pp. 21-22.

[463] Burnes, II, pp. 150-71.

[464] Gommans, p. 31.

of 500 persons with a long chain of beasts of burden, camels and wagons.

Finally it is difficult to quantify the volume of trade that passed between these countries. Jahangir in his memoirs refers to the transit duty (*sair jihat*) collected at Kabul annually amounted to 1,23,000,00 *dams* (Rs. 30,75,000), which he abolished at the time of his accession. The amount given by the emperor indicates that the volume of trade passing through Kabul route alone was quite large.[465] And though Kabul had very little of its own products (fresh fruits, some horses and some woollen goods) that it could furnish for outside markets but the gain from the above traffic and trading activities of merchants had provided Kabul with a means of regular and substantial income.[466] At the beginning of the 19th century, Alexander Burnes believed about 24,000 camel-loads of merchandise annually reached Kabul from Hindustan.[467] According to G.T. Vigne, besides the Luhanis, there were five or six other caravans which annually passed through Hindu Kush to Bukhara.[468] The Aleppo caravan usually consisted of loaded camels reaching Kabul twice or thrice a year.[469] Almost

---

[465]   *Tuzuk-i-Jahangiri*, pp. 21-22; See *Waqiyat-i-Jahangiri*, in Elliot and Dowson, *The History of India as told by its own Historian*, reprinted, New Delhi, 2001, VI, pp. 290-91.

[466]   H. K. Naqvi, *Urbanisation and Urban Centres Under the Great Mughals*, Shimla, 1972, p.81.

[467]   Burnes, II, p. 416, 429-432. Burnes was in Bukhara in 1832 and published his account in 1834.

[468]   Vigne, p. 70.

[469]   J. H. van Linschoten, *The Voyage of John Huyghen van Linschoten to the East Indies*, from the old English translation of 1598, ed. A. C. Burnell and P. A. Tiele, Hakluyt Society, London, 1885, vol. II, p. 316.

all the 19th century travelers visiting Kabul refer to the fact that the place was vibrant and lively; the shops full of goods and the *bazaars* buzzing with activity.[470]

2. Local Trade:

A substantial part of what Kabul produced was absorbed by the local demand.[471] The principal articles carried from the western part to the east were woollen, fur, madder and other fine articles of dress. From the east were carried loongis, silk, Multani chintz, mixed silk and cotton cloths of Bhuwalpur, together with indigo and some cotton.[472]

The Hazaras to the west of Kabul produced a kind of cloth from camel wool called *borak*. They sent it to the plain areas of the country. They also sent cattle and sheep. Ghee was also supplied by them, and they received salt, thread needle and other commodities, in return. Its need of corn, to feed it population was met by supplies drawn from Ghazni and Logar districts; rice was brought from Logar, Jalalabad, Lamghanat and Kunar.[473]

Iron was found in the mountains north of Kabul near Ghorband; these iron ore was brought in great quantities to Charikar, to be worked up for the market in Kabul.[474] Salt was scarce in Kabul and was brought from salt range. Timber came

---

[470]   Burnes, III, pp. 315-65; Elphinstone, I, pp. 232, 383; Raverty, pp. 659-60; Mohan Lal, p.102; Vigne, pp. 425-41.

[471]   Elphinstone, I, p. 386.

[472]   *Ibid.*

[473]   *Baburnama*, I, p. 210; Adamec, p. 316.

[474]   Rici, Commentary, A.D. 1610, cited by Wessels, Early *Jesuit Travellers*, p.17.

from Kurram and fruits from Daman Koh which produced them in abundance.[475] Wheat and barley were produced in Daman Koh and were then carried to the *sarkar* of Kabul.[476]

There were no date trees in the Kabul city but dates were sent to the city from south-west and south-east.[477]

3. Means of land transport

A land locked region, Kabul was deprived of navigable rivers, and the roads were quite unsuitable for wheeled carriages. Commerce in Kabul was necessarily carried on with the help of beasts of burden. It is worthy to note that bulk of merchandise and other commodities were carried on the back of packed animals. The various means of land transport were camels, horses, mules, ponies, asses, and bullocks. Among them camels were found to be the most suitable for the commercial purpose because of their strength and endurance.[478] The male camels were called *bughdi* and the female *jammaza,* they were known for their swiftness. Abul Fazl writes that camels were swifter than an arrow.[479] The *bughdis* were mainly used for carrying burdens. When the camels were loaded and travelled, they were generally formed into *qatars* (strings), each *qatar* consisted of five camels. The first camel of each *qatar* was called *peshang*; the second, *peshdara*; the third, *miyana qatar*;

[475]   Adamec, p. 316.
[476]   *Ain,* I, pp. 594-5; *Khulasat-ut Twarikh*, p. 86.
[477]   Burnes, I, p. 154.
[478]   *Ain,* I, p. 146; Elphinstone, I, p. 189.
[479]   *Akbarnama*, III, p. 44. Akbar in 1572-3 proceeded towards Gujarat on a she-camel.

the fourth, *dumdasht*; the last, *dumdar*.[480] It is mentioned that merchandise from Agra to distant places were sent in large camel- caravans.[481] The camels loaded with fruits fresh or dried came to India from Turkistan through Kabul.[482] The camels could easily pass the desert areas than the other animals of transportation.

The merchandise was carried on the backs of the camels which were owned by merchants and the carriers of the city. The merchants usually organized themselves in *qafilas*[483] because of the danger of theft, loot and plunder. Therefore, the merchants generally travelled in *qafilas* and sometimes waited for days to form a *qafila*. Insecurity on the routes and passes was a strong deterrent. Jenkinson noted that even though a caravan was assured safety, it was sometimes robbed by thieves.[484] The camels hired from particular tribes usually made their journey in company with the tribe to which they belonged and sometimes others were also attached to them for better safety. Each caravan had a hereditary chief called *qafila bashi* (a Turkish term meaning 'head of caravan'). He was assisted by eighty men and was to keep peace; settle disputes,

---

[480]   *Ain*, I, 146.

[481]   *E F I, 1618-21*, pp. 74-90; Withington, *Early Travels*, pp. 217-218; Pelsaert, p. 31. He states that in the beginning of 17th century, about 14,000 camels annually passed from India to Persia via Lahore-Qandahar route.

[482]   Manucci, II, p 391.

[483]   Henry Yule and A. C. Burnell, Hobson Jobson, *A glossary of Colloquial Anglo-Indian Works and Phrases*, ed. William Crook, London, 1903, p. 142. *Coffylen*- that is companies of people and camels.

[484]   Purchas, XII, p. 26.

appoint and post-guards, and collect money required paying the custom duties.[485]

Next important animals for carrying burden were mules and asses. The mule possessed strength of a horse and patience of an ass, and though it had not the intelligence of the former it had not the stupidity of the latter. The mules possessed more common sense than any other animal as they were known for not to forget the way it had once travelled.[486] They were well suited to the use of lower segment of population.

Like camels the mules were formed into *qatars* of five and had the same names, except the second mule of each *qatar,* which was called *bardast* instead of *peshdara*. The mules were the best animal for carrying loads and baggage and travelling over uneven ground as they had soft hooves.[487] Asses were used for carrying grains and manure from one place to other. In certain parts they were used in ploughing the land.[488]

During 16th and 17th centuries inferior horses were used for transport purposes. Horses in great number laden with dry fruits and other commodities used to pass through Kabul annually. The horses were employed for transport by merchants trading between Turkistan, Hindustan, and Khurasan.[489] Ponies were also used in carrying goods. A strong and useful breed of ponies, called *yabus,* was reared especially about Bamian. The *Yabu* a short and hardy animal was mostly

[485]   *Ibid.*, pp. 378-382. The *Qafila bashi* was more common with the Tajiks than with the Afghans, who often marched together without any chief or any regulation.

[486]   *Ain,* I, p. 152.

[487]   *Ibid.*

[488]   Elphinstone, I, pp. 189, 402.

[489]   Angus Hamilton, p. 243.

used as a beast of burden. Indeed this variety of horses was the chief means of transport throughout Kabul.[490] They were used to carry baggage and could bear a great load, but were not able to stand a long duration of hard work as mules.[491] The caravans going to Turkistan, however, rested on horses or ponies, probably on account of the mountainous routes.[492] All the merchandise was carried from one place to another by beasts of burden. There were specialized tribal communities who were trained in transporting merchandise from one place to another.[493]

4. Horse Trade:

Horses were needed for military purposes, as cavalry, and as a means of transport. It was the military role that determined the Mughal's demand for horses. Therefore, the demand for Central Asian horses never slackened in India.

Bernier, the French traveller (1658-67) put the figure at twenty-five thousand annually.[494] Towards the end of the seventeenth century, Manucci stated that Indian traders purchased horses of Balkh and Bukhara at Kabul numbering 1,00,000.[495] The trade in horses was considerable, both in

---

[490] H.W. Bellow, *Afghanistan – A Political Mission in 1857,* London, 1920, p.11.

[491] Elphinstone, I, pp. 189, 402.

[492] *Ibid.*, pp. 378-80.

[493] Elphinstone, I, p. 378.

[494] Bernier, p. 203.

[495] Manucci, II, pp. 390-91. The figure given by him appears an exaggerated one.

terms of number as well as value. Even during the fourteenth century Ibn Battuta found it very profitable.[496]

Babur tells us that there were no good horses in Hindustan.[497] A great number of horses were annually sold in Hindustan. The Kabul horses were in great demand in the Indian markets. All these horses, however, came from Central Asia. No horses were bred at Kabul (only by the rich for their own use). There were two types of horses mostly dealt in, one rather small but very stout, the other much larger and more valued on that account, although not so serviceable except for war. In most of Balkh and Bukhara the *Turki* or Turkomani breeds were sold and purchased.[498]

Throughout the Mughal period, horses had been by far the most significant import item from Kabul. The great breeding country in the Central Asia was Balkh, and from that place as also from the Turkoman country, lower down the Oxus River, a great proportion of the exported horses were brought. Kabul merchants mainly purchased their horses in Balkh and Bukhara. In these markets many of the horses were brought down by the Bukharian merchants from the surrounding steppes, where well-bred Turkomani horses were especially famous for their strength and endurance.[499] Ibn Battuta, writing in the 14th century informs us that the steppe land of Southern Russia was known for Tartari horses. These horses were exported to Hindustan by the traders who made a handsome profit out of it,[500] when these merchants reached

---

[496] Ibn Battuta, p. 145.
[497] *Baburnama*, II, p. 518.
[498] Elphinstone, I, p. 386.
[499] Burnes, II, pp. 271-275.
[500] Ibn Battuta, p. 145.

Kabul with their horses they fed them with forage. Forage for cattle was plentiful in this region. Grass was found to a great extent and was much liked by horses.[501] Kabul merchants in return for their merchandise purchased good breed *Turki* horses to sell them in India.[502] There they were taxed seven silver *dinars* (a silver *tanka*, the coin of 170 grain) for each horse.[503]

Nicolao Manucci writes that "Kabul abounds in good horses called *Turki* and it had a garrison of sixty thousand horses. The reason for this is that Kabul was situated near the kingdom of Persia".[504] Marco Polo describes that there were many fine horses in the kingdom of Persia. During eighteenth century, however the horse trade with Persia was secondary to the overland trade with Central Asia. As the Persian horses were imported by sea or through the Qandahar-Multan-Lahore route, here they are not discussed in detail.[505]

Even during Humayun's reign horses were purchased by the imperial establishment *sarkar-i-khasa sharifa*. The best quality horses were reserved for king's service. Among them some were selected for royal stable and some for the imperial officers accordingly to their rank and the remaining few were chosen to be given to the kings of other dominions.[506]

---

[501]   Burnes, II, p. 335.

[502]   Mohanlal, p. 45.

[503]   Simon Digby, p. 35.

[504]   Manucci, I, p. 59; II, p. 426-427.

[505]   *Marco Polo*, II, pp. 82-83. Marco Polo describes that there were many fine horses in the kingdom of Persia. These horses were taken by the merchants to Hormuz and other ports where they were purchased by those who carried them to Hindustan. Most of them fetched handsome amount for the merchants.

[506]   *Akbarnama*, I, p. 242.

It appears from the writing of Abul Fazl that the commerce in horse was conducted under the state control. A place was assigned where except for few trusted and privileged merchants, all the horse dealers were required to stay along with their horses; and an official designated *amin-i-karwansara* was appointed to keep watch over them. A clerk was appointed to keep records and an experienced man to determine prices.[507] From Monserrate's account it transpires that in spite of these control and restrictions, there was no state monopoly and horses were sold through open auction. The emperor or rather his officials purchased horses in same manner as private bidders. Monserrate writes "there is a law that no horses may be sold without the king's knowledge or that of his agents. Akbar allows auctions to be freely held, but bought up all the best horses for himself, without however interfering with the bidding or taking offence of anyone tried to outbid him".[508] Monserrate also tell us that horses were also purchased in exchange for slaves.[509]

On account of the large profits of the horse dealer Akbar enforced a tax of three rupees for every Iraqi, *Mujannas* and Arab horses imported from Kabul and Persia and two rupees for every Kabul horses.[510] Abul Fazl informs us that Akbar was very fond of horses and there were twelve thousand in the royal stables. According to him, the cavalry horses, both imported and those of the indigenous breed were divided into seven categories. *Arabi*, Persian, *Mujannas* (resembling Prsian and mostly *Turki*), *Turki*, *Yabu* (a small horse like mule), *Tazi* and

---

[507] *Ain*, I, pp. 140.
[508] Monserrate, pp. 207-208.
[509] *Ibid.*; Bernier, p. 122.
[510] *Ain*, I, 162.

Jangla.[511] Even during Aurangzeb's reign we find all the same classification, except the Arab horses were not mentioned. But Arabian horses were very much in use during that period too, as we find them mentioned in the contemporary records.[512]

The *Tazi* (imported from *Iraq-i-Ajam* i.e. Persian Iraq and Fars) were considered of much value during the Sultanate period, but their value depreciated during the sixteenth and seventeenth centuries. They were referred to as *bahri* or sea-borne because they were imported overseas.[513] *Turki* horses bred in Khurasan and Turkistan had then become the most valuable breed. One of the factors which contributed to the success of *Turki* breed was its easy availability. They could reach the sub-continent more easily overland than the Persian or Arabian thorough bred from the far off Middle East by sea. As we have already noted that they were referred as *bahri* or sea-borne.[514]

According to Alexander Burnes, writing at the first quarter of the nineteenth century, explains that the horses sent to Hindustan were reared about Balkh and the eastern parts of Turkomania or on the bank of Oxus River. They were considered inferior to the horses from Bukhara and Merve. These horses were sold cheap.[515] He further goes on to say that very few of the genuine Turkoman horses were ever sent across Hindu Kush. The horses sent into Hindustan from Kabul

---

[511]   *Ibid.*, pp. 140.

[512]   *Ibid.*; Cf. W. Irvine, *The Army of the Indian Moghuls: Its Organisation and Administration,* Delhi, 1962, p. 51.

[513]   Marco polo, I, pp. 83-84, 264.

[514]   *Ibid.*

[515]   Burnes, II, pp. 271-275.

were of inferior and distinct breed.[516] Vigne informs that the Tarkoman breed horses were well-built and were sent to distant places. They were about 16 hands high.[517]

India had always been deficient in raising sturdy horses. The most favoured horses coming from Central Asia were in great demand for the Mughal armies and nobility, which were annually taken through Kabul, since Kabul lay astride the main route to Central Asia.[518] Owing to the increase in the size of the military organization of the Mughals during the 16th century, it can be presumed that the period must have seen a proportional increase in the import of horses.

Tavernier has mentioned that the horse trade through Kabul was voluminous as well as profitable. The trade in horses annually amounted to more than 60,000 rupees.[519] Throughout the Mughal period, Central Asia remained the principal source of supply of horses; they all came through Kabul to Hindustan. Babur informs us that ten to seven thousand horses came to Kabul every year.[520] It appears from the *Dobistan-i-Mazahib* that the Sikh Guru also took interest in the horse trade. In 1643-44 Sada a disciple of Guru Har Rai, brought from Balkh three *Iraqi* horses, twenty-five *Turki* horses and one camel besides many valuable articles. All the three *Iraqi* horses were seized by the *qiledar* of Ghorband by the order of Shahjahan.[521] During the seventeenth century the

---

[516]   *Ibid.*

[517]   Vigne, p. 203.

[518]   William Foster, p. 168.

[519]   Tavernier, I, p. 75-77.

[520]   *Baburnama*, I, p. 202.

[521]   "Mobad", *Dabistan-i-Madhahib*, tr. D. Shea and A. Troyer, Lahore, 1973, p. 284; *Sikh History from Persian Sources*, ed. J.S.

demand increased enormously and the horse traders sometimes purchased as many as a hundred thousand Central Asian horses at Kabul.[522] For encouraging the import of horses and to provide security to the merchants, *sarais* were constructed where they could stay with their flocks of horses.[523]

During the eighteenth century the bulk of the supply was provided by pastoral nomads. The Turkoman or *Turki* breeds chiefly the war-horses were bought cheap and were prepared for market by letting them graze on the natural pastures. The merchants bought them during summer from the area north of Hindu Kush either through middlemen at the fair or directly from the breeding nomads themselves. In general the horses were bought in a rather bad condition for only about one quarter of the Indian sale price, in order to fatten them at their own pastures or *Maidan* around Kabul. There were extensive meadows both at Kabul and Ghazni.[524] During October and November these Afghan merchants joined the caravans of *Powinda* trading nomads and moved towards Hindustan. At the end of the eighteenth and the beginning of the nineteenth century a duty of 40 rupees per horse was to be paid by the merchants which was approximately 10% of the selling price. All the merchants trading between Kabul and Peshawar were taxed, according to Burnes about sixty rupees per horse.[525] Thus, we find an established rhythm and pattern of the eighteenth century overland horse-trade. Once the merchants

---

Grewal & Irfan Habib, Delhi, 2001, p. 75.

[522] Bernier, p. 203; Manucci, II, p. 391.

[523] *Ain*, I, p. 140.

[524] Elphinstone, I, pp. 386-388; Gommans, pp. 89-90; Mohanlal, p. 45.

[525] Burnes, p. 418.

crossed the Sulaiman Mountains the horses were made to feed on the waste of Jalandhar Doab and the Lakhi Jungle in the north of Bhatinda. In autumn these horses arrived at the Indian market from Central Asia.[526]

As far as the overland horse trade is concerned, we may say that it stood in a complementary relation to the transportation of horses by sea.[527] Whenever the land route was disturbed by political unrest, importation by sea could provide a viable alternative and vice versa. When compared to the overland trade the overseas trade had always been safe. But one cannot deny the fact that the cost of overseas transport of horses was considerably higher than the transport through the overland passage. Since overland transport was easier than the oversea trade, *Turki* or *Tartari* horses from Afghanistan and Central Asia were cheaper and could find more outlets.[528]

5. Trade Routes:

In order to meet the demands of the large volume of interregional and foreign trade, there was a need for a network of routes and a developed transport system. It is to the credit of the Mughals that we find an elaborate network of routes linking all the commercial centers by the beginning of the 17th centuries.

---

[526] Gommans, pp. 89-93.
[527] Bernier, p. 203. Before eighteenth century the so called *'Bahri'* or 'sea' horses had usually come from Fars, Iraq or Arabia in large numbers.
[528] Marco Polo, p. 264.

The Mughal emperors constructed new routes of commerce and maintained the long-established one.[529] Abul Fazl towards the close of the sixteenth century, records that there were no less than seven routes that were frequented by the merchants between Kabul and Turkistan or Bukhara (the principal emporium of Western Turan during Mughal period) and five routes between Kabul and Hindustan, commonly used for transport.[530] The passes and valleys between Kabul and Hindustan provided commercial communication between the two countries.[531]

Situated at the cross roads of the overland routes that connected north-western India with Central Asia, Kabul was the principal entrepot of this region during the Mughal period. Its commercial importance was further emphasized because of the domination of Indian Ocean by the Portuguese, so that the traders whether Indian or Central Asian who wished to avoid dealing with these sea masters resorted to this route. Kabul retained much of its importance when during the reign of Akbar the journey to Kabul was made easier by making the road across in the Khyber Pass fit for vehicular traffic,[532] which facilitated the commercial traffic. Akbar made the Khyber Pass the safest and preferred route between Kabul and Hindustan, by widening the road and building a series of caravansarais

---

[529] Manucci, I, pp. 114-115. He notes that since the time of Humayun many *sarais* had been built upon the royal highway throughout the Empire from one end of it to the other.

[530] *Ain*, I, p.590; *Baburnama*, I, p. 206.Towards the beginning of 16th century, Babur states, four roads reached Kabul from Hindustan side. The Karappa road, it seems, was not traversed during Babur's time.

[531] Masson, II, p. 288.

[532] *Ibid.*; Akbarnama, III, pp. 359-61.

all along it to provide safety to traders and travelers.[533] The Afghan tribes often blocked the pass and harassed the caravans passing through it. The Mughal emperors tried to pacify the Afghan and Baluchi tribes by offering them material incentives in return of assurance of safety on trade routes. The Afghan chiefs were often appointed to act as Mughal officials and guard the Pass.[534]

South of the Khyber route from Peshawar to Kabul was an alternative route via the Kurram valley. The next important link between India and Afghanistan, south of Kurram, was the Tochi valley. It had been utilized in the past for sudden raids from Ghazni in spite of the difficulties in it. The Tochi and the Gomal route south of it must be regarded as highways to Ghazni but there is no comparison between the two as regards their facilities and amount of traffic they carried. All trade to Ghazni was condensed into the narrow ways of the Gomal. Trade in the Tochi hardly extended farther from the villages at its head.[535] The Gomal Pass was always used by merchants who traveled between Hindustan, Kabul and Turan, a 120-mile long caravan path from the Derajat plain to northeastern Afghanistan was a difficult and longer route across the mountains.[536] The commercial viability of this route during

---

[533] *Akbarnama*, III, p. 519. See also Wayne E. Begley, "*Four Mughal Caravansarais Built During the Reign of Jahangir and Shahjahan*", ed. Muqarnas, New Haven, Yale University Press, 1983, I, pp. 167-69.

[534] *Tabaqat-i-Akbari*, II, p. 602; *Tuzuk-i-Jahangiri*, p. 157; *Early Jesuit Travellers in Central Asia 1603-1721*, ed. C. Wessels, p. 14.

[535] *Gates of India*, pp. 135-6.

[536] Dale, p. 52. Like the Bolan it was also named for the principal river that carved a pathway through the Sulaiman range to the Indus plain. Traveler entered the eastern end of the Gomal

sixteenth and seventeenth centuries was largely established because of its use as the principal migratory path for a number of Afghan nomadic clans and the *powindas*.[537] Among them the most important tribe to utilize the pass was Lohanis. When these trading nomads and merchants reached Ghazni, they turned off to northeast towards Kabul. The Lohanis traded between Kabul and Bukhara as well as Samarqand. But it was a difficult route and there was a constant danger of threat and harassment by the Waziri tribe of Afghan.[538] Babur was warned against following the Gomal Pass when he was returning back to Kabul in 1510, because of the high water in the Gomal River and "uncertainty of the Gomal road".[539]

The distance between Ghazni and Kabul was 40 *kos*.[540] From Kabul a route went to south western direction to Qandahar via Ghazni. According to the *Chahar Gulshan* the stages on this route were: Charasia, Sufed Sang, Daghchan, Dehnau, Sujawand, Haft Asia, Shashgaon, ShehDahan, and fort of Ghazni.[541] There was an alternative route from Kabul to Ghazni which passed through Maidan and joined the above

---

Pass west-northwest of Dera Ismail Khan and first followed the Gomal and Kundar rivers southwest through the Sulaiman range at which point they would turn northward along the Gomal in the direction of Ghazni.

[537] Raverty, pp. 483-504.

[538] *Ibid,* 501; Vigne, pp, 67-104.

[539] *Baburnama,* I, p. 235. It was not safe because of the Afghan menace.

[540] Tavernier, I, p. 74.

[541] Rai Chaturman Saksena, *Chahar Gulshan or Akhbar-i-Nawadir,* MS Bodl. Eliot 366, f. 140 b.

mentioned route below Sujawand. The trade route from Kabul to Qandahar via Ghazni passed through hilly areas.[542]*

There were seven routes frequented between Kabul and Turkistan.[543] During seventeenth century the caravans reached to Balkh from Kabul through Charikar and Parwan route in three or four weeks and a little more if they went through the hills. Alexander Burnes took the Charikar route in 1837.[544] Owing to extreme heat in the desert the merchants were forced to travel in nights. The merchants were often attacked by the Turkoman tribes on the route. Jenkinson has mentioned that a caravan, just ten days journey from Bukhara was destroyed in 1558, "that had come from India and Persia".[545] There was an alternative route to Turan or westward to Ottoman cities from the west of Kabul, which passed from Khurasan via Bandar Abbas and Kirman.[546]

From 1586-87 onwards in order to provide better facilities to traders the Mughal emperors started establishing a large number of caravansarais and sarais or rest-houses well placed along the main land-routes.[547] Abul Fazl mentions, "The

---

[542] Tavernier, I, pp. 73-74.

* For detailed description of the route and passes see chapter 1.2.

[543] *Baburnama*, I, pp. 204-6; *Ain*, I, p. 590.

[544] Burnes, II, pp. 150-71

[545] Jenkinson, *Early Voyage and Travels*, II, p. 93.

[546] Dale, pp. 43, 44.

[547] For the *sarais* under Sher Shah, see Abbas Khan Sarwani, *Tarikh-i-Sher Shahi*, Ms. India Office, (Ethe 219) 218, f. 218; Rizqullah Mushtaqi, *Waqiat-i-Mushtaqi*, Ms. Bri. Mus., Or. 1929, R. N. 3, Deptt of History, pp. 96-97. According to the *Waqiat-i- Mushtaqi*, written some time before 1581, Sher Shah built *sarais* at the distance of one *kuroh* in every direction of his

gracious sovereign cast an eye upon the comfort of travelers and ordered that in the serais on the high roads, refuges and kitchens should be established, and the articles of food should be in readiness for the empty-handed travelers".[548] Abul Fazl goes on to record that from 31st regnal year Akbar started raising funds from his nobles for establishing different type of public works such as a well, a reservoir a garden or a caravansarai.[549] In the traveller's accounts of sixteenth century and onwards we find repeated references to the existence of a large number of sarais in different parts of the Mughal India. William Finch, who visited Kabul in 1608 and 1611, described it as "a great and faire citie.... with two castles and many sarayes".[550] Arif Qandahari, writing about 1580, refers to these *sarais* as *chaukis* located at a distance of five *kurohs*.[551] In the account of 48th R. Y. (1603-4) of Akbar it is stated that in the *sarais* or *ribatat* located on roads, *langarha* (residential quarter) and *matbakha* (kitchens) were established to supply *khwurdani* (edibles) of various types to *rah-nawardan-i-bi-maya* (indigent wayfarers).[552] In these *sarais* there were a number of *nigahban* (watchmen) under a *shuhna* (officer). These *sarais* had a walled enclosure with a

---

dominion.

[548] *Akbarnama*, III, p. 825

[549] *Akbarnama*, III, p. 516. The nobles, according to the number of his years, had to give one rupee, or a *dam* or a *muhar* for some good object.

[550] Finch, p. 168' Masson, II, p. 263. He states that there were some fourteen or fifteen caravansarais or *sarais* for the accommodation of foreign merchants.

[551] Arif Qandahari, *Tarikh-i-Akbari*, edited and Annotated by Muinuddin Nadwi, Azhar Ali Dihlavi and Imtiyaz Ali Arshi, Rampur, 1962, p. 44.

[552] *Akbarnama*, III, p. 824.

single gateway. Within this enclosure were located a number of *khanhas* (houses) for the accommodation.[553]

Even Jahangir who is remembered for his observation of nature and patronage of painting built many caravansarais on major trade routes. He ordered that more "sarais.., mosques and dig well" should be built "which might stimulate population and people might settle down in those sarais".[554] Many other bridges and caravansarais at either end of the Khyber route were built during Shahjahan's time under the supervision of his engineer Ali Mardan Khan, and some along the routes leading to Badakhshan through the Hindu Kush mountains. Alexander Burnes who traveled from Kabul to Balkh described about the network of caravansarais, built by the Mughal emperors across the mountains to Balkh.[555] Thus by the seventeenth century the Mughals had a system of communication between the most distant provinces which enabled them to have favorable conditions for trade and economic development throughout the entire region.

---

[553] Iqtidar Alam Khan, The *Karavansarays* of Mughal India: A Study of Surviving Structures', in *Indian Historical Review*, vol. xiv, no. 1-2, July 1987-Jan 1988, pp. 111-116; See Ravindra Srivastava, "The distribution of *Sarais* and Mughal trade-routes in Uttar Pradesh", paper presented at the Indian History Congress, 1976, Paper on Medieval Indian History, Calicut, 1976, pp. 2-10.

[554] *Tuzuk-i-Jahangiri,* trans. I, p.8.

[555] Burnes, II, p. 109. Some of these were built during Aurangzeb's time, who was governor of Balkh.

6. Merchants and *Bazaar:*

Kabul was a large commercial centre, and a meeting place for merchants from India, Persia and Central Asia. During 16th and 17th centuries Kabul was the commercial hub of the merchants involved in intra-Asian trading network. Merchants from a wide variety of ethnic and racial backgrounds were based in, or had trade settlements in Kabul. The city of Kabul enjoyed considerable prosperity during the Mughal rule, profiting from the great commercial intercourse that passed through it.

The merchants who imported goods from foreign countries to Kabul often made a huge profit. Kabul was well situated at the crossroads of the overland routes that connected north-western India with Persia and Central Asia.[556] The merchants from Mughal India who conducted trade between Iran and Turan or beyond during the sixteenth and seventeenth centuries went to those areas through Kabul. There are references of merchants from Central Asia and West Asia who used to come down to Lahore, Agra, and Delhi through Kabul.[557] Indian merchants who conducted trade in Kabul, purchased beavers (castor), skin, musk, and rubies etc. these articles were brought there from Balkh and Badakhshan and other Central Asian cities.[558] This clearly reveals the extent of commercial activity in Kabul.

Among the foreign merchants trading in Kabul were Turani, Irani, Armenian and Afghan merchants.[559] When

---

[556] Masson, II, p. 288.

[557] Pelsaert, p. 31; *E F I, 1634-36*, p. 38 (Agra); *Khulasatu-t Twarikh*, pp. 39-41 (Delhi).

[558] Manucci, II, p. 426.

[559] *E F I, 1646-51*, pp. 220, 335-36.

in 1598 Akbar was about to leave Lahore, a rich merchant
came there from Khita (Northern China) via Kabul.[560] These
merchants came to India to purchase Indian commodities and
to sell their goods.[561]

The most important among the Indian merchant groups
who traded overland through Kabul in Iran and Turan in
the sixteenth and seventeenth century, were the Multani and
Gujarati *baniyas*, Afghans and Marwaris. They had their own
rules and regulations regarding their business.[562] It is evident
from the sources that thousands of merchants from Mughal
India resided semi permanently in Iran and Turan. Many
Muslim Multanis were active in the textile trade in Samarqand
and Bukhara in the sixteenth and seventeenth century. Daria
khan Multani, son of Shaikh Sadi was apparently one of the
richest and most influential merchants of the sixteenth century,
as his name or *nisba* suggests was a Multani but settled in
Samarqand. He brought Indian textile artisans to Samarqand,
where they manufactured cloth using yarns and wool produced
there. The Indians merchants were trading in Samarqand is
evident from a collection of sixteenth century documents
from the office of the *qazi* of Samarqand, *Majmua-i- Vasaik*,

---

[560]   Father Fernao Guerriro, *Jahangir and the Jesuits,* tr. C.H. Payne,
London, 1930, p. 119-20. Xavier wrote from Lahore to Goa
in 1598, the journey, he said easily accomplished, though the
distance was great; throughout the journey they were free from
molestation, for justice was very strictly administered in those
part and robbers were never pardoned.

[561]   *Ibid., 1637-41,* pp. 134-35; Manrique, II, p. 180.

[562]   Tavernier, p. 74; for the Baniya class see Irfan Habib, "Merchant
communities in pre-colonial India" in *The Rise of Merchant
Empires Long-Distance Trade in the Early Modern World, 1356-
1750,* ed. James D. Tracy, New York, 1990.

discovered by R. G. Mukminova.[563] Daria Khan traded not only in textiles but also in extremely fine variety of wool, which was used for manufacturing Kashmiri shawls.[564] Another influential merchant was Khwaja Ibrahim Multani, some of them had the name or *nisba* as Lahori which suggests they belonged to Lahore.[565] It is conceivable that nearly all the Hindus [Multani] trading in Iran, Turan or Russia were Panjabi Khattris and that most of Muslims [Multani] were Afghans or Pashtuns.[566] Mountstuart Elphinstone reported that Khattris were found throughout Afghanistan and as far as Astrakhan functioning as "bankers, merchants, goldsmiths and sellers of grain.[567] The Indian merchants from their bases in Central Asian cities had a far-flung commercial network which extended to the cities of cis-Syr Darya region, Kazakhstan steppes and also with China.[568]

Another merchant group who trade in this region in the eighteenth century was Jain *baniyas*, they were not Multanis but were Marwaris, the natives of Marwar areas of Rajasthan.[569]

---

[563] R. G. Mukhninova, pp. 219-31.

[564] *Ibid.*, p. 65.

[565] *Ibid.*, p. 62; Dale, p. 55. *Nisba* is derived from an Arabic word *Nasaba*, meaning to relate, to link, to trace, i.e. ancestry, is often suffixed to names to indicate origin, residence etc. Thus Multani, Bukhari, Isfahani, etc.

[566] Rajat Kanta Ray, "The *Bazar*: Indigenous Sector of the Indian Economy", in Dwijendra Tripathi, ed., *Business Communities of India*, New Delhi, Manohar, 1984, pp. 241-67.

[567] Elphinstone, p. 317.

[568] *Ibid.,* p. 113; *Jahangir and the Jesuits,* pp. 119-120.

[569] Surendra Gopal, *Indians in Russia in the 17th and 18th Centuries*, New Delhi, Indian Council of Historical Research, 1988, pp. 7-8. See Dale, p. 60. The Marwari *nisba* was and is used as a collective designation for Hindu and Jain commercial castes

In 1504-5 Babur speaks of his men's killing of Khwaja Khizr Nuhani [Luhani], "a well known and respected Afghan merchant". He was a prominent *powinda* merchant. Luhanis, settling near Ghazni were one of the principal *powinda* (pastoral nomads) tribes that traded between India, Kabul, Iran and Turan. During the expedition of same year he also talks of the seizure of "white cloths, aromatic roots, sugar and high-quality horses bred for trade" from Afghan merchants on the roads.[570]

In 1634, the author of the *Mazhari-i Shahjahani* informs us that merchants from plains went into the hill country, along with their goods such as cloth, food grains and weapons and brought back felt, carpets, camels, horses, oxen and sheep.[571] The merchants who traded between Kabul and Central Asia had to make their trips between mid-April and mid-November because in winter snow blocked the lofty peaks of Hindu Kush passes, three of which exceeded 10,000 feet.[572] The Kabul merchants imported about two thousand camel-loads of goods from Hindustan annually, out of which half of the quantity as sent to Turkistan.[573]

A great part of the trade conducted with India via the Bolan Pass and Jalalabad was controlled by Hindu merchants and

---

such as the Hindu Agarwals and the Jain Oswals who originated in Marwar.

[570] *Baburnama,* I, p. 235; Vigne, p. 54. G. T. Vigne, who accompanied a Luhani caravan through the Gomal Pass in 1836, says that "they traded then as now and their merchandise was of the same description".

[571] Yusuf Mirak, *Mazhari-I Shahjahani,* ed. Sayyid Hasamuddin Rashidi Karachi, 1962, p. 239.

[572] Burnes, II, pp. 150-71.

[573] *Ibid.,* p.429.

bankers. The centre for their financial exchange was Shikarpur on the Indus, a small entrepot at the eastern entrance of the Bolan Pass.[574]

The merchants usually organized themselves in *qafilas* or caravans for safety.[575] Heavily armed they marched through the Sulaiman Mountains to Hindustan. They traveled in such large groups that they were relatively safe from attacks by various bandits and plunderers. These merchants reached Kabul at the beginning of June and then set out for Central Asia. In exchange for their merchandise they exported horses and a great quantity of fruits (both fresh and dried).[576] Again these merchants brought various articles along with the silk of Bukhara in considerable quantities to Kabul. It was then exported to Hindustan.[577] The merchants of Turkistan brought wool (*Pushm*) to Kabul where it was manufactured into a coarse kind of shawl.

All these tribes followed a firmly set pattern of migration, moving in a fixed order to India during autumn and returning to Kabul in the same pattern in spring. The merchant waited till they formed a caravan and they moved out. The delay and irregularity in forming a caravan much hampered the free movement of merchants and goods.

Some of the merchants also kept camels of their own while some hired out. Camels hired from a particular tribe usually made their journey in company with the tribe to which

---

[574]   *Indian merchants and Eurasian trade*, p. 24

[575]   Elphinstone, I, p. 380.

[576]   *Ibid.*, pp. 415-416.

[577]   *Ibid.*, p. 439. The silk of Bukhara was chiefly produced on the bank of Oxus. Almost all the Turkomans were engaged in rearing silk-worm during the month of summer.

they belonged. Even individual merchants travelling in the direction, generally attached themselves to these tribes for safety.[578] In Kabul both the caravans of merchandise from Hindustan and those from Central Asia arrived simultaneously during the summer months of June and July. Without much loss of time the merchants could again leave Kabul for the Indian market in October and for Bukhara in August. Usually, the Bukhara merchants, traveling via Balkh, Tashkurghan or Qunduz would arrive there in October at which time they had to await the arrival of the Orenburg caravans some time during November or December.[579]

The merchants of Kabul were generally Tajiks, Persians and Afghans. During the Mughal rule Afghan played a major role in the Indo-Persian and Indo-Turanian trade, since they occupied the principle over-land routes that connected Mughal India with Safavid and Uzbek territory.[580] They belonged to the upper classes of the society and lived comfortably but not ostentatiously.[581]

The merchants had to pay taxes on their merchandise, though the levy was normally moderate 2.5 to 3% but the Mughal government derived significant revenues from customs duties on both imported and exported goods. The fiscal system was not oppressive for the merchants, and favoured trade and commerce. In order to ensure free flow of traffic Akbar had remitted all imposts on goods in transit over land routes. He also abolished the commercial taxes *baj* and *tamgha* in 1581.[582]

---

[578] Elphinstone, I, pp. 378-380.
[579] Gommans, p. 31.
[580] Stephen Dale, p. 61.
[581] Elphinstone, I, p. 335.
[582] Cited in Dale, pp. 37-38. *Tamgha* was used as an all inclusive

The collection of *sair jihat* (transit duty) from *balda*-i-Kabul in 1595 amounted to 31,896.02 rupees,[583] but this amount at the death of Akbar reduced to 3,07,500.[584] Jahangir continued the policy and completely abolished the duties on the Kabul routes. He mentions, "as I had remitted in my dominion custom duties amounting to *krores*, I abolished also all the transit dues (*sair jihat*) in Kabul. These brought 1,23,00,000 lakhs of *dams*. From Kabul large sums used to be derived every year from customs, which were in fact the chief revenue of that place. The remission greatly benefited the people of Iran and Turan".[585]

During the reign of Shahjahan the total annual revenue amounted to 10, 53,595.4 rupees.[586] Similarly Aurangzeb had also issued a *farman* forbidding the levy of cesses on traders and merchants in the course of their journey on land routes.[587]

The cess on trade was fixed at two and half percent. However, the taxation system was not uniform, and varied from one community to other. In certain instances, the Armenian merchants were taxed at twenty percent and the baniyas, ten percent of their sales and purchases in Kabul.[588] Abul Fazl refers to the tax on sale and purchase, he states that half percent of the value should be charged from the purchaser, one and half percent from the seller and half percent from both

term for urban taxes while *baj* referred to city custom duties.

[583] *Ibid.*

[584] *Tuzuk-i-Jahangiri*, pp. 21-22.

[585] *Ibid.*.

[586] *Dastur-al 'Amal Shahjahani wa Shuqqajat-i 'Alamgiri (1701-2)*, MS. Add. 6588, f. 23 a.

[587] Khafi Khan, pp. 89-90.

[588] Burnes, II, pp. 440-441.

on account of *inam*[589](which was probably brokerage); in all two and half.[590] Under Jahangir and Shahjahan, the official rates for all legal levies also remained at one in forty.[591] But Aurangzeb during the eighth regnal year enforced a general regulation with regard to market dues and all other legal levies and the rates prescribed were two and half from Muslim and five percent from Hindus and in case of foreigners three and half.[592] This rate was implemented throughout the empire and collection at higher rate was prohibited. Two years later the levy prescribed for Muslims was abolished and Muslims goods throughout the empire were declared custom free.[593] But all this caused a set back to the government revenue, it was found that a large number of Hindus were transporting their goods under the names of their Muslim friends and thereby evading custom collection. Consequently, Aurangzeb in 25th year of his reign through another regulation, set aside the exemption given to the Muslims and reimposed the older regulation of two and half percent.[594] Bazaar merchants were taxed at the rate of approximately five percent of gold coins and two and half percent of silver coins of cash on hand. Taxes on external trade varied according to whether merchants came from "friendly" i.e. Muslim countries, in which case they were taxed at the rate of five percent; other could be taxed at double this rate.[595]

---

[589]   *Akbarnama*, III, p. 394.

[590]   *Ain*, I, p. 204.

[591]   *Tuzuk-i-Jahangiri*, pp. 206-07.

[592]   *Akhbarat*, dated 13th Rabi, 10th year of Aurangzeb; *Mirat*, I, pp. 258-9;

[593]   *Mirat*, I. p. 265.

[594]   *Ibid.*, pp. 298-9.

[595]   *Gardens of eight paradises*, p. 194.

Babur informs us that a large proportion of the revenue of Kabul probably came from commerce; as Kabul lay astride the main trade route between India and Central Asia as well as India and Persia.

To Kabul caravans came from Kashgar, Ferghana, Turkishtan, Samarqand, Bukhara, Balkh, Hisar and Badakhshan. Kabul is an excellent trading centre; if merchants went to Khita (north China) or Rum (Anatolia) they might make no higher profit. Down to Kabul every year came 7, 8, or 10,000 horses and up to it, from Hindustan come every year caravans of 10, 15 or 20,000 heads of houses, bringing slaves (*barda*), white cloth, sugar-candy, refined and common sugars and aromatic roots. Many a trader is not content with a profit of 30 or 40 on 10. In Kabul can be had the products of Khurasan, Rum, Iraq and China; while it is Hindustan's own market.[596]

Bazaar:

During the Mughal period we come across a number of markets, such as *bazaar-i-Khas* (the main market) also known as *bazaar-i-chowk* or *chauraha*, *katra*, *mandi (joba)*, *ganj* (grain market), *dariba* (a short lane or street)[597], *nakhas* (cattle market), *peth* (*hat*), fair and seasonal markets. Among these the first six were permanent while the other three were occasional or seasonal.[598] *Bazaar-i-khas* or *kalan* was established at the principal streets of the city. In a big city there were separate

---

[596] *Baburnama*, I, p. 202.

[597] Steingass, p. 508. *Dariba* is derived from an Arabic word meaning a lane and street

[598] At Agra, see Monserrate, p. 31; Finch, p. 182; for Lahore Manrique, II, p. 191.

shops for each commodity. In these *bazaars* all sorts of goods and commodities such as food grain, cloth, fruits and other item of necessity were available.[599] Kabul had a *bazaar* consisting of nearly 2000 shops. Both sides of streets contained shops.[600] Of the various *bazaars* in the city of Kabul, the two principal, almost parallel to each other, were the *Shor bazaar* and the *Darwaz-i-Lahori*.[601] The former extended east and west from the Bala Hissar while the latter stretched from the *Darwaza-i-Lahori* and terminated at the *chabutra*. The *chahar chhatta* or four covered arcades was the most magnificent of the Kabul *bazaars* located towards the western end of the *bazaar* of *Darwaz-i-Lahori*.[602] *It was once the finest bazaar* of Kabul and the structure is ascribed to Ali Mardan Khan.[603] The four covered arcades of equal length and dimensions were separated from each other by square open areas, originally provided with wells and fountains. This type of *bazaar* was in vogue throughout Persia.[604]

Everything that was brought to the city for sale was taxed.[605] The articles taxed in the markets were cloth, leather, oil, food grain, fish and other product from water, horses, camel, cow etc.[606] The taxes levied on these goods were termed

---

[599] *Baburnama,* I, p. 202; for different commodities in the *bazar* of Agra, see Mundy, II, p. 216.

[600] Burnes, II, p.335.

[601] Masson, II, p.267.

[602] *Ibid.*, Elphinstone, II, p.143.

[603] Raverty, p. 65. *Lahori Darwaja* was situated towards east of Kabul city.

[604] Masson, II, p. 268.

[605] *Khulasatu-s Siyaq*, f. 13 b.

[606] *Siyaqnama*, p. 307; *Dasturu-l 'Amal-i-Alamgiri*, f. 28 b.

as *hasil-i-sair* or *mahsul-i-sair*.[607] For the collection of various taxes known as *sair* or *sair-jihat* (transit duty) the *bazaars* of big cities were formed into several separate *mahals* collectively known as *mahalat-i-sair* or *mahalat-i-sair balda*.[608] The number of *sair mahals* depended upon the size of the city. In Kabul there were seven *mahals*, namely—*bazar, mandi, peth nakhas, chabutra-i-kotwali, dar-ul zarb, jihat bazar* and *bargadi* (probably a market for grass and leaves).[609]

Abul Fazl informs us that Akbar in the 27th R. Y. appointed several market inspectors to check oppression and irregularities in buying. These market inspectors collected half per cent from the purchasers and one per cent from the sellers and kept half of the collection with themselves as honorarium.[610] A *chaudhary* was selected from amongst the merchants by the government for each *bazaar* who was to act as the head of traders.[611]

These *bazaars* had a fine appearance. It was quite impossible to move from one part of Kabul to another without passing along a *bazaar* consisting of double lines of shops.[612] Every trade had its separate *bazaar* and all of them were busy all day long.[613]

---

[607]   Khwaja Yasin, f. 66 b.

[608]   For an excellent discussion on *bazar* see M.P. Singh, pp. 138-168.

[609]   *Dastur-al 'Amal Shahjahani wa Shuqqajat-I 'Alamgiri (1701-2)*, MS. Add. 6588, f. 23 a.

[610]   *Akbarnama*. III, p. 396.

[611]   *Akhbarat*, dated 11th Muharram, 20th year of Aurangzeb; Mundy, II, p. 147.

[612]   Vigne, pp.159-160; Mohanlal, p. 42.

[613]   Burnes, I, p. 145; II, p. 335.

The shopkeepers and artificers were divided into thirty-two trades, each of which had its own chief called *cudkhoda,* who had to manage all transaction between traders and the ruler.[614]

The cattle-market called *Nakash* where horses, elephants, camels, cows, buffaloes, oxen, donkeys goats etc. as well as slaves were sold, was situated north of the river and west of the Pul Kishti in the Andarabi quarter.

There were two grain-markets or *mandi,* a place where corn was brought from other places for sale in the city. One near the *chahar chhatta* called *Mand-i-Kalan* and the other between *Shor bazaar* and *Lahori Darwaza* known as *Mand-i-Shahzada.* Usually a *mandi* was named after the chief commodity sold there. There might be a number *mandis* in a city and in each a separate commodity was to be sold. In *mandis* the commodities were sold and purchased in bulk and not in retail.[615]

The quarter called *Shikarpuri* was the fruit market of Kabul. Several varieties of fruits were brought there from the adjacent countries and were distributed among the retailers of the city. In the same manner, were the markets for wood and charcoal.[616]

The shops rose over each other, in steps to elevation.[617] The shops displayed a profusion of all variety of fruits and other items. The *bazaars* of Kabul were bustling with activity and were marked by an abundance and huge variety of goods. There were a large number of shops of dried and fresh fruits.

---

[614] Elphinstone, I, pp. 336-337.
[615] *Mirat* Supplement, pp. 166-7, 182.
[616] Masson, II, pp. 268-269.
[617] Mohanlal, p. 42.

The winter fruits such as the grapes, pears, apples and quinches were even available in the summers, in abundance.[618]

It is apparent that *suba* of Kabul being strategically situated at the intersection of a vibrant, and expanding, trading network extending from the plains in northern India to Central Asia and Iran, derived considerable revenues from inter-regional trade, and remained all through the period, indispensable for the organization of overland trade between India and Central Asia. The *suba* produced several fruits and agricultural commodities for export, and these had considerable demand in the markets in northern India, Central India and Iran. Kabul could with some justification, lay claims to relative prosperity in our period, and much of this prosperity it seems came from trade and commerce.[619]

---

[618]   Burnes, I, p. 145.
[619]   Thevenot, p. 80; Masson, II, p. 270.

Chapter – V

Pastoralism

1. Pastoral Nomads and Economy:

In most of Afghanistan, pastoralism existed side by side with agriculture. The pastoral tribes, pasturing their herds over large areas of grassland and desert of Central Asia, subsisted mainly by cattle-breeding and commerce based upon it.

Given the relatively low area of arable, the Afghans, in the south-east of Kabul, particularly the area around Sulaiman mountain, which was of considerable mercantile importance, depended largely on pastoral existence based on the raising of sheep and goats. The eastern Afghan tribes who may have been expelled from earlier western Afghan homeland in the fifteenth century, but by sixteenth century they had settled near Ghazni. The eastern Afghans combined agriculture with pastoralism. But they were mainly shepherds, and the land reserved for pasture was more extensive than the land employed in agriculture. The pastoral tribes remained in the plains in winters and retired to the hills in summers.[620]

---

[620] Burnes, II, p. 415. Alexander Burnes reports that the caravans of Luhanis, a pastoral tribe of Afghans living eastward from Ghazni to the Indus were the principal carriers of trade between Kabul and Hindustan; Vigne, pp. 111-112, 117. The pastoral

In Kabul region the largest nomadic group was the Ghilzai Afghans, with a small number of Kirghiz, Turkoman, Baluch and Aimaq tribes. Though the small sections of the Ghilzai tribe were settled in the plain and undertook agricultural pursuits, but the majority of the tribe was pastoral in their habits of life. They moved with seasons from the lowlands to the highlands with their families and flocks and their black hair tents. They never settled either in villages or cities. In pastoralism a much larger area was required to feed a family than in agriculture. The proprietary rights under pastoralism were restricted to the cattles, and did not extend to the land, or its products. Apparently, it was an economy mainly depending upon animal husbandry.[621]

According to Andre Wink, "Real nomadism involves the entire community and typically is a form of long-distance movement of people, animals, and dwellings. This is characteristic of all nomadism, even though we can distinguish different types according to the patterns of movement or modes of livelihood that are favoured. Nomads can move cyclically or periodically, and they can be either hunters-and-gatherers, pastoral nomads, traders-and-service nomads or a combination of these".[622]

Durrani also cultivated a little area. They left the charge of their land to the *bazgar* (cultivator) when they were absent from their country.

[621] Elphinstone, II, pp. 302-4.

[622] Andre Wink, 'India and the Turko-Mongol Frontier', in *Nomads in the Sedentary World*, ed. Anatoly M. Khazanov and Andre Wink, Great Britain, 2001, p. 212; Cf. Anatoly M. Khazanov, *Nomads and the Outside World*, tr. Julia Crookenden, London, 1994, p. 37. Khazanov writes that "the character of the pastoral migration of different groups of nomads varies considerably,

The pastoral economy involved nomadism, as the herdsmen led an erratic life, moving vertically from one region to another with the flock of animals such as sheep, goat, horses and camels, in search of pasture.

The need of suitable pasture for the livestock mainly determined the character of pastoral migrations among nomads rather than just mobility. They move to higher elevation in summer and down to the semi desert in winter. Such seasonal movements meant there could be no permanent settlement but only movable houses or camps.[623] Their summer station was called *ilak* and the winter station *kishlak*.[624] *All the shepherds lived in kizdis* or black tents. But those to the upper Helmand, following a Central Asia tradition lived in *yurt* (abandoned camping site or a specific kind of a felt tent). *Yurt* was circular and framed construction, covered with felt. They were portable, normally provided with a doomed roof and are extremely strong.[625] The *kizdis* were composed of course black camlet, sometimes single or sometimes double, which

---

even amongst nomads within one region. Regularity and stability vary; cycles (interseasonal and in-season pastoral migration) vary; distance varies; directionality varies, it can be both vertical and horizontal, either linear or nonlinear; economic priorities vary, whether for food and or water and or temperature, pollution of the locality, etc."

[623] See Nomadic Societies in *History of Civilization of Central Asia,* V, p. 344.

[624] Elphinstone, II, p. 88.

[625] *Ibid.,* I, pp. 305-6; *Civilization of Central Asia,* V, p. 344. Felt is made of wool (generally of that which is shorn off the camlet, carpets and other woolen manufactures). It is made by women. The common colours are grey and black. The Uzbek tent is called *khirgah,* Elphinstone, II, pp. 192-193.

provided good shelter from weather. The camps of pastoral tribes consisted of ten to fifty tents; one with hundred tents was usually a large camp. According to their number they were pitched in one or two lines. The tent of chief was in the middle of the line. A large camp was called *khail* and a small one *keelee*.[626]

The fodder requirements of the herd, the necessity of providing it with water and the best way of protecting it from the cold in winter were the basic factors in the economic life of the pastoral nomads. The amount of time spent in camps, the direction of migrations, number of pastoral migrations and distance of the latter all depended on these factors.[627] Though the nomad's mobility threatened the sedentary population, in some ways nomadism contributed to the efficiency and mobility of the rural economy. The Afghan nomads provided the settled areas of Kabul region with transport opportunities and commercial communication system. The nomadic tribes wandering between Central Asia and India were closely linked with the cosmopolitan cities and the producer and consumer lands of South and Central Asia.

The Afghan nomads rarely cultivated the land but were almost wholly occupied in the care of their flocks. They had plenty of wealth in the form of cattle. Defining the life of steppe nomads, Qasim Khan, the Qazaq, as recorded by Mirza Dughlat, said: "We are men of the desert and here there is nothing in the way of riches or formalities. Our most costly possessions are our horses, our favourite food their flesh, our most enjoyable drink their milk and the products of it. In our

---

[626]   *Ibid.*, II, pp. 112-113.
[627]   Khazanov, p. 50.

country there are no gardens or buildings. Our chief recreation is inspecting our herds".[628]

The nomads and semi nomads, generally called *kuch*[629] in Afghanistan, mostly kept sheep and goats. The produce of their animals viz. dairy products, hair and wool were exchanged or sold in order to purchase grain, vegetable and other products of sedentary population. In this way an extensive network of exchange had developed along the routes annually followed by the nomads. Cattle-breeding was adopted by them because of the limitations imposed by nature. However, it was not an easy job and needed as much rigorous labour as was require in agriculture. In a flock, subsequently joined by other merchant and travellers, the nomads migrated from the Indus valley to Ghazni, Kabul and beyond to the pastures of Qarabagh. In October-November they returned to the South following the same route. They left most of their families and cattle behind in the summer camp in the Derajat or the winter camps near Ghazni. They dispersed across the cities (*qasbas*) of Kabul in the summer and of India in the winter. They travelled in such a large group under *qafila bashi* that they were relatively safe from attacks of plunderers.[630]

---

[628] Haydar Dughlat, tr., p. 276. Qasim Khan of Qazaq tribe told to the Moghul Khan, Abu Said in 1531. There could be no better picture of the life of steppe nomads.

[629] *Kuch* a Persian word means a wandering tribe and robber. See Steingass, *Comprehensive Persian English Dictionary*, Delhi, p. 1973, p. 1059.

[630] Gommans, pp. 29-31. Similar to the *Powinda* movement between North India and Afghanistan, the Qazaq nomads wandering between Bukhara and Southern Russia traveled Southward to the summer pastures and northward to their winter pastures. It was the case of "vertical" migration.

We should keep in mind that the pastoral nomads were not only shepherds but also traders, a great deal of the trade with Central Asia was transmitted through them, who traversed the pastures between the Amu Darya and the Indus valley and hence deep into India.[631] Alexander Burnes reports that the caravans of Luhanis were the principal carriers of trade between Kabul and Hindustan. Many of the Ghilzai clans were almost wholly engaged in carrying trade between Kabul and India and many countries of Central Asia.[632] These trading nomads were known as *powindas,* a name probably derived from the Pashto word *pawwal* and the Persian *puyudan* meaning respectively 'to graze' and 'to roam'.[633] They were chiefly composed of the Ghilzai and Lodi tribes of which Luhanis, Nasiris and Niyazis were the most marked subgroups. The several clans travelled with their families and flocks and dependents as well as beast of burden, numbering many thousands. During autumn season they assembled in the plains of Zurmat and Gardez to the east of Ghazni and left for Indian markets with their merchandise, leaving their families and flocks to pasture there. They moved in long files of camel and made return journey in the beginning of spring. The pastoral tribes brought down various productions of their country such as fruits, madder, asafoetida, wool and woolen fabrics, furs, drugs together with horses, raw silk, shawl, &c. from Bukhara. They

---

[631]   *Ibid.* Apart from individual merchants, a great deal of the trade of Kabul with Hindustan as well as Central Asia was transmitted through the pastoral nomads, who traversed the pastures between the Indus and Amu Darya.

[632]   Burnes, II, p. 415.

[633]   Raverty, pp. 484-485.

took back cotton goods, chintzes, brocades, silks and muslins &c. of Indian manufacture.[634]

Almost all the nineteenth and twentieth century sources confirm that Luhanis were one of the principal powinda tribes that traded between India, Kabul, Iran and Turan. They had traded between India and Kabul at least since tenth century. According to Vigne, "their annual trek took them from the steaming Derajat plains in April and May to their summer highland pastures west of Sulaiman range or in their terms Khurasan".[635] Babur mentions about the Lohanis in his memoirs. His troops attacked them and captured their flocks, cloths, camels and horses bred for trade.[636] Every year thousands of *powindas* together with other merchants and travelers migrated in tribal formation from the Indus valley to Ghazni, Kabul and beyond. Most of them made use of the Gomal Pass through the district of Dera Ismail Khan on their way to India.[637] In October-November they returned to the South in same manner leaving most of their families and cattle behind in summer at Derajat or in the winter at Ghazni.[638] The *Powinda* caravans were led by a chosen *qafila bashi,* mostly from the dominant tribe.[639] The poor who were

---

[634]	Denzil Ibbetson, *Punjab Castes,* Delhi, 1993, pp. 65, 76. In 1877 the number of these traders was 76,400; H. W. Bellew, p. 104.

[635]	Vigne, pp. 54, 69. He accompanied a Luhani caravan through the Gumal Pass in 1836, the first traveler who is known to have left an eyewitness account of Luhani migrations; Dale, p. 62-63.

[636]	*Baburnama*, I, p. 235.

[637]	Raverty, pp. 497-98.

[638]	Gommans, pp. 28-30.

[639]	Elphinstone, I, p. 380.

not able to carry on their own trade, took other's good on retail price or hired their camels. This also cannot be denied that the pastoral nomads were usually poorer than those who were settled agriculturists.

While it is evident that the nomad traders played a considerable role both in the local and overland trade, it is hard to estimate the exact proportion of trade controlled by them. In early 1830s, Mohanlal observed that the Luhanis provided Kabul and Bukhara with Indian and English goods consisted of 600-700 camels.[640] Vigne is of the opinion that besides the Luhanis, five or six caravans crossed the Hindu Kush for Bukhara each year.[641]

The *powindas* were involved for many centuries in the caravan trade between India and Central Asia and Iran. They assumed this role because the caravan routes coincided with the routes of their pastoral migrations. Luhanis are mentioned selling horses in 1599 and supplying grain to Dara Shikoh's army before Qandahar in 1653.[642] These Afghan nomads rented dromedaries, drove flocks, guarded caravans, and engaged in trade themselves, particularly horse trade a crucial commodity in Indian markets.[643]

The pastoral economy of the nomads was almost self sufficient and was closely connected with sheep and cattle.

It was a general practice that a mixed species-composition of herd usually pastured separately. However, it was not uncommon (particularly in winter) for different species to

---

[640]   Mohanlal, pp. 45-46.
[641]   Vigne, p. 70
[642]   *Akbarnama*, III, p. 1160; Raverty, II, pp. 488-89.
[643]   *Nomads in the Sedentary World*, p. 215.

be pastured on a rotational basis on the same land.[644] The specificity of the species-composition of herds of Afghan nomads was determined by the leading role of two species: camels and sheep. The variety of plants which sheep ate was very wide and included many different kinds of plants which were unfit for large stock. Also important is the fact that sheep could get at fodder in pasture covered with snow up to 15-17cm. deep.[645] These people were quite busy in the spring season and required twice the number of shepherds. During this season they had to take care of their lambs and to shear their sheep. Again in the end of autumn the sheep were sheared.[646]

The pastoral tribes were stratified according to wealth that mainly depended upon the number of animals one owned. The rich had a good number of camels which were employed in carrying their baggage or merchandise at the time of traveling from one place to another. The poor among them used bullocks and asses.

There are references in sources that the taxes were paid in the form of sheep.[647] It was sheep which formed a standard unit of wealth. Abul Fazl informs us that in the localities (south-eastern) the Afghan tribes paid their taxes in the form of sheep.

---

[644] Khazanov, pp. 46-47. In contrast to Arabia and Sahara, among the Afghan nomads there were no pure camel-or-horse herders, nor were there any pure sheep-breeder.

[645] *Ibid.*, pp. 46-47.

[646] Elphinstone, II, pp. 117-118. In spring grass is plenty in all parts even in the worst part of Durrani country.

[647] See Irfan Habib in *Evolution of the Afghan Tribal System,* p. 301. In an around Qandahar province where pastoralism was the principal means of sustenance taxes were paid in the form of sheep.

In 1595 the annual tax paid in the form of sheep amounted to 45.775 and 45 Baluch horses.[648]

As for the utilization of ecological zones is concerned, pastoral nomads utilized several ecological zones which were separated by other zones, in which agriculture was usually undertaken. Nomads themselves never utilized these zones, but had to travel across them during pastoral migrations, thus creating complication for both sides. There were certain instances when nomads shared either fully or partially the same zone with agriculturists. In this situation co-existence was usually characterized by nomads pasturing their livestock on fields which were harvested.[649]

2. Horse Breeding:

The bulk of the supply of horses was produced by the pastoral nomads. The capacity to produce both war-horses and cavalry was one of their major assets.[650] During 16th and 17th centuries the horse claimed the first notice of all domestic animals. A considerable number of horses were bred in Afghan dominions. Babur tells us that good meadows were found on all the four sides of Kabul, which had grass suitable of horses.[651]

The environmental condition of Central Asia with plenty of pasturage and grasses was very favourable to the

---

[648] *Ain*, I, pp. 588-89.

[649] Khazanov, pp. 33-36.

[650] Gommans, p. 22-23. In Central Asia pastoralists can keep large herds of horses, which was not possible in India.

[651] *Baburnama,* I, p. 204. He says mountain slope of eastern as well as western Kabul had grass *buta kah aut* (grass), which was very much liked by horses.

development of the *equine-race*. The fodder produced there was more sweet and nutritious than that of Indian more moist and temperate climate. It produced in the horses of this region a higher temperature and better condition of blood, as well as a peculiar elasticity and strength of nerve and muscle perfectly wonderful.[652] Although it was possible to raise horses in India, these were of inferior quality and insufficient in number. When compared with Persia and Turkistan, India had a shortage of good and extensive pastures. In India the facilities for horse-breeding were relatively meagre. There was a shortage of extensive pastures in India, since the best soil was mostly reserved for cultivation. Apart from the shortage of space, the greatest drawback was the want of appropriate fodder grasses. The best Indian breeding grounds for horses were on the north-western fringe of the subcontinent.[653] But the country bred horses from this region had consistently been regarded as inferior to those brought down from the highlands of Afghanistan or from Central Asia.[654] The main breeding centre in the region was Balkh and it was from here and the Turkoman country lower down the Oxus that the bulk of those exported were bred.[655]

The Turkoman horses were celebrated all over Asia. The Turkoman or *Turki* horses were a modification of the Arab breed, and as good in every respect as the famous horses of

---

[652] Ferrier, p. 94.

[653] *Ain*, I, pp. 140.

[654] Simon Digby, *War-Horses and Elephant in the Delhi Sultanate A Study of Military Supplies,* Oxford, 1971, p. 26; Gommans, pp. 81-85.

[655] Elphinstone, I, p. 387; II, p. 182. The province of Balkh was famous for strong and active breed of horses.

the desert. They differed, however, in respect to height, and their form was more developed. According to J. P. Ferrier their outline was not pleasing to eyes. He also reports that Timur introduced new blood by dispersing amongst the tribes 42,00 mares, which he had selected in Arabia from the very best breeds. Later on Nadir Shah renewed this cross with 600 mares, which he confided exclusively to the Tekiens.[656] Their horses were known for powers of endurance and were trained to carry their rider and provision for seven or eight days together approximately at the rate of eighty to hundred miles a day. They fed them barley alone and piled *numuds* upon them at night to sweat them, until every particle of fat was removed. Consequently their flesh became firm and hard. They were trained to run every day and quick walk as well as gallop for forty or fifty miles, without ever drawing bridle or showing any symptom of fatigue.[657] Some of these horses were very handsome and when they were in good condition and well groomed, they certainly had a good figure.[658]

According to Alexander Burnes, the *Turki* horses were a large and bony animal, more remarkable for strength and stamina than symmetry and beauty. The stamina and stay quality rendered it particularly valuable on long marches and

---

[656] Ferrier, pp. 94-95

[657] James B. Fraser, *Narrative of a Journey into Khorasan in the years 1821 & 1822*, with a new Introduction by Edward Ingram, OUP, New York, 1984, p. 269-72; Cf. Ferrier, p. 95. I saw one of these animals go from Tehran toTabreez, return, and again reach Tabreez in twelve days; the distance is four hundred and twenty miles. But from this three days must be deducted; the horse having been allowed twenty-four hours rest after each journey.

[658] *Ibid.*

heavy duty. He also goes on to explain that the horses sent to Hindustan were reared about Balkh and the eastern parts of Turkomania or on the bank of Oxus River. They were considered inferior to the horses from Bukhara and Merve. These horses were sold cheap.[659]

Green fodder was found on these steppes only in the spring and during this season the Turkoman refrained from making any expedition until the end of July. During this period their animals rested and from the month of August up to the winter they were kept upon dry food, which consisted of barley mixed with dry chopped straw, Lucerne, *sainfoin* or clover-hay. If the horses had to go for an expedition they were put upon half forage.[660] A Turkoman horse was never kept in stable. He was always picked in the open air, clothe with felt rugs, with the exception of the period they were at grass. They were made to exercise everyday and worked well for twenty and twenty-fife years. These horses resisted cold as well as heat and were accustomed to drink at all time even when they were full of perspiration.[661]

Though the horses were bred in Afghan dominions, they were not quite as good. The Kabul dealers often bought inexpensive and frail horses from the horse markets of Balkh, Bukhara and Khurasan or the breeding plains around it. They then fed them at their own pastures, and once they became strong and agile, sold them with huge profits in India.[662] In the horse market of Bukhara, the Bukharian merchants brought the stock from the surrounding steppes where the

---

[659]   Burnes, II, pp. 271-275.
[660]   Ferrier, pp. 94-95.
[661]   *Ibid.*
[662]   Elphinstone, I, pp. 386-88.

well-bred *Turki* horses especially renowned for their strength and endurance were found. But it is quite a mistake to believe that horses in these parts were sold at low or even at moderate price. Horses of best breeds were purchased at 350*l.* to 400*l.* sterling. Even good *yabus* bred in that part were sold for 30*l.* to 40*l.* sterling.[663] In fact the good *Turki* horses were never sent to India for cavalry purpose and those sent were just better than the inferior ones.

The horses in these parts were so numerous that there was hardly a man in Turkistan who didn't have at least one. Even the beggar in Balkh, it was believed could afford at least one horse.[664]

Even during the Mughal period the main breeding areas which provided Hindustan with the bulk of its supply of war-horse remained more or less the same as was during the Sultanate period. The area beyond the North West Frontier was collectively known as *Mulk-i-Baldasta* (the high land) and there the superior horses could be raised because there was enough food to maintain them. Although the soil and climate of these regions was less favourable to settled agriculture, they were blessed with a high quality of natural grass. Babur informs us that the hills and slopes of those of eastern and western Kabul had grass (*aut*) called *buta kah* grass, was very suitable for horses.[665]

The horses from the north-west of India were known as *Buldasti,* referring to *Mulk-i-Baldasta*. A good breed of the Indian kind was also found in Bannu and Daman and excellent

---

[663] Fraser, pp. 272-73.
[664] Elphinstone, II, p. 193.
[665] *Baburnama*, I, pp. 221-222.

variety of *Tazi* were bred between Jhelam and Indus. The *Yabu* was reared about Bamian.[666] The *yabus* or large ponies were also quite remarkable. Though they were not superior to their best breed, in their power of sustaining fatigue, but were stout, compact, spirited beast and more within the reach of poorer classes.[667]

There were extensive meadows around Logar and Ghazni and the one, called, Nuwur, particularly near Ghazni supplied a force of 20,000 cavalry. Forage for cattle was most plentiful.[668] Horses of excellent breeds were produced in some districts of Kabul. The breed was annually becoming greatly improved owing to care and judicious breeding. The ability to breed good horses was of much use as the Afghans sought employment as cavalry soldiers.[669]

Babur furnishes information about the plunder of "flocks, cloth and horses bred for trade" in Afghan villages by his troops during the expedition into Kohat and Bannu in 1504-5. During the same expedition he also talks of the seizure of "white cloths, aromatic roots, high-quality horses and horses bred for trade" from Afghan merchants on the roads and of his men's killing of Khwaja Khizr Nuhani, "a well known and respected Afghan merchant".[670]

The *Afsan-i-Shahan,* a 17th century text, states that, "the Afghan traded in horses. They brought from *Vilayat* (Afghanistan) and fatten and rear them at Baywara (Jalandhar

[666] Elphinstone, I, p. 189; II, p. 109. Horses and mules were also bred, particularly in the country of the Ishaqzais.
[667] Fraser, p. 271.
[668] Burnes, II, p. 335.
[669] See Irfan Habib, in *Evolution of the Afghan Tribal System,* p.301.
[670] *Baburnama,* I, p. 235.

Doab, Panjab), since all things were cheap at Baywara whether grain or green stuff and then spreading them in Hindustan, sold them. Their home was in Roh (Hilly Country). This was the source of livelihood of the Afghan there".[671]

3. Sheep:

The nomadic economy was closely connected with sheep and so their breeding was required for the acquisition of wealth. In Kabul pastoral tribes bred sheep along with horses, camels, cows, buffaloes and goats. The sheep constituted the main wealth of the nomadic tribes of the country. There were large herds of sheep.

The great stock of the pastoral tribes was sheep. The long tail sheep called in Persian *dumba* was the most important. It was remarkable for its tail, fat and healthy.[672] The tribes also kept goats but took less interest in them. In some parts one third of the flock consisted of goats, in others they only had a few goats to lead the sheep in grazing.[673] But the hair and meat of goat were inferior to that of sheep. On the whole the importance of goats was secondary to that of sheep, although in certain regions (particularly desert region) goats were more important. Khazanov says, "the goat is known to be a somewhat inferior equivalent of the sheep".[674]

The sheep bred in south of Kabul were generally the fat-tailed sheep. They were known as *siahbandi* which were the

---

[671]   Muhammad Kabir, *Afsan-i-Shahan*: Br. Mus., Add. 24, 409, f. 5 a; Cf. *Evolution of the Afghan tribal System*, p. 305.

[672]   Elphinstone, I, p. 190.

[673]   *Ibid.*, II, p. 117.

[674]   Khazanov, pp. 46-47.

best fat-tailed sheep all over the region. Some of the sheep were called the *dumbi* or large-tailed sheep with long ears, a small plums, and very good looking animal. It was of dark reddish-brown colour.[675]

The northern zone of central Asia was known for the flock of sheep. The Uzbek, Tajiks and other northern tribes kept a great number of sheep. The quality of northern sheep was not so fine as those known as *siahbandi*. Northern sheep were of black colour and their wool was inferior to that of white wool of sheep in southern and western Afghanistan. These sheep were physically strong and heavier than the southern white sheep. A large number of sheep were bred in Ghazni and Hazara country.[676]

During the spring the pastoral tribes sent out the flocks even in night. It was the busiest time and they required twice the usual number of shepherds. During this season they had their lambs to take care and their sheep to shear. They sheared their sheep again in the end of autumn.[677]

The sheep were driven to the hills or wastes in the morning and return at night. During summer the nomads moved to the hills with their flocks in order to get pasturage, where they lived in tents, but during winter they found plenty of herbage in the plain.[678]

[675]   Vigne, p. 109.
[676]   Moorcroft and Trebeck, II, p. 483.
[677]   Elphinstone, II, p. 117-118.
[678]   *Ibid.*, II, p. 109.

4. Camels:

On the whole one of the most important animals in Kabul was camels. Amongst the Afghan nomads camels were used primarily for transport and most particularly as beast of burden, on which they carried their tents and baggage; while for the Bedouin nomads of Arabia camel-herding was an important source of food.[679] The tribes sold the male and kept the female for breeding. Most of the traffic of Kabul was carried by camels.[680]

The most valuable possession of the pastoral tribes was their camels. In the desert region, mainly amongst the Turkoman and certain groups of Qazaks the camel was of essential importance. The Qazaks and Kirghiz for the most part herded Bactrian or hybrid camels and Turkoman herded dromedaries. There were two principal sorts: the dromedaries (those with one hump), and the Bactrian, those with two humps. The former were found mostly in the sandy and dry parts of Kabul. They were tall and long-legged animal. The dromedary was light and swift but was less powerful as a beast of burden. The Bactrian camel or two humped camel instead of one was called *ushree* in Turki. It was very rare in Kabul and was brought in from the Qazaq country north of Bukhara. They were very stout and covered with shaggy black hair. In size it was lower than the common camel or dromedary. They could bear greater burdens. These camels had the capacity to march with ease for fourteen successive hours.[681] The *bughdi*

---

[679]   Khazanov, p. 28.

[680]   *Ibid.*

[681]   Burnes, II, p. 178.

camel found in the south-west of Khurasan resembled the one mentioned above, but unlike them the *bughdi* was as tall as the dromedary.[682]

There was also a third sort which was bred between these two. It was greatly preferred because of being uncommonly patient, docile and strong. It grew to a very large size with short stout bony legs. It had a large quantity of shaggy hair upon their neck, shoulder, haunches and on the crown of the head. The colour of these, as of both the other breeds, varied from a light gray to a brown colour, more or less dark.[683]

For Kabul country which had mountains on all the four sides, camels were found to be the most suitable beast of burden.[684] In Kabul, the camel was an animal of first importance. In this region the basic use of the camel was as a mean of transport. However, camels were also used for milking. The camels in Kabul were often covered with eruptions and almost destitute of hair. On the other hand, the camel of Bukhara had a sleek coat, as fine as that of a horse and shed their hair in summer; from which a fine water-proof cloth of close and rather heavy texture was manufactured. It was known as *urmuk* and retained the natural colour of the camel.[685]

5. Cattle and Other Beasts of Burden:

Although the greatest part of the flocks of the pastoral tribes consisted in sheep, they kept other animals as well in

---

[682]   *Ibid.*, pp. 189-190

[683]   Fraser, p. 273.

[684]   Elphinstone, I, pp. 378-88.

[685]   Burnes, II, pp. 176-177.

herds or flocks. On an average, 60 percent of the animals were sheep, 13 percent horses, 4 percent camels and 12 percent cattle.[686] But it is to be noticed that sheep were rare in Bajaur, upper Swat and Buner.[687]

The oxen in Kabul were everywhere used for tillage, and in few parts for carrying burdens. All over the Kabul country the ox was used to plough the land. They were inferior to Indian variety in many respects. They were imported from the western India. No herds of oxen were found in this region, except in a place close to Sistan.[688]

Though the buffaloes were found in many parts of Kabul but they were rare, because of the hot and moist climate of the country.[689]

They also keep asses to carry their light luggage. But they were limited in number. The Ass was not a common animal in this country, but it was stronger and bigger than the Indian variety. Mules were very common and of a superior breed but they were for the most part confined to the hilly districts. Asses and mules were also employed in carriage. During Akbar's reign the mules were bred only in Pakhli, which was one of the *sarkars* of Kabul and its neighbourhood, as rearing and breeding of this animal was considered derogatory by the commoners in India. But according to Abul Fazl this attitude changed after Akbar started taking interest in them.[690] Elphinstone informs us that in the west of Panjab were found some better mules and that west of Indus were better than the former and they

---

[686]   *History of the Civilization of Central Asia,* V, p. 375.
[687]   Elphinstone, II, p. 6; II, pp. 190-191.
[688]   *Ibid.,* II, pp. 5-6, I, p. 190.
[689]   *Ibid.,* p. 190.
[690]   *Ibid.*

continued to improve as one went further westward.[691] Mules were also bred in the country of Ishaqzais. The poor used mules for carriage.[692] Mules were generally imported in large number from Western and Eastern Iran.[693] The Iranian Shah sent mules as gift to Jahangir. If we are to believe Withington in the royal stable there were 1,000 mules,[694] while Pelsaert gives their number at only 260.[695] They were very costly and superior mules were often sold at Rs. 1,000 per head.

6. Wool:

Wool yielding was quite important as sheep, camels and hairy goats rearing was common in this region. Wool obtained from these animals was worked to produce woollen coverlets (*takya-namad*), rugs, blankets and several other woollen goods.[696] But it was the fleece of sheep that met the commercial demand of wool. It was an old cottage industry and continued to be important in the 16th century. In India its production was inadequate and fine wool had to be imported from Kabul and Central Asia.

The wool of the white fleeced sheep formed an important item of export for Kabul. Besides woollen coverlets or

---

[691]   *Ibid.*, I, p. 189.
[692]   *Ibid.*, II, p. 117.
[693]   *Ain,* I, p. 152; Thomas Roe, *The Embassy of Sir Thomas Roe, 1615-19, as Narrated in his Journals and Correspondence,* ed. William Foster, London, 1926, New Delhi, 1993, p. 259.
[694]   Hawkins in *Early Travels*, p. 104.
[695]   Francois Pelsaert, *Remonstrantie*, tr. by B. Narain and S. R. Sharma, 'A *Contemporary Dutch chronicle of Mughal India*', Calcutta, 1957, pp. 34-35.
[696]   *Ain*, I, p. 51; Khafi Khan, I, pp. 199-200.

takya-namad, several other varieties of woollen goods were sent to India.[697] Indian wool was not of fine quality. Abul Fazl informs us that woollen goods were costly.[698] All the sheep in this region were of the fat-tailed variety and were remarkable for the predominance of the rufus-brown colour of their wool. From their skin were made *postins* or sheep skin coats. It was a cotton dress for the all classes of people.[699]

The sheep and goats of Bukhara were known for their celebrated skins. These flocks grazed on furze and dry grass. All the sheep were of the *dumbu* kind, with large tails. Some of them yielded in season so much as fifteen pounds of tallow. The sheep looked deformed from its size and felt uneasiness after that. The sheep which produced the jet-black curly fleece was in demand everywhere. These kinds of sheep were usually not found everywhere and were sent to Persia and other countries. When the curly fleece was removed they lost the peculiarity in their fleece and appeared like any other sheep. The people attributed this curly fleece to the nature of the pasture and believed that the grass called '*boyak*' and by the Persian "*ronass*" which was long kind of bent changed the nature of the animals.[700] The skins of the male lambs were most highly prized. They were killed within five or six days after birth never later than a fortnight. A very few were procured from premature birth in the ewes; and skin of such were as fine as velvet, but not curled. These were called '*kirpuk*' and exported to other countries. The other kind was called

---

[697]   *Ibid.* Woollen coverlets (*takya-namad*) were brought from Kabul and Persia

[698]   *Ibid.,* II, p. 183, 285.

[699]   Moorcroft and Trebeck, II, p. 165.

[700]   Burnes, II, pp. 173-174.

'*danudar*' which was curled and exported to Persia, Turkey and China. Garments made from their wool were exported to other countries where they fetched a very high price.[701] They used to make carpets and felts for domestic use from the wool and hair of their cattle.

The wool (*pushm*) of Turkistan was sent to Kabul, where it was used to make a coarse kind of shawl. The articles made from *pushm* were coarse and lacked fineness. *Pushm* was procured from the Qazaqs and wondering tribes in Bukhara, who were long ignorant of its value and used it in the common ropes by which they used to bind their horses and cattle. The lamb skins of Bukhara were in high demand in India. The Kabul merchants purchased them for ready money. They could only be procured at Karakul, a small district that lies between Bukhara and the Oxus. They were exported to Persia, Turkey and China, but chiefly to Persia.[702]

The goats also yielded wool and many stuff were prepared out of it. The wandering tribes were earlier unknown of its value and prepared out of it a rope to bind their horses and cattle. The goat wool was imported to Kabul and then to India. Usually they were of black colour and of normal size. The stuffs prepared from it were good but far surpassed by those of Kashmir, which were manufactured from the wool of Tibet.[703] This wool was of black colour. Their size was quite normal and was of a dark colour. They differed from those of Tibet, which was a small and pleasant animal.

---

[701]   Burnes, II, p. 175.

[702]   *Ibid.*, II, p. 440.

[703]   *Ibid.*, pp. 175-176.

To conclude, pastoralism co-existed with agriculture in Kabul, and while it is impossible, given the dearth of sources, to estimate the relative share of each to local economy, we can safely assume that pastoral economy was the lifeline of Kabul, and was just as important as the agricultural sector. Given the rich pasture, Kabul enjoyed a wide variety of livestock which sustained itinerant tribal communities earning their livelihood in pastoralism. The pastoral communities were also linked to trade and commerce, and played a crucial role in transporting commodities, in particular fruits and food grains, from one place to other.

THE TRIBES OF KABUL

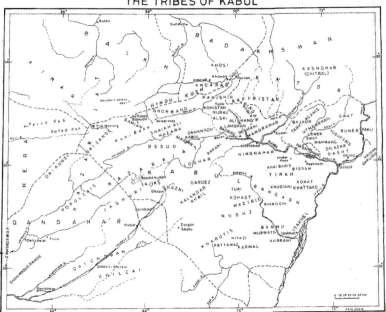

Chapter – VI

Tribes In Kabul: Organization, Politics And Culture

1. Tribal Organization:

The Afghans or Pathans (Pashtun) have played an important role in medieval Indian History. The Afghans have known to have subsisted for centuries at the corridor between Iran and the Indian sub-continent, and from the fifteenth century they appear in sources as divided among numerous tribes, with some, such as the Lodi becoming rulers to Northern India (1451-1526). However, it has been difficult to reconstruct the history of the Afghan tribes in their own homeland, where one has to piece it together largely from sundry incidental references in Indo-Persian sources, collated with local tradition.

Looking into the details of the Afghan tribes, we find a clear distinction between those who inhabited plains on the one hand and the highlanders on the other. The former can again be broadly divided into the Western and the Eastern Afghans. Among the Western Afghans, the Abdalis (popularly known as Durranis) were the most important, while among the Eastern Afghan there were 'Berdooranee' or Bar Durrani ("upper" Durrani) who were so called by Ahmad Shah Abdali to distinguished them from the Abdali Durrani who remained at Qandahar. There in the middle of 18th century they made themselves the ruler of the country since came to be known as Afghanistan.[704] The Eastern Afghans mainly consisted of the Yusufzais and kindred tribes of Peshawar plain and mountain valley to the north of it.[705]

Towards the close of the sixteenth century, Abul Fazl in his *Ain-i-Akbari* provides a detailed account of the Afghan tribes. He not only gives a number of names of Afghan tribes settled in both Kabul provinces, but is also the first to give the traditional explanation of the rise of the Afghan tribes, in which common ancestry played an important role.[706]

Abul Fazl tells us that the traditional progenitor of the Afghan race was a person from Bani Israel, called Afghan – who had three sons: Sarban, Gharghasht and Batan. They became the ancestors of the three tribal federations (*ulus*). Genealogical tradition sought to accommodate the Afghan to a common ancestor named Abdur Rashid alias Qais. The same person was named Afghan as quoted by Abul Fazl.[707]

From the descendants of Sarban, Gharghasht and Batani arose as sub-divisions various tribe. Abul Fazl goes on to list them all under each of the three original tribes. The Yusufzais, Mahmands and other eastern Afghan tribes considered Sarban

---

704   Elphinstone, II, p. 2. The term *Ber-Doorani* means upper-Durrani.

705   *Punjab Castes,* p. 63.

706   *Ain,* I, p. 591; See Irfan Habib, 'Evolution of the Afghan Tribal System', in *PIHC,* 62nd session, Bhopal, 2001, p. 302.

707   *Ibid.*; Khwaja Nimatullah, *Tarikh-i-Khanjahani* or *Makhzan-i-Afghani,* ed. S.M. Imam Al-Din, Dacca, 1960, II, pp. 548, 650. Qais was the contemporary of the Prophet Muhammad and was 37th in descent from Saul, King of Israel.

their forefather (Qais's eldest son); Gharghasht was reckoned to be the ancestor of the Afridi, Khattak and the Kakars dwelling in the area east of Qandahar and in Baluchistan; Batani gave rise to the Ghilzai, Niyazi, Lodi and Sur (1539-1555). Abul Fazl records that the Ghilzai, Lodi and Sarwani were not really descendants of Batan, through agnatic lineage, but were sons of Batan's daughter born out of an illegitimate union with a Ghor chief Mast Ali called Mati.[708] This tradition is also recorded in the seventeenth century work of Niamatulla entitled *Makhzan-i-Afghani* probably completed about 1613 (Nimatulla was a scribe at the court of the Mughal emperor Jahangir).[709]

Though the lineage and tradition of common descent were carefully preserved, they were divided into several bodies, distinct and separate from one another. They were torn by the feuds of clans against clans and often families against families. Throughout their history they failed to establish any compact nation. The tribe was divided into numerous clans and these again into septs. They all were alike distinguished by the name of a common ancestor by the addition of the word *Zai* or *Khel*.[710]

---

[708] *Ain*, I, p. 591. See also *Punjab Castes*, p. 65. The Ghilzai were the most famous of all the Afghan tribes till the rise of the Durrani power, while the Lodi section gave Delhi the Lodi and Sur dynasties. The Sarwani never rose to prominence, and are now hardly known in Afghanistan.

[709] N'imatullah, II, pp. 548, 650.

[710] Bellew, p. 111. The Sufix *Zai,* a Persian word meaning 'born of', but Ibbetson writes it is the corruption of the Pashto *Zoe* meaning 'son'; while *Khel* is an Arabic word meaning an association or company; *Punjab Castes*, p. 61.

The word *Ulus* or clannish commonwealth was applied to a whole tribe or to one of this independent branch. *Ulus* was divided into several branches, each under its own chief, known as *Malik*, who was subordinate to the chief of the *Ulus*, called Khan. He was always chosen from the oldest family of the *Ulus* and acted as the chief of the whole tribe. He was seldom more than their leader in war and their agent in dealing with others. The Khan possessed influence rather power. The real power belonged to the *Jirga* or tribal assembly, a democratic council composed of all Maliks.[711] The Khan presided in the principal *Jirga* and internal government of *Ulus* was carried by him. At the time of emergency, the Khan acted without consulting the *Jirga* but in important matters, the sentiments of the whole tribe were ascertained before a decision was taken. Elphinstone observed in 1809 that amongst all the tribes of Afghans the clannish attachment was towards the community as a whole, and not to the chief of the community.[712] The *Jirga* was essentially an instrument for intertribal consultation and action. A *Jirga* comprised Khans, Maliks or elders, assisted by Mullahs, who heard judicial cases.[713] A *jirga* was a sort of primitive aristocracy, not an institution of democracy.

Although they were collectively bound to one another by common descent, the various clans and groups of clans formed distinct communities, governed by separate chiefs, with rival and opposing interests, which developed into continual feuds and jealousies. But in their relations with the foreigners, internal feuds and disturbances would be put aside and the

---

[711]   Elphinstone, I, pp. 213-215.

[712]   *Ibid.*, p. 217.

[713]   *Ibid.*, pp. 218, 222.

entire community would act together against the perceived common enemy.

2. Afghan Tribes:

Throughout history Kabul has been the abode of a variety of ethnic groups such as Turks, Aimaq, Arabs,[714] Pashais, Parachi, Tajiks, Barakis and Afghans.[715] According to Adamec there were few Pashais left, "now obscure and nearly forgotten". The Parachis mostly lived in Kabul and the Barakis, a tribe of Tajiks inhabited Logar and parts of Butakhak.[716]

The Hazaras and Nikdari tribes were based in the mountains west of Kabul and in the mountains to the northeast were Kafiristan populated by Kitur (Gawar) and the Gibriks.[717] The Pathan or Pashtun traditionally was the Afghan par excellence, ritually distinct from all the other ethnic groups inhabited chiefly in the southern part.

---

[714] *The Baburnama, Memoirs of Babur, Prince and Emperor*, tr. Wheeler M. Thakston, New York, 1996, pp. 172-73. The Turks were Turco-Mongolian tribes and the Arabs of Kabul were brought by Timur. They spoke only Persian and lived chiefly in the Jalalabad district.

[715] *Baburnama*, I, p. 207.

[716] Adamec. pp. 91, 635, 647

[717] *Baburnama*, I, p. 207. See Thakston's trans. pp. 172-74. Gibrik is the name Babur gives as one of the Kafir groups. Over time and also because of the "paganism" of the region, 'Gibar' could easily have been transformed into 'Kafir'. Cf. Sir George Robertson, The Kafir of the Hindu-Kush, London, 1896, p. 75. In his study of late nineteenth century Robertson says that the Gibriks were also known as Ramgulis, who inhabited the most western part of Kafiristan.

It is significant to note that the first mention of individual tribes in the Afghan homeland is made by Babur. He places all the Afghan tribes to the south of Kabul. Towards the close of the sixteenth century Abul Fazl in his *Ain-i-Akbari* furnishes a much more detailed account than Babur's incidental references about Afghan tribes.[718]

The entire north-western frontier region was inhabited by the numerous Afghan and non-Afghan tribes. Amongst the various Afghan tribes of this region, the following were prominent: Dilazak, Yusufzais, Mahmadzai, Afridi, Bangash, Ghilzai, Waziri and Orakzai among others.

H.W. Bellow is of the opinion that though the term Afghan and Pathan are used as synonymous it was not one and the same. In fact they belong to different race and origin.[719] Although Babur specifies so many Pathan tribal names, he nowhere mentions them as Pathan, Pakhtun or Pashtun. Even among the various languages spoken in Kabul; he mentions Afghani as the language of Afghanistan.[720]

As for their 'original home' our early information about the Afghans put them in an area around southern and south-eastern Afghanistan. They remained in this region since early medieval times, but by the sixteenth century they had expanded considerably into the areas northward. In the 6th and 7th century's records, the Afghans are mentioned, inhabiting the Sulaiman Mountains east of Ghazni. In Huan Tsang's account they are referred to as a tribe (A-po-kin) located in the northern part of the Sulaiman Mountain.[721]

---

[718]   *Ibid.*; *Ain,* I, p. 591.

[719]   H.W. Bellew, pp. 24-25.

[720]   *Baburnama,* I, p. 207.

[721]   Thomas Watters, On Yuan Chwang's *Travels in India 629-645*

Similarly, the *Hudud-i-Alam* a Persian work on geography describes them as settled in Farmal district which was not far from the Sulaiman Mountain or Takht-i-Sulaiman.[722] The famous medieval scholar Al-Beruni (d.1050) describes them as the inhabitants of the same mountain range.[723] Ibn Battuta, the Moroccan traveller, in the 1330s noticed their settlements in Kabul, which was then just a village. He describes them as "Persians called Afghans", probably because they spoke Persian, and says that they inhabited the territory between Kabul and the Indus.[724] On the evidence of Ibn Battuta, Irfan Habib believes that they were based in the mountains west of Sulaiman Range, i.e. Takht-i-Sulaiman on the NWFP-Baluchistan.[725]

Since the early medieval times, these Afghan tribes remained in and around this territory but by sixteenth century they had also migrated considerably into areas northward. Therefore we find that both Babur and Abul Fazl place the Afghans in the territory eastward from Kabul to the Indus. In 1504 Babur noted that they (Afghans) were well-established in the region of Laghman, Hashtnagar, Swat and Bajaur. The

---

A.D., ed. T.W. Rhys Davids and S.W. Bushell, London, 1905, II, p.265; Cf. Evolution of the Afghan Tribal System, p. 300.

[722] V. Minorsky (tr.), *Hudud-i-Alam, The Regions of the world*, London, 1937, pp. 30, 91, 251-252; Raverty, p. 5. The highest peak of Sulaiman mountain was called Takht-i-Sulaiman which is also called *Koh-i-Siyah* by the people inhabiting that area.

[723] Alberuni, *Alberuni's India an account of the religion, philosophy, literature, geography, chronology, customs, laws, and astrology of India about A.D. 1030*, tr. E.C. Sachau, Delhi, 1964, I, p. 208.

[724] *The Travels of Ibn Battuta*, III, p. 590.

[725] Evolution of the Afghan Tribal System, p. 300.

Yusufzais were based in Kohat. Many of these Afghans had occasionally confronted with Babur's troop.[726]

The eastward movement of the Afghans seems to have continued throughout Babur's period and beyond. In 1519, the Afridis were reported as recently having settled around the Khaibar region. At that time the Karlanris, (who would later settle in Bajaur) and the Usman- Khel, (who would later settle at the Peshawar border) were still dwelling further west in the region of Ningnahar.[727] A tradition of such northward migration can also be seen in respect of the Yusufzais.[728]

The Mughal historians Abul Fazl and Muhammad Kazim give a fairly cogent account of the migrations of the Yusufzais.[729]

The original home and the native places of this large tribe of Yusufzais were between Qandahar and Qarabagh i.e. south of Ghazni. From there they migrated to the district of Kabul and became powerful during the middle of the fifteenth century. At that time Kabul was ruled over by Babur's uncle, Mirza Ulugh Beg (1469-1502). Mirza Ulugh Beg massacred a large number of them and those who survived moved eastward into Lamghan (Laghman) then onward to Kashghar (Chitral), finally settling in Swat river basin and Bajaur (Panjkora valley). In and around this region, where we now find them, these Yusufzais emerged as the dominant class overthrowing the local chief called "Sultan" who claimed an ancient lineage.

---

[726] *Baburnama,* I, pp. 207, 217, 221, 230-32.
[727] Raverty, pp. 53, 125, 223.
[728] *Baburnama,* I, pp. 230-231. The Yusufzai tribes of Afghan then inhabited the Kohat territory.
[729] *Akbarnama,* III, p. 475; *Alamgirnama,* II, pp. 1039-40.

They retained their speech, their tribal organization and their marauding practices.[730]

Elphinstone writing in the early decades of the nineteenth century records the tradition that the Yusufzais had been expelled from Gerra and Nushki in the neighbourhood of Qandahar about the end of the thirteenth or beginning of the fourteenth century.[731] The Afghan migration to these areas led to the displacement or subjugation of the local population. Soon after they settled in the neighbourhood of Kabul and migrated to their present home in the sixteenth century; there they clashed with the Dilazak (an Indian race)[732] whom they gradually ousted. The Yusufzais slew and deported the Dilazaks in large numbers so that the district was almost cleared of them.[733] Thus by the end of the reign of Jahangir the occupation of this tract by Yusufzais was completed.

---

[730] *Akbarnama,* III, p. 475.

[731] Elphinstone, II, pp. 9-11; Raverty explains that Nushki is not a place we know today in Baluchistan close to Kalat, but a locality now named Mashaki, some thirty miles south of Ghazni. Thus there can be no doubt that the original seat of Yusufzais towards the beginning of 14th century was in the neighbourhood of Qandahar.

[732] Bellew, p. 65.

[733] Elphinstone, II, pp. 10-11. The Dilazaks were Karlarnis, the progenitor of their tribe being one of the sons Karanalary. They were divided into two great divisions said to be descended from Dilazak two sons – Yaqub and Loraey. According to him, lower part of Bajaur as far as Jhelam belonged to the Afghan tribe of Dilazaks. Jahangir also refers to Dilazaks. Raverty, pp. 220, 383-385.

During the sixteenth century the Yusufzais also overcame a class of people called Hindkis, whom they treated as a subjugated race.[734]

The Yusufzais proved themselves to be the most formidable enemies of the peace of the country and the safety of the roads. Highway robbery was the hereditary profession of these hardy people. The region they lived in yielded too scanty a sustenance for their fast growing numbers and the gains through agriculture were far too modest when compared with the fortune to be led by plundering the rich traders as well as travellers passing through the hills.[735] The Yusufzais dwelt in a very strong mountainous tract of this region, to which access was difficult. Although a part of this region was plain, most of it was studded with hill and defiles. Babur informs us that these areas also contained *dasht* or steppes plain.[736] The Indus surrounds them on two sides and on the other two sides by the river Kabul and the northern hilly regions. Abul Fazl writes that the length and breadth of this territory was 30 and 15-20 *kos* respectively.[737]

There have been various estimates of the Yusufzais population. Nimatullah informs us that early in the seventeenth century (1613), they were called *nuh lakh* or nine lakhs.[738] Elphinstone estimated their numbers including *faqirs*

---

[734] Bellew, p. 67; Adamec, vol., 6, pp. 254-55. Hindkis was the name given to the Hindus who lived in Afghanistan. The Yusufzais converted them to Islam and called them Hindki in contradistinction to Hindus.

[735] *Akbarnama*, III, p. 475.

[736] *Baburnama*, I, pp. 218, 223.

[737] *Akbarnama*, III, p. 476; Raverty, p. 193.

[738] Nimatullah, II, p. 577.

and dependents as not more than 700,000. He writes that the Afghan reckoned them at 900,000; but more numerous than them were their *faqirs* 'villeins' who were labourers for Yusufzais.[739] Raverty estimated their population at 200,000 families, not far from the estimates of Nimatullah and Elphinstone.[740]

Besides the Yusufzais, the most numerous and powerful of all the Eastern Afghans, there were other border tribes. The most famous names among them are – Afridi, Khattaks, Ghilzai, Orakzai, Bangash and Waziri etc. Elphinstone records that Karlanri, who was adopted by grandson of Sarban was the traditional ancestor of most of the border tribes such as Usman khel, Orakzai, Khugiani and Waziri.[741]

The Ghilzais were a race of probably Turkish origin, who were settled in the Siyah-band range of the Ghor mountains where they mixed with the Persian blood. They first rose into prominence during the time of Mahmud of Ghazni, whom they accompanied in his conquest of India. Later on they conquered the area between Jalalabad and Kalat-i-Ghilzai. In the beginning of the 18th century they revolted against their Persian ruler and declared themselves independent under Mir Wais. But a quarter of a century later they were reduced by Nadir Shah. The Lodi Afghans, the Surs the Niyazis and the

---

[739] Elphinstone, II, p. 27. *Faqirs* were labourers and shepherds attached to the individual Yusufzai peasants, who were their *Khwand* or master. The *faqirs* were placed outside the tribe and not entitled to participate in the *Jirga* or tribal assembly. They had liberty to move from one master to other.

[740] Reverty, p. 193.

[741] Elphinstone, I, p. 210.

Nuhanis were all allied to the Ghilzais.[742] To them belonged almost all the tribes of pastoral traders termed as *Powindas,* who were mainly engaged in carrying the trade between India and Kabul and the northern parts of Central Asia.[743]

Prior to the Afghan's migration to the Kabul river valley, the Tajiks had formed the dominant population around Kabul, Lamghan and Ningnahar. Before the advent of the Ghilzais sometimes in the late sixteenth century the Logar valley, located south of Kabul had also been a Tajik stronghold.[744] They were remnants of the old Persian inhabitants of Afghanistan.[745] The Tajik lived mostly around towns. They constituted the principal part of the population round Kabul city and Ghazni; while in the mountainous parts of Kabul, and in the region of Hazaras, those of the southern Ghilzais and Kakkar, there was scarcely a Tajik to be found.[746] They were styled as *Farsiwan* as well as Tajik by the Afghan people. The word is now loosely used to express all Pathans who speak Persian.[747]

Babur informs about the existence of the Mahmand tribe of the Afghans in Kabul. They inhabited the area east of Jalalabad along the Kabul River.[748] The Bangash Afghan inhabited the upper Bangash. In the Bangash territory Babur places the Afghan tribes called Khugiani, Khirilchi, Turi and

[742]   *Ibid.,* p. 591.
[743]   *Punjab Castes,* pp. 64-65.
[744]   *Baburnama,* I, p.207: Raverty, pp.100, 682.
[745]   *Punjab Castes,* p. 64.
[746]   Elphinstone, I, p. 408.
[747]   Raverty, p.453; *Punjab Castes,* p. 64.
[748]   *Baburnama,* I, p. 221; *Khulasat-ut-Twarikh,* p. 85.

Landar.[749] He reports that the Kurani, Kiwi, Sur, Isa Khel and Niyazi tribes cultivated the territory of Bannu.[750]

Abul Fazl has noted that the *sarkars* of Dawar, Bannu and Isa Khel[751*] were peopled entirely by Afghans, principally by the Shiranis, Karranis and Waziris.[752] The Shirani Afghans were settled in the mountains about the Takht-i-Sulaiman. They were by descent Sarbani Afghans. The Tarkalani Afghans had made the territory of Mandrawar their homeland.[753]

Apart from these Afghan tribes, there were certain other non-Afghan tribes, among them Kafirs and Hazaras, played an equally important role in the history of this region. The following section deals with the non-Afghan tribes in Kabul.

3. Non Afghan Tribes:

i) The Kafirs:

Babur informs us that the Kafirs were one of the major ethnic groups in Kabul.[754] They were very different from the Afghans because of their language and culture.

---

[749] *Baburnama,* I, p. 220; Ibbetson, III, pp. 168, 245 Khugiani inhabited on the strip of land lying between Kabul and Laghman.

[750] *Baburnama*, I p. 233 *Bannu* was a fertile region because of the Bangash or Kurram River.

[751] * Although, Abul Fazl mentions it as a *sarkar* but they too were Afghan tribe which inhabited the area along the Indus River and found there even during the 19th century.

[752] *Ain*, I, pp. 586-87.

[753] *Baburnama,* I, p. 341.

[754] *Ibid.*, p. 207. To the north-eastern mountains were the places of the Kafirs, such as Kitur (Gawar) and Gibrik. *Kafir* is an Arabic

The Kafiristan or "Land of the *Kafirs* or Infidels" was bounded on the north by Badakhshan and Qunduz, on the west by Andarab and Khost and the ranges above the Najrao and Panjshir valleys of the Kabul province. On the east it extended towards Chitral proper and Lower Chitral and in the south it was bounded by *darra* of Kunar, Lamghan and their dependencies.[755]

There was an extensive region embracing the eastern parts of the Hindu Kush range that was outside the area claimed by the Mughals. A tract within this area was known as Kator or Katur, which was chiefly peopled by Kafirs. It was first mentioned in Sharfuddin Yazdi's *Zafarnama*. No Muslim conqueror except perhaps Timur ever set his foot on Kator. The author of *Zafarnama* reports that Timur on his way to India advanced to Parian and then to the Khawak Pass. He attacked the Kafirs of Kator from the latter place. He repaired the celebrated fort in Parian and ordered a pillar of marble to be set up and inscribed with the account of this expedition.[756]

---

word signifying the infidel. This appellation has been applied to the South African in the same manner as to the people of Kafiristan; Cf. Raverty, p. 132.

[755] *Baburnama,* I, p. 207; Vigne, pp. 234-235.

[756] *Zafarnama,* II, ff. 8-19. Since the infidels dwelt in narrow passages and precipices and there was no road to get to them owing to the deep snow, the expedition was not entirely successful; *Akbarnama,* I, p. 283. The Parian fort was later on repaired by Humayun and was given the name of Islamabad, when Humayun was returning to Kabul in 1548 after a campaign in Badakhshan; Cf. Robertson, p. 75.

Mirza Haidar Dughlat states that Kator lies in the district of Khost on the northern slopes of Hindu Kush, between south and south-east of Qunduz and was near Kafiristan.[757]

Babur tells us that the north-eastern mountain of Kabul *suba* was inhabited by the Kafirs. According to him the territory of Kafiristan extended from the vicinity of Panjshir to Chighan Sarai and Kator which he spelt as *Kawar* or *Gawar* was a part of it. He further says that the *tuman* of Alingar of the Kabul province was close to the Kafiristan of Kator and that the Alingar river came down out of that district.[758] In the mountainous tract of Alasai and Najrao, lying north-east from Kabul and behind it in the same mountains all the inhabitants were Kafirs.[759]

Abul Fazl tells us that the *sarkars* of Pakli, Swat, Buner and Bajaur touched the border of Kator in the north. It is thus apparent that he considered Kator as embracing the region represented by Kafiristan on modern maps.[760] Therefore, we find that the area of Kator extended probably also to Chitral or Kashghar (not to be confused with the Kashghar in China)

[757]   Dughlat, pp. 103-104.

[758]   *Baburnama*, I, pp. 210-212, 214. He says that the Pech river issued out of Kator the Pech valley produced plenty of grapes.

[759]   *Ibid.*, p. 220. Alasai was 4-6 miles (2 or 3 *shari*) east of Najrao, p.213. The Kafirs of Najrao burnt the *chilghoza* instead of lamps to get light or fire; *Ain*, I, p. 593.

[760]   *Ibid.*, pp. 585-592; *Akbarnama*, III, pp. 515, 642-684. In 1581, Akbar, on his way to Hindustan after his campaign against his brother Mirza Hakim, reached Jalalabad. From that place he sent a detachment of troops to penetrate as far as the skirt of the mountains of Kator or the country of the *Kafiran-i-Siyah-posh*. Zain Khan Koka in pursuit of Jalala Raushanai penetrated into the country of the Kafirs lying east of Bajaur. In these operations some of the Kafirs assisted Akbar's troops.

which is mentioned in the *Ain-i-Akbari* as situated in the north of Buner, Swat and Bajaur.[761]

Though the name of Kator was applied to a tract within Kafiristan, but during the mid sixteenth to about mid-nineteenth century the rulers of Chitral were also called Kator. W. Moorcroft and G. Trebeck also noted that the rulers of Chitral were known to the Afghans as the "Raja of Kator".[762]

According to Raverty, the length of Kafiristan from Lamghan to Chitral was over one hundred *Kuroh* and from Kunar to the frontier of Badakhshan was about eighty *kuroh* in breadth.[763] The country of Kafirs was rough and difficult and it had snowy mountains, deep pine forests, and small but fertile valleys, where plenty of grapes were produced.[764]

The *tuman* of Panjshir was a thoroughfare for the Kafir highwaymen and they obtained a livelihood from it. On account of being so near, the people of Panjshir paid perquisites to them. In 1526, when Babur advanced towards Hindustan to conquer it, the Kafirs attacked Panjshir and slew a large number of its people.[765]

The territory of Chighan Sarai was situated in the mouth of Kafiristan; though its inhabitants were *Musalman,* they

[761] *Ibid.,* p. 585; Elphinstone, II, pp 388-89. He mentions Chitral as being a part of Kaushkaur; but now the name is applied to the territory of Chitral exclusively.

[762] Moorcroft and Trebeck, II, p. 269; *Civilization of Central Asia,* V, p. 237.

[763] Raverty, p.132; *The Gates of India,* pp. 102-3, 133. He records "all the wild mountain district west of the Kunar are held by Kafirs still….., Laghman and Kunar both spread their plains to the foot of the mountains of Kafiristan".

[764] Burnes, I, pp. 200-201; II, pp. 210-211.

[765] *Baburnama,* I, p. 214.

mixed with the Kafirs and followed their custom and practices. That is why they were called *neemcha musalman* (half bred in custom).[766]

Babur says that "the Kafirs are wine-drinkers, never pray and fear neither God nor man. They were heathenish".[767] Alexander Burnes who visited Kabul in the early 1830s reports that the "Kafirs appear to be the most barbarous people, eater of bears and monkey and fighting with arrows and scalping their enemies". He further describes them as aborigines of Afghanistan and in no way connected with the reputed descendants of Alexander the Great as has been stated by some authors.[768] According to G.T. Vigne, they had grey eyes, light brown hair, and quite fair complexion and that they were descendants of the Greeks of the Bactrian dynasty.[769] Sir George Scott Robertson, who visited the Kafir's country towards the close of the nineteenth century, found no Greek or Christian affinities beyond as he puts it, a fondness for wine and goats.[770]

The Kafirs consisted of two great sects or divisions. Those who were dressed in white garment (or white clad infidels) – called *Safed-posh* in Persian and *Spin Kafiri* in Pashto. The other sect was dressed in black (or black clad infidels) – called *Siyah-posh* in Persian and *Tor Kafiri* in Pashto. It should be kept in mind that they were so called owing to their attire. Otherwise, the Kafirs were celebrated for their beauty and

---

[766] *Ibid.,* See also the footnote.

[767] *Ibid.,* I, pp. 210, 212, 213; See also *Ain,* tr. H.S. Jarrett, Delhi, 2006, p. 410, footnote.

[768] Burnes, II, pp. 210-212.

[769] Vigne, pp. 236-237.

[770] *The Kafirs of the Hindu Kush,* pp. 157-170.

European complexion. One division wore a sort of garment of black goat-skins while the other dressed in white cotton. Mounstuart Elphinstone writing in 1815, reports that the Kafirs were remarkable for fairness and beauty of their complexion.[771] On one occasion Alexander Burnes came across a Kafir boy, and describes him thus: "his complexion, hair and features was quite European; his eyes were of bluish colour. Few words of his language were Indian".[772]

The Kafir had no general name for their nation, for they were all divided into tribes, though not according to genealogy, but by geographical position. The *Siyah-Posh* Kafirs, roughly speaking, peopled the northern half and the east of Kafiristan. The *Safed-Posh* Kafirs who occupied the centre and the south-east of the country consisted of three tribes: the Wai, the Presun and Ashkund. The Wai inhabited the south-east of Kafiristan called Waigal. The Presun inhabited an inaccessible valley at the centre. They were entirely different from the *Siyah-posh* Kafirs on the one hand and from the Wai and Ashkund on the other. They were known for their peaceful disposition and lack of interest in martial skills. These people could be easily plundered without much difficulty. The Ashkund were found to the south-west of Presun.[773]

The Kafir rarely inhabited the valleys, but all their dwellings were placed on the mountain side. The Kafirs who were remarkable mountaineers also carried on mixed agricultural and pastoral pursuits. Their country though mountainous was fertile and produced grapes in abundance.[774]

---

[771]   Elphinstone, II, pp. 375-376.
[772]   Burnes, I, pp. 165-166.
[773]   Grierson, VIII, Part, II, pp. 29-31, 45, 59, 68.
[774]   C. Wessels, p. 15.

Babur informs us that in the district of Badrao Kafirs grew corn.[775] Their flocks and herds were very large. The poor kinsmen tended to look after the herds.[776]

Their society was tribal and oligarchal. Their women were known for their beauty. The Kafir women wore silver ornaments and many cowry shells. Both male and female used ear-ring, rings round the neck and bracelets sometimes of silver and often of brass. The age of marriage was from 20 – 30 for the males and 15 – 16 for the women.[777] Mutamad Khan tells us that in their society monogamy was the norm. They did not have more than one wife, except when the first wife was barren or the husband be displeased with her or if the wife refused to live with the husband.[778]

There were in the Kafir tribes, slaves as well. The male and female slaves of this race were exceedingly faithful and well-natured towards their masters. It was a common practice that the powerful men seized the children of weak ones and sold them to *musalman* or kept them for their own use, however, they were not ill-used.[779]

The Kafirs placed their dead ones in coffin and deposited the coffins in caves and cavities of the mountains. They made neither lamentation nor mourning; indeed they carried their corps to its last abode with great drum beating.[780] But Elphinstone records that the womenfolk lamented and from

---

[775]   *Baburnama,* I, p. 221; Elphinstone, I, p. 130; II, p. 5.
[776]   Vigne, p. 238.
[777]   Elphinstone, II, pp. 381-384; Raverty, p. 141.
[778]   *Iqbalnama-i-Jahangiri*, pp. 268-269.
[779]   Vigne, p. 236.
[780]   Raverty, pp. 131-132.

time to time the body was kept down and their women used to weep over it.[781]

The Kafirs were very fond of wine. They also ate cheese and fruits but consumed comparatively little bread. Both men and women consumed wine to great excess.[782] Babur tells us that wine was so commonly used that they kept a leather bag called *khig* at their neck and drank wine instead of water. He further informs that the wine of Kafiristan was not of a high quality because they boiled it. Strong wine of Kafiristan was sent to neighbouring areas.[783]

As far as the religion of Kafirs was concerned they believed in one God, which they called Imra. But there were a large number of secondary deities as well, which according to them represented great men of former days.[784] Mutamad Khan confirms that these idols were made of stone or wood and always represented men or women.[785] Their temples were kept well ornamented and their idols were adorned with gold and other ornaments. Benedict Goes states that they never entered their temples unless clothed in black.[786] The faces of their idols were washed with the urine of a cow and goat when they sought a blessing. Animals were also to be sacrificed to their God.[787]

---

781 Elphinstone, II, p. 382.

782 Vigne, p. 236.

783 *Baburnama,* I, pp. 211, 212-213. They drank wine both pure and diluted out of large silver cups; Vigne, pp. 337-338. He states that he tasted the wine of Kafiristan; it was not of bad taste but required clarifying.

784 Elphinstone, II, p. 377.

785 *Iqbalnama-i-Jahangir,* pp. 268-269.

786 C Wessels, p. 15.

787 Elphinstone, II, pp. 377-379; Raverty, p. 131.

Regarding the languages of Kafirs, it was till lately assumed that as there were two main groups of Kafirs, viz. the *Siyah-posh* and the *Safed-posh*, there were, therefore two languages in Kafiristan corresponding to these two groups. But Grierson says that the languages of Kafiristan consisted of four languages such as Bashgali (Kati), Wai-ala, Presun or Wasi-veri and Ashkund.[788] They belonged to the Indo-Iranic branch of Indo-European languages.[789]

It appears that the *Siyah-Posh* Kafirs, who, roughly speaking, peopled the northern half and the east of Kafiristan, all employed various dialects of a language, apparently resembling Bashgali (the speech of the people inhabiting the valley of the Bashgal River).[790] It was also called Kati. It seems that they all were at once able to understand each other and converse fluently or without hesitation.

The Wai and the Presun tribes used different languages which were mutually unintelligible, and both of which were unintelligible to the *Siyah-posh* Kafirs. These tribes were unable to converse with each other without the help of interpreters. The language of Ashkund, which according to George Robertson was the most difficult to understand, was probably allied to the Wai.[791] Elphinstone reports that all the languages of Kafir country had some connection with Sanskrit.[792]

---

[788] Grierson, pp. 29-31.

[789] *Civilization of Central Asia,* p. 724.

[790] Grierson, pp. 29-31. The centre of the Kati speaker is the village of Kamdesh (Kamgrom), which is located in the Bashgal valley.

[791] *The Kafirs of the Hindu Kush,* pp. 74-78. He says it was most difficult to get any information of this language; Grierson, pp. 29-31, 68. Regarding Ashkund he writes, we knew nothing about this dialect except the word means 'bare mountain'.

[792] Elphinstone, II, p. 376; *Colliers Encyclopedia,* ed. William T.

The Kafirs were always at war with their Muslim neighbours. The latter also detested them and frequently attacked their territory. The arms of Kafirs were bows and light arrows of reeds with barbed head which they sometimes poisoned. They wore a dagger of a peculiar shape on the right side and a sharp knife on the left. Their common mode of warfare was surprise attacks and they often undertook remote and difficult expedition. They considered it a matter of glory to slay a *Musalman*.[793] The *Siyah-posh* Kafirs were famous for their valour and fearlessness and in a fight with the *Musalman* preferred to die. For them it was an eternal disgrace to return wounded. They considered their chief occupation to be that of carrying on war with races other than own.[794] These turbulent people used to hide themselves in their upland villages, amidst their magnificent woods and forests. They often made surprise attacks in the passes and routes and killed traders and travellers.[795]

Towards the end of Akbar's reign in 1603, the Jesuit, Benedict Goes started his journey from Lahore to Kashghar. In his account of the journey he writes that in the country of

Couch, New York, 1956, II, pp. 355, 491.

[793] Elphinstone, pp. 385-386; Vigne, p. 235.

[794] Raverty, pp. 130-131; Vigne, pp. 234-235.Such was the animosity that exists towards the *Musalman,* that when a return from a foray was expected, the young Kafir girls put walnuts and dried fruits into their bosoms and advanced to meet the men returning, who flourished their long knives, with the heads of their victim upon the points. Those who had killed a *Musalman* had then a right to snatch the walnut and fruits from the girl's bosoms

[795] *Ibid.*; Vigne, pp. 234-235.

Kafirs no *Musalman* was allowed to enter and if one did get in he was punished with death.[796]

In spite of these characteristics, the Kafirs were in general a harmless, affectionate and kind-hearted people. Even to *Musalman* they were kind when they admitted them as guests.[797]

In 1895, the Afghan Amir, Abdur Rahman captured Kafiristan and made it a part of Afghanistan. Many Kafirs were captured and converted to Islam and their country was renamed *Nuristan* ("Land of Light").[798] The tribe was not exterminated and survived, but in the process of their continued subjugation, lost their distinct identity and culture.

ii) The Hazaras:

In the Kabul *suba,* the Afghans and Hazaras were the main groups among the inhabitants.[799] Amongst the non-Afghan population of Kabul *suba*, the Hazaras have also played an equally important role in the history of this *suba.*

The Hazaras occupied a very extensive area of country, extending from the borders of Kabul and Ghazni to those of Herat in one direction and from the vicinity of Qandahar to

---

[796] *Jahangir And the Jesuits,* pp. 126-134.

[797] *Ibid.,* p. 387.

[798] *Gates of India,* p. 269.

[799] *Ain,* I, p. 591.

* Being an Arabic plural of Hazara now often also called Hazaristan.

that of Balkh in the other.[800] The area is known as Hazarajat or Hazaristan.

The author of *Rauzat-us Safa* tells us that Changhiz sent his youngest son Tulai to conquer Khurasan and in particular to devastate the great cities of Merv, Nishapur and Herat. All the inhabitants of these cities were slaughtered. The following year he sent an army of 80,000 men to kill the whole population of Herat and Afghanistan. He ordered his men to spare no living creatures, not even cats and dogs.[801] It appears that the largest number of ancestral Hazaras had settled in this country during the thirteenth century by Chaghatai, Changhiz Khan's son or by Manku Khan, his grandson, on the lands of Ghorid, who had been largely exterminated during the Mongol invasions. Juwaini reports about 1259, 'the children and grandchildren of Changhiz Khan are more than ten thousand, each of whom has his position (*muqam*), territory (*yurt*), army and equipment'.[802] The descendants of Changhiz Khan and his officers dominated *Ajam* for a century and a half till Timur replaced them by his own set of officers. The Hazaras, therefore, were the relatives of Mongol warriors,

---

[800] *Ain-i-Akbari*, I, p. 591. He defines the limits from Ghazni to Qandahar and from Maidan to the vicinity of Balkh; *Badshahnama*, II, p. 401; Cf. Erskine, p. 216. Hazaras—who inhabit the hills that lie along the upper course of the Helmend river, nearly as far as Kabul; *An Atlas of the Mughal Empire*, Sheet 1 A-B

[801] Muhammad Bin Khwand Shah alis Mir Khwand, *Rauzat-us Safa*, Tehran, 1339, V, pp. 36, 37, 38-39. The only inhabitants of Nishapur left alive were forty artisans who were taken to Turkistan.

[802] Alauddin Ata Juwaini, *Tarikh-i-Jahan Gusha*, ed. Mirza Abdul wahhab Qazwini, Gibb, Memorial series, 1911-1912, I, p. 31.

serfs and descendant of Mongol feudal lords themselves related to Changhiz Khan's commanders. It is more probable that they represented many of the tribes and races incorporated in the Mongol army.[803] Abul Fazl also declares them to be the offspring of the Mongols. He says that "the Hazaras are the descendants of the Chaghatai army sent by Manku Khan (grandson of Changhiz Khan) to the assistance of Halaku Khan (brother of Manku Khan).[804]

The Mongol origin of Hazaras is attested by their high cheekbones and sparse beard, which readily distinguish them from Afghan and Iranian neighbour.[805] Furthermore, the word Hazara is said, to be the Persian equivalent of the Mongol word *ming*, meaning 'thousand', the term originally was used to refer to the Mongol military unit of 1,000.[806] The Mongol regiments were so styled from the number of men they usually contained. The term was applied to these people in consequence of their

---

[803] S.A. Mousavi, *The Hazaras of Afghanistan*, Great Britain, 1998, pp. 24-25.

[804] *Ain*, I, p. 591; *Khulasat-ut Twarikh*, p. 87.

[805] Elphinstone, II, p. 202; Burnes, I, p. 178. In physiognomy they resemble Chinese, with their square faces and small eyes. They are Tartar by descent; Persy Sykes, *A history of Afghanistan,* London, 1940, I, p. 15.

[806] Raverty, pp. 66-67. The word *Ming* is the Turkish equivalent of the Persian word *hazar; History of Civilization of Central Asia, A.D. 750 to the end of the fifteenth Century,* ed. M.S. Asimov and C.E. Bosworth, Unesco Publication Paris, 1998, IV, p. 326. The decimal system was traditional among the Mongols was adopted by Timur also. The army was divided into *tumen* (ten thousand); *mingliks or hazar* (thousand); *yuzluks* (hundreds) and *onluks* (ten).

having been left there as military colonists in detachments of a thousand fighting men each by Changhiz Khan.[807]

The descendants of Halaku, who exercised authority in Persia after him, were known as 'Ilkhans'. The last ruler of Ilkhanate dynasty was Abu Said (1316-34), and Malik Chopan was his premier officer who led his army into eastern Khurasan and settled there. The Dai Chopan, a major Hazara tribe, was named after him.[808] Following the fall of Ilkhanate, shortly after the death of Abu Said (1334 year of Timur's birth), there was a power vacuum in the Persian Empire.[809] In early 1381 Timur overran the city of Herat, Khurasan and all eastern Persia and laid claim to the provinces of Qandahar, Garamshir and Kabul. Several other cities terrified by Timur's success, submitted to him.[810] Timur, after a great slaughter also established his power over the Persian city Mazendaran, with its capital at Astrabad, which was governed by a descendant of Shaikh Besud, an Ilkhan officer. The Besudis,[811] another major Hazara tribe was named after him. Under his son and

---

[807] Elphinstone II, p. 208; H.W. Bellew, *The Races of Afghanistan*, Delhi, 1980, p p. 114. He says that Changhiz Khan left ten such detachments, nine of them in the Hazaras of Kabul, and the tenth in the Hazaras of Pakli to the east of the Indus; Cf. *Punjab Castes*, p. 66.

[808] *A Comprehensive History of India*, ed. M. Habib and K.A. Nizami, V, Part, I, reprinted, Delhi, 2006, p. 95; Mousavi, p. 25.

[809] *History of Central Asia*, IV Part, II, p. 256, 329; Sykes, I, pp. 231-2. Halaku Khan founded a dynasty known as that of the Ilkhans

[810] Sharfuddin Yazdi, *Zafarnama,* ed. Maulvi Muhammad Ilahabad, Asiatic Society of Bengal, Calcutta, 1887-88, II, ff. 310-11, 316-17, 320, 325-327, 353, 375-78.

[811] *Ibid.*, I, 325, 433-34; Mousavi, p. 25.

successors, Shah Rukh, (1405-48) troops and officials were sent into the area, and it is probable that some of them remained when the Timurid returned north of Oxus to Samarqand on the death of Shah Rukh in 1447.[812]

In 1469-70 Sultan Husain Mirza (1469-1506) (Sahib-i-Kiran Sani), the grandson of Umar Shaikh Mirza, son of Amir Timur succeeded in establishing himself upon the throne of Herat and Khurasan.[813] He in 1471-72 made Amir Shujauddin Zulzun (a noble of Herat) of the Arghun family governor of Ghor and Zanimdawar.[814] The region of Ghor, Garamshir

---

[812]   Khan Muhammad Atif and Hamid Afaq Qureshi, *Amir Timur Beg 1336-1396 (English Rendering of Molana Sharfuddin Ali Yazdi's Persian Zafarnama*, I, Lukhnow, 2008, pp. 238-39.

[813]   *Comprehensive History of India,* V, p. 131. During Sultan Husain reign Herat became a real seat of learning. The last Price of the house of Timur in Central Asia. His sons were displaced by the Uzbeks.

[814]   Mir Khwand Shah, *Habib-us Siyar,* ed. Ghyasuddin, Bombay, 1857, IV, pp. 180, 191; Raverty, p. 580. It is a mistake to suppose that the Arghuns were descendants of the Changhiz Khan. Babur did not consider Shah Beg's brother Muhammad Mukim the Arghun (son of Zulnun Beg), a suitable match for the daughter of Abd-ur Razzak, son of his uncle Ulugh Beg. And this marriage was one of the causes of Babur's enimity towards the Arghuns. Had these Arghuns been descended from the Changhiz Khan, they would have been superior in rank to Babur, who was a Barlas and descendant of Amir Timur. Babur and his descebdants always styled the Arghuns 'Beg' instead of 'Khan', which they never would have done had the latter been of the family of the Changhiz Khan. Cf. *Baburnama*, p. pp. 195-96. Mirza Ulugh Beg, son of Abu Said Bahadur, who held Kabul and other territory adjoining, having died in 1501-2, Mirza Abd-ur Razzak, his son who at that time was very young, succeeded. In the following year, Muhammad Mukim made a dash upon Kabul from Qandahar and ousted him from

and Zamindawar at that time was predominantly inhabited by the Hazaras and Nukdari tribes.[815] Amir Zulnun in 1478-79 attacked into the tract occupied by them and was successful against them.[816] During many expeditions undertaken by Badi-uz Zaman (son of Sultan Husain Mirza) Zulnun Beg utilized the services of Hazara tribesmen. When Badi-uz Zaman marched from Herat to attack Khurasan, Zulnun Beg joined his sovereign from Qandahar side and recruited many of the Hazara tribesmen in his army. They succeeded in subduing the territory of Khurasan and carried away along with them a large number of sheep and a good deal of other booty.[817]

By the time another Timurid, Babur, captured Kabul at the beginning of the sixteenth century; the Hazaras were a distinct people, dwelling in the mountainous region to the west of Kabul. He in his memoirs referred to them living from west of Kabul to Ghor and towards the west of Ghazni.[818] Babur reports that he imposed on the Sultan Masudi Hazara a large tribute in horses and sheep as they were refractory and often were reluctant in paying tributes.[819] "The Hazaras", he

---

the government. When Babur captured Kabul, Muhammad Mukim was in possession. He gave up the place and later was permitted to return to his brother at Qandahar.

[815] *Habib-us Siyar*, IV, p. 392.

[816] *Ibid.*, pp. 392, 237; *Humayun Nama*, p. 5. Zulnun Beg Arghun, a descendant of Ilkhan of Persia ruled over Ghor, Sistan, Zamindawar and Garmshir. He made Qandahar his capital. His son Mukim's capture of Kabul raised their reputation temporarily.

[817] *Habib-us Siyar*, IV, pp. 348-49.

[818] *Baburnama*, pp. 207, 205 (see footnote), 214 Ghorband, 218 (Ghazni); Charles Masson, II, p. 295. The Hazara district between Kabul and Bamian are collectively called Bisut.

[819] *Baburnama*, p. 228.

says, "down to the time of my arrival in Kabul had been guilty of numerous insolent things and depredations; I therefore, decided to make an expedition against them". This expedition was executed during 1506 in mid-winter and resulted in the slaughter of some of the Hazaras. According to him he collected as many as 4 Babur captures a flock of sheep from the Hazaras* to 500 sheep and from 20 to 25 horses.[820]

During the winter of 1552-53, Humayun set out from Kabul for Qandahar by way of Charkh and the Kharwar Kotal. It was in this neighbourhood that the Hazara people dwelt here and there. Dawa Beg Hazara clan was in the fort of Tiri, when Humayun arrived there he gave him horses and sheep.[821] Towards the close of the sixteenth century, the Hazaras of this area helped Akbar in his fight against the Jalala Ansari, the Raushanai, against whom bodies of troops had been constantly sent for the last ten years or more, who had kept Ghazni in a state of constant ferment, and in endeavouring to capture whom, Zain Khan Koka had been for years occupied. [822]

The Mughal control over the Kabul-Qandahar route via Ghazni depended upon the loyalty of the Hazaras. Until 1622 the Mughal succeeded in maintaining some sort of authority over them. The capture of Qandahar by the Safavids in 1622 weakened the Mughal control over the

[820] *M.S. Randhawa, *Paintings of the Baburnama*, National Museum, New Delhi, 1983, p. 40, Plate, XII.
Baburnama, pp. 251-53.
[821] Bayazid Bayat, *Tazkira-i-Humayun-o-Akbar*, ed. M. Hidayat Hosain, Bib. Ind., Calcutta, 1941, pp. 128-130; *Akbarnama*, I, p. 242; *Ain*, I, p. 593. Charkh was a village of the *tuman* Loghar.
[822] *Akbarnama*, III, p. 776.

Kabul-Ghazni-Qandahar route and also their hold over the Hazaras, living to the west and south of Kabul astride the Uzbek-Mughal frontier. Following the fall of Qandahar, it appears that the importance of above mentioned route declined and so also the traffic out of the tolls on which the loyalty of the Hazaras used to be purchased.[823] Ghazni, lying about a hundred miles south-west of Kabul was now the most important Mughal held city in the Hazara dominated region. It was also important because of the easy passage it provided to Kabul through a rugged and mountainous area.

The Persian capture of Qandahar made it clear to the Uzbeks that it was the Mughals against whom the military preparations of the Safavids had been directed. Prior to this, there existed good relations between Jahangir and the Uzbeks. And both Imam Quli and Nazar Muhammad had been attacking and plundering the territory of Khurasan from 1614-1617.[824] After 1622, the ties between the Mughals and the Uzbeks also got disturbed and we find in 1625 Nazar Muhammad sent an ambassador Nazir Mirza Bashi to the Persian court[825] It appears that all this political situation invited the attention of the Uzbeks under Nazar Muhammad, who found it a good opportunity to subvert the Mughal rule south of the Hindu Kush. As Kabul provided no easy access from its north, their strategic plan was to attack Kabul from

---

[823]   M. Athar Ali, *Mughal India: Studies in Polity, Ideas, Society and Culture*, Delhi, 2006, pp. 320-22; Elphinstone, II, p. 213. Mounstuart Elphinstone also found them inhabiting the plains about Muqur and Qarabagh to the west of Ghazni.

[824]   Iskandar Beg Turkman, *Tarikh-i-Alam Ara-i- Abbasi,* Tehran, 1314, pp. 588-91, 677-78.

[825]   *Ibid.*, p. 715.

the south by seizing Ghazni. In 1624, Uzbeks under the leading command of Yalingtosh marched towards Ghazni by penetrating into the Hazara country and started mounting pressure upon the Hazara clans encamped there. The forced Hazara leaders approached the governor of Kabul, Khanazad Khan who was governing on behalf of his father, Mahabat Khan and sought his protection. Khanazad Khan fortified Kabul and put it into a state of defence. He sent a strong force to help the Hazaras. Khanazad Khan marched with 20,000 cavalry against Yalingtosh who was 40 *kos* away from Kabul. In the beginning the Uzbek army with 30,000 horses pressed the royal troops hard but Khanazad Khan with his artillery skills caused a great havoc and killed some 3 to 4,000 men, Yalingtosh Nephew was also among the slain. This loss on the part of Uzbeks provoked Yalingtosh, who in order to subdue Kabul, again collected a large army consisted of *Almans* (a nomadic Turkish tribe)[826] and Uzbeks and marched towards Ghazni. A forceful battle was fought at Sheer (a village five miles from Ghazni), Khanazad Khan with his efficiency inflicted a crushing defeat upon the Uzbeks and Yalingtosh fled away. Khanazad Khan returned to Kabul with many horses and much booty, together with 3-4,000 Uzbek prisoners. Shahjahan increased Khanazad's rank to 5,000 *sawar* and sent

---

[826]   Lahori, II, pp. 515-16, 618.

many presents. [827] Pelsaert, the Dutch chronicler, has also given a very detailed account of this attack.[828]

The Hazaras as a people differed entirely from the Afghan in appearance, language and manners. Among all the major ethnic groups of the Kabul *suba*, the Hazaras were the only members of the *Shia* sect of Islam.[829] This difference in religious belief naturally contributed to the hostility that existed between the Hazaras and their neighbours. They held the Afghans in detestation for following the opposite sect, and they often insulted, if they did not persecute every *Sunni* who entered their country. All Hazaras were considered heretics by the Afghans who pride themselves on being orthodox '*Sunni*' musalman.[830]

The region they lived in was difficult and mountainous throughout and for the most part soil was poor. The rugged mountains and the severity of climate as well as the barren land made husbandry difficult for them. But according to Welfred Thesiger on the southern slopes of the Koh-i-Baba range (the heart of Hazarajat) there were many springs and streams in all the valleys. He found that every fold in the ground to which

---

[827]   Mutamad Khan, *Iqbalnama-i-Jahangiri*, Nawal Kshor's Litho. Lucknow, 1870, III, pp. 207-9; Jahangir, *Tuzuk-i-Jahangiri*, ed. Saiyyid Ahmad, Ghazipur and Aligarh, 1863-64, pp. 386-7; Shah Nawaz Khan, *Maasir-ul Umara*, ed. Abdu-r Rahim and Ashraf Ali, Bib. Ind., Calcutta, 1888-91, I, p. 740.

[828]   Pelsaert, *Contemporaray Dutch Chronicle of Mughal India* or *A Dutch Chronicle of Mughal India*, tr. and ed. Brij Narain and S.R. Sharma, Calcutta, 1957, pp. 66-67. He believes that the Uzbeks were intending a direct attack on Kabul, and Ghazni was merely on their way.

[829]   Vigne, pp. 126-27.

[830]   Elphinstone, II, p. 212; *The Races of Afghanistan*, p. 116.

water could be conducted was cultivated. They cultivated two types of wheat—irrigated wheat and *lalma* or rain-grown wheat. Besides they also grew barley, peas, lentil, broad beans, lucerne and clover as fodder for their animal.[831] Many of the Hazaras possessed large flock of sheep and goats and some small, black, humped cattle. Nearly all the ghee (clarified butter) that was sold in Kabul came from the Hazarajat, and from the flocks of the Hazaras, and not from those of the nomad Afghan tribes, or *kuchis*.[832] The Hazaras also made felt (*namad*) and *barak* a special cloth made of camelhair. They chiefly depended on the flesh of sheep, oxen, and horses and other products of their flocks such as cheese and ghee as grain was very scarce.[833] A few of them drove cattle, sheep (big-tailed) and goats down to Kabul, where they fetched high price. There were no mules in this country and they owned no camels, since it is too cold for these animals in the winter.[834]

Several Hazara families called *khanwar* and *dadrau* (literally meaning joint family or household) made up a large unit called the *tol* or *tolwar*. Every *tol* had its own chief, known as the *malik*. Several *tol* in turn made up a *tayefa*, a more complex unit than the *tol*. Every *tayefa* had a head known as the *arbab* or *khan*. The *arbab* or *khan* was generally prosperous and enjoyed a high socio-economic status. The highest unit in

---

[831] Welfred Thesiger, 'The Hazaras of Central Afghanistan, in the *Geographical Journal*, vol. 71, No. 3, London, 1955, pp. 313-17. The writer went to Afghanistan in summer of 1954 from southern Iraq, during this journey he travelled in Deh Zungi, Besud and in a corner of Yakwalang.

[832] *Ibid.*; Cf. *Ain*, I, p. 591.

[833] Elphinstone, II, p. 208.

[834] Thesiger, p. 316.

the social hierarchy of the Hazaras was the *qaum,* made up of a conglomeration of several *tayefas.*[835]

Following is the Socio-ethnic structure of the Hazara society.

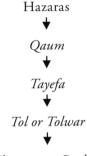

Hazaras
↓
Qaum
↓
Tayefa
↓
Tol or Tolwar
↓
Khanwar or Dadrau

Every Hazara *qaum* had its own powerful leader known as *beg, mir* or *sultan.* The head of a *qaum* was in full control of the socio, economic and political life of his people. His power was absolute in his tribe. Every individual member of the Hazara society was genealogically related to a *tol, tayefa* and *qaum.* The Hazaras were divided into tribes (*qaum*). The most important of which were the Dai Zangi, Dai Kundi, Dai Mirdad, Jaghuri and Besud. It is interesting to note that Hazara *qaums* and *tayefas* were named either after the area which they inhabited or after one individual such as Dai Chopan or Bihsud, consequently, all Hazaras can be traced back to Amir Chopan, (Dai Chopan is named after one of

---

[835]   S.A. Mousavi, *The Hazaras of Afghanistan*, Great Britain, 1998, pp. 46-47. *Qaum* an Arabic word is synonymous with 'nation', however in Afghanistan it is used to refer to a smaller unit, and the term *millat* is used to mean 'nation'. Therefore the Hazara *Qaum* should not be confused with it.

the landlords close to Abu Said, known as Amir Chopan, who led his army into eastern Khurasan and settled there, whom they regarded as having first brought their ancestors to the area of Girisk)[836] or Baba Besud (the Besudis, another major Hazara tribe were named after Behsud/Besud, one of Changhiz's relation).[837]

Amongst the tribes Dai Kundi occupied the large region bordering the Aimaqs area; Dai Zangi occupied the area North West of Bamian and to the south of western part of the *Koh-i-Baba*; Dai Mirdad to the east of Dai Zangi and Dai Chopan to the area of Girisk and Jaghuri inhabited the area to the west of Ghazni and Qarabagh. Besuds were found to the south of the Helmand river. Shaikh Ali Hazaras were found in Bamian and south of Ghorband valley and towards Yak Walang.[838] (See Map)

The Hazaras were often at war with each other, so that there was scarcely a Hazara tribe which was not at war with their neighbour. But two or three *sultans* united among themselves when it was a foreign war.[839] The Hazaras had a reputation for physical strength endurance and deceptive in their common intercourse.[840] They were generally a brave and

---

[836] R. Leech, 'A Supplementary Account of the Hazarahs' in the *Journal of the Asiatic Society of Bengal*, Vol., XIV, No. 161, Calcutta, 1845, p. 333 quoted in Mousavi, p. 25.

[837] *Ibid.*, p. 25, 54; *Ain*, I, p. 591. Abu Fazl gives the name of Behsudi in his list of several wild tribes who by that had become settled colonists; Elphinstone, II, pp. 211-212.

[838] *Ibid.*; Masson, II, p. 218; L.W. Adamec, *Historical and Political Gazetteer of Afghanistan,* Graz (Austria), 1985, VI, pp. 106, 143, 252, 711.

[839] Elphinstone, II, pp. 211-212.

[840] *Ain*, I, p. 591.

hardy race and had many of the warlike characteristics of the Gurkhas. They were of fairer complexion.[841]

The Hazara women were very beautiful. The women enjoyed a status not inferior to their husbands and very much consulted in all her husband's measures. They were never ill-treated. The wife managed the house, cared for the property and had her share of the honours. [842]

As far as their language is concerned, Babur testifies that many of the Hazaras spoke Mongoli up to his time.[843] The Hazaras speak Persian (*Farsi*) though with their own accent known as *Hazargi*. *Hazargi* is the mixed dialect of *Farsi*, Mongolic and Turkish with its own oral but not written tradition. No books have ever been written in *Hazargi*. The dialect of Hazara differs greatly from that of other *Farsi* speakers because of the influence of the Turks and Mongols.[844]

4. Relations with the Mughal State:

The disturbances created by the wild and turbulent Afghan tribes living all along the border and in most parts of Kabul were a source of great concern to the Mughal state.

The Afghans were a turbulent people, always fighting and intriguing. 'Never in all their history it was claimed, had the Afghans been subjected to any empire. They fiercely resisted the Mughal emperors and neither Akbar nor his successor really managed to rule over them. The control was nominal

---

[841]   Bellew, p. 116.

[842]   Elphinstone, II, p. 209.

[843]   *Baburnama*, p. 207.

[844]   *Mousavi*, pp. 81-82. *Hazargi* is composed of 80% *Farsi*, 10% Mongolic and 10% other languages.

and whatever success they had was short lived.[845] The strong sense of independence was the hallmark of Afghan character. One Afghan had eloquently expressed to Elphinstone, "we are content with discord; we are content with alarm; we are content with blood; but we never will be content with a master".[846] The Afghan race failed to establish any large and compact state, or even any enduring confederacy of tribes. Fighting among the Afghan tribes was a common occurrence. The internal feud among various tribes and even members of the same tribes was due to two important factors of the Afghan code of conduct: revenge (*badal*) and honour (*nang*). Nothing could prevent an Afghan to compromise on these two issues. They were united only under the threat of a common danger and always separated on the death of a successful leader.[847]

Kabul in 1504, at the time of Babur's conquest, was infested with numerous Afghan tribes, which enjoyed independence sufficient enough to embarrass any who sought a way to Hindustan from Kabul. Babur on his way from Kabul to Hindustan faced these refractory Afghan tribes. Babur admits that all the tribal area which he specifies as 'Bajaur, Swat, Parshawar and Hashtnagar', although they had once been part of the principality of Kabul, had now been entirely occupied by Afghan tribes and was no more the parts of the *suba*.[848]

Shortly after the capture of Kabul, Babur decided to attack the territories of Kohat, Bangash and Bannu. He reports that the Afghan tribesmen of these areas never paid taxes

---

[845]   Sarkar, III, p. 143.
[846]   Qouted in J.A. Robinson, *Notes on Nomads Tribes of Eastern Afghanistan*, Quetta, 1934, p. 8.
[847]   Elphinstone, II, p. 19.
[848]   *Baburnama,* I, p. 207.

willingly.[849] Babur had no time to bring these tribesmen to obedience as he was busy with the conquest of Qandahar, Balkh and Badakhshan. He was anxious to suppress "the Bangash thieves", once their preoccupations in Qandahar were over.[850]

Many years were to elapse before Babur could subdue these tribes. He admits that the most prominent and forceful tribes among the eastern Afghans were the Yusufzais, partly for the reason that in their country, he spent more time. During one of his campaigns against the Yusufzais, much before his conquest of India, Babur married Bibi Mubarika, the daughter of the powerful Yusufzai chief, Malik Shah Mansur, possibly hoping that the alliance would win her tribe's allegiance.[851] The Yusufzai tribe at that time occupied the Swat and Bajaur valleys and the plain (*samah*) of north Peshawar. This tribe had migrated to this region at the time of Ulugh Beg during 16th century from the Qandahar area and settled there.[852]

The first serious attempt to enforce peace with the border tribes was made by Akbar.

In July 1585 Mirza Hakim died, and so finally enabling Akbar to incorporate Kabul in his dominion. On his way back to Hindustan when Akbar was at Attock a group of chiefs of Afghan tribes and few others petitioned before Akbar

---

[849] *Ibid.*, pp. 230-31.

[850] *Ibid.*, p. 220. The Afghan highwaymen such as Khugiani, Khirilchi, Turi and Lander inhabited the *tuman* of Bangash.

[851] *Baburnama,* I, p. 375; Gulbadan Begam, p. 10. Malik Mansur Yusufzai, the father of Afghan lady Mubarika, came in and paid his respect. His Majesty took his daughter in marriage and allow him to go; Elphinstone, II, p. 11.

[852] *Alamgirnama,* pp. 1039-40; Elphinstone, II, pp. 9-11.

complaining against the Yusufzais; they were always molesting and plundering caravans of traders and travellers on the way from Kabul to Hindustan and vice-versa.[853]

Akbar was now determined to bring under his direct rule all these Afghan tribes of the North western region and surrounding mountains, which had never admitted allegiance to Babur, Kamran and Mirza Hakim or to any of the government who had ruled whether at Kabul or from Delhi. Abul Fazl informs us that Akbar realized that the backbone of tribal resistance was in the Yusufzai and the Mandar countries and so long as they maintained a defiant attitude, there could be no possibility of unhindered operation in Kabul or in the Uzbek country. He further states that in a short span, the country of Swat, Bajaur and Buner were cleared of the evil doers. A large number were killed and many were sold as slaves in the markets of Central Asia and Persia.[854]

In 1585 Akbar appointed Man Singh as *subedar* of Kabul and dispatched Zain Khan Koka (Kokaltash) in that direction with the object of making inroads upon the Yusufzai tribes. Zain Khan began his operation by penetrating in the Yusufzai territory, that had three thousand families there. The difficulties started when he advanced further into the interior, in the region between Peshawar and the Swat river, this region was the home of 40,000 families of the Mandar tribes. Though Zain Khan tried to subdue them, but even by 1585 his success was limited and the district of Buner was still out of the Mughal control.[855]

[853] *Akbarnama*, III, pp. 485-86.
[854] *Ibid.*, pp. 485-86.
[855] *Ibid.*, pp. 481-82; Raverty, p. 259.

Zain Khan asked for reinforcements. Akbar sent Raja Birbal and Hakim Abul Fath in that direction. The three armies under Zain Khan, Birbal and Hakim Abul Fath joined at Chakdara, a fort built by Zain Khan Koka during his recent operation.[856] Dissensions however broke out among the three generals. On February 1586, the three armies marched from Chakdara to Karakar Pass and encamped at Kandak. Next day they advanced further and encamped half a *kos* away from the defile. The battle commenced on the third day a number of tribesmen were captured. Despite the warning of Zain Khan Koka, the imperial army proceeded further through the narrow pass. There was confusion among the imperial forces. On 16th February 1586, the tribesmen suddenly attacked from all side. The incautious imperial army suffered losses. These operations against the Yusufzai tribes were a terrible disaster and an army of 8,000 men including Raja Birbal was cut down in a Swat defile. Abul Fazl, taking the official line, says that only 500 men of Akbar's army perished in the battle.[857] But there are other sources which provide a much higher figure for casualties on the imperial side. Badauni records that at least 8,000 men from Akbar's army lost their lives during that fateful night.[858] According to Khafi Khan that number of those killed was approximately 40 to 50,000. He asserts that everyone in Birbal's force was killed and that Zain Khan and Hakim Abul Fath escaped because they were not there.[859]

After much difficulty Zain Khan Koka and Hakim Abul Fath succeeded in reaching the imperial camp at Attock

[856]   *Akbarnama*, III, p. 483.

[857]   *Ibid.*, pp. 485-86.

[858]   Badauni, II, pp. 361-62

[859]   Khafi Khan, I, p. 191.

Banaras in a sorry plight. Akbar was quite remorseful at the death of Raja Birbal his prime favourite and for two days did not admit Zain Khan Koka and Hakim Abul Fath to his presence.[860] On the third day news arrived that the Yusufzai were advancing against the Mughals. Akbar sent Prince Murad and also Raja Todar Mal as his councellor and guide, not only to punish the Yusufzais but also to reduce them to complete obedience and submission. Zain Khan and Hakim Abul Fath also received orders to join the Prince's army. Shortly after, Man Singh too was recalled from Jamrud with his troops to strengthen the battle against the Yusufzais.[861]

The Emperor finally subdued these turbulent tribesmen by a strict blockade and in 1588 the Afridi's and the Urakzais agreed to keep the Passes open in return for allowances.[862] It was at this point of history that we hear of Khattaks (the later leader of Afghan rebellion). In 1586 Akbar appointed them as the guardians of the king's highway. This tribe had an interest in warding off the continual forays of the powerful Yusufzais and served well in the operation against them.

The Yusufzais were the hereditary enemy of these large and warlike tribes, as the boundary of these two clans met in the middle of the Peshawar district. The Khattaks occupied the southern part of the Peshawar district and much of Kohat and Bannu. The Yusufzais had also murdered Khushhal Khan's father. Therefore, Khushhal Khan after his release in 1666 readily accepted Mughal offer to fight in the campaigns

---

[860] Badauni, II, pp. 361-362. He writes, "Many grandees were killed in this disaster but his Majesty cared for the death of no grandee more than that of Birbal.

[861] *Akbarnama*, III, p. 487.

[862] *Ibid*, pp. 640-642.

against the Yusufzais.[863] In Swat Zain Khan was quite successful. His campaign lasted nearly eight months during which time he gradually built a series of forts from where he could render these mountainous passes safe.[864] Throughout these campaigns Akbar had kept himself at Attock watching keenly the work of his generals in these hilly regions.

In spite of reinforcement sent to these generals and their penetration into the tribal areas, the tribes, chiefly the Yusufzais and the Afridis, could not be completely subdued. The Mughals carried out campaigns up and down Bajaur and Swat for five years from 1587 to 1592, but without any real, lasting success. Mughal historians claim that the rebels were entirely overcome and compelled to evacuate and in large numbers fell into the hands of the Mughal troops. But we cannot ignore the fact that even in 1593 'the rebel' were strong enough to besiege the Mughal commander in Peshawar, which was only relieved by a special effort on the part of Zain Khan.[865]

There is other and a clinching evidence that confirms that Swat, Buner, Bajaur and the hill tracts never came under imperial control. In the *Ain-i-Akbari* Abul Fazl includes these areas in the *sarkar* of Swat under Kabul Province.[866] Raverty says that the Mughal ruler never obtained a permanent footing

---

[863] Badauni, II, pp.350-1; *Alamgirnama,* p.1042 Khushhal Khan Khattak was first an official Mughal army then an implacable foe of Aurangzeb.

[864] *Akbarnama,* III, pp. 529, 533. He caught and imprisoned Kalu, a wicked man of Yusufzai tribe while many of his men were killed.

[865] *Ibid.,* pp. 639-41.

[866] *Ain,* I, pp. 585-86.

in these parts and their communications were continually interrupted.[867]

After Akbar's time no serious endeavour was made by any of his successors to bring Swat or any of the rest of the mountainous regions under administrative subjection, and even in *samah (samah* in Pakhtu has much the same significance as *dasht* in Persian – meaning plain country) control remained weak.[868]

The problem of the north-west frontier grew worse during the reign of Aurangzeb. In order to keep the north western passes open and safe for traffic Aurangzeb first tried to win over the hillmen by providing them cash stipends, but in vain. The Mughal Emperors paid subsidies to various border chiefs which under Aurangzeb amounted to an annual expenditure of 6,00,000 rupees.[869] During his time the Yusufzais and the Afridis rose in arms against the Mughals in 1667 and in 1672 respectively. The Yusufzais revolted under the influence of a local *Mulla* Chalak. One of their leaders, Bhagu, a man of obscure origin proclaimed himself as king of the whole tribe with the title of Muhammad Shah and induced the different clans to unite. Uniting under one leadership they decided to establish their independence.[870]

Under the leadership of Mulla Chalak, a body of five thousand Afghans captured the post of Chhachal in the Pakli

---

[867]   Raverty, pp. 203-4.

[868]   *Ibid.*, pp. 215, 258. The *Samah* consisted of the entire territory lying between the district of Hashtnagar and the Indus from west to east, and the mountains surrounding Swat and Buner and the River of Kabul.

[869]   *Alamgirnama*, II, pp. 1041-42; *Ma'asir-i-Alamgiri*, p. 41.

[870]   *Alamgirnama*, II, p. 1041.

division. The fort of Chhachal was the seat of Shadman, a local chieftain, who with other Mughal officers was entrusted with the defense of the Attock area. Here the Yusufzais started to levy tax on the peasantry, and their success attracted more of their clansmen and they raised the standard of rebellion. They began to plunder and tribal encroachments on imperial territories near Attock started.[871]

Aurangzeb took measures of defense and ordered Amir Khan the *subedar* of Kabul to dispatch a contingent of thirteen thousand men under Shamshir Khan to operate against the rebels from Kabul. Kamil Khan, the *faujdar* of Attock was ordered to call up all *faujdars* and *jagirdars* near the Indus and subdue the Afghans. Muhammad Amin Khan, the *Mir Bakhshi*, son of Mir Jumla was ordered to go there from the imperial court with ten thousand picked troops and other officers carefully selected by the emperor himself, including 500 royal horsemen (*ahadis*). But before their arrival Kamil Khan left Attock with Khushhal Khan Khattak and marched towards the ferry of Harum in order to cross the Indus there but Shamshir Khan had already dispersed the rebels. Muhammad Amin Khan then marched towards the Shahbazgarhi (the site of an Ashokan inscription), and sent a force against the tribes of Bajaur. He entered the Swat valley, destroyed the village of Hijaz and returned to Ohind in October 1667. Here he was ordered to return to court. The command was now placed in the hands of Shamshir Khan, who was given an additional *mansab* of 2000.[872]

---

[871] *Ibid.,* II, p.1042; *Akhbarat,* 10th R.Y., sheet, 3, 4.
[872] Khafi Khan, II, pp. 237-46.

A well contested battle was fought in which, in spite of their numerical strength; the Afghans lost to the Mughals. The Afghans were defeated with heavy losses of lives. A tower of their heads was raised. They were pushed back to Mansur on the Panjshir river. Three hundred tribesmen, including several headmen (*maliks*) were captured and imprisoned and many were slain and drowned in the river.[873]

Five years later in 1672, Afridi rose in rebellion irritated, by the action of the *faujdar* of Jalalabad and induced several other tribes to join hands with them under the leadership of Ajmal Khan.[874] In 1672, the imperial army under Muhammad Amin Khan, the *subedar* of Kabul marching towards Kabul from Peshawar after passing the winter season there had entrenched at Ali Masjid. At Jamrud they found that the Afghans had blocked the way ahead and cut off the water supply. The Afridis slew and captured over ten thousand Mughals and secured twenty million worth of cash and goods and obtained further big sums as ransom for the captive officers and their families.[875]

According to Khushhal Khan Khattak, the Afridis had inflicted a loss of forty thousand men on the Mughal armies. Everything was lost, including Muhammad Amin Khan's own wife, mother, sister and daughter and the families of the nobles and officers serving under him. Later most of the women

---

[873] *Alamgirnama,* II, pp. 1044-45; Khafi Khan, II, pp. 230-31.

[874] *Ibid.,* II, p. 232; *Ma'asir-ul-Umara,* I, p.281. The name of Ajmal Khan appears constantly in Khushhal Khan's poems and other works as the heroes of the Pakhtun of those days.

[875] Khafi Khan, II, pp. 232-233.

were ransomed, but Muhammad Amin's wife, in bitterness of disgrace refused to return and became a recluse.[876]

The disaster of the Mughal forces encouraged the Khattaks, under their leader Khushhal Khan, who fought for long against Mughals during Aurangzeb time. The Khattaks under him joined the Afridis, and there was a general rising in the entire north-west, which took long to be suppressed.[877] Muhammad Amin Khan was replaced by Mahabat Khan, whom Aurangzeb considered fit for the governance of the refractory and dangerous tribes on his frontier.[878] Ajmal Khan, the Afridi chief and Khushhal Khan jointly attacked the fort of Nawshera and overthrew the imperial forces at Khapakh. Though Mahabat Khan had sought to prevail on Khushhal's loyalty as a Khattak vassal, but the latter turned down that offer and went into active opposition. Ultimately, the Emperor himself conducted operations from Hasan Abdal in 1674, and by skillful diplomacy succeeded in bringing the situation well in hand by the end of 1675.[879]

Aurangzeb's policy towards the border tribes was to set one tribe against another, and to subsidize their chiefs, into keeping peace on the frontier. He ordered to strengthen the Mughal forts on this line of communication. The tribesmen defied the strength of the Mughals for nearly three years before

---

[876] *Ma'asir-i-Alamgiri,* pp. 117-118. For the detailed description of Khushhal Khan. See Elphinstone, I, p. 196.

[877] *Alamgirnama,* p. 1042; *Akhbarat,* year 10, sheet, 9.

[878] *Ma'asir-ul-Umara,* III, p. 616, 593. Muhammad Amin Khan was sent off to Gujarat as *subedar* Mahabat Khan who had been the *subedar* of Kabul thrice before, was recalled from the Deccan and sent to Kabul as viceroy for the fourth time.

[879] Khafi khan, II, pp. 237-46.

the Afridis made terms of peace with Aurangzeb. He left the North-west frontier in December 1675. Amir Khan, who was appointed the *subedar* of Kabul in 1677, ruled this *suba* till his death in 1698, was remarkably successful in maintaining friendly relations with the Afghan Chiefs.[880]

By that time Khushhal had left the leadership of his tribe to his eldest son, Ashraf Khushhal who was imprisoned and sent in 1683 as a state prisoner to Bijapur, where he died in 1689.[881] Later on, his son Afzal acted as tribal aide to Shah Alam, Prince Muazzam. According to the records of the last ten years of Aurangzeb's reign, no parts of Kohat and Bannu district were subjected to effective Mughal domination. When in 1707 news of Aurangzeb's death reached there, Afzal was with Shah Alam at Attock and was left in change of the highway to Peshawar, his family's long standing responsibility.[882] The Mughal could never develop a well-defined and coordinated policy for the suppression of the tribes in the region of Kabul and other places in Central Asia. This was one of the reasons for the ease with which Nadir Shah invaded Northern India in 1739.[883]

5. The Raushanai Movement:

In the history of this region, the Raushanai – a popular Islamic revivalist movement occupies an important place.

---

[880]   *Ma'asir-i-Alamgiri,* pp. 157, 170, 270, 394; *Akhbarat,* 39th R.Y. and 40th R.Y.

[881]   Raverty, p. 435.

[882]   *Ibid.,* pp. 435-439. Muhammad Afzal Khan, the grandson of Khushhal was the author of the *Tarikh-i-Murassa.*

[883]   *Seir Mustaqherin,* III, p.300.

This socio-religious movement of 16th century appears to have attracted the attention of historians a number of times. But in these works focus have been directed on the religious aspect of this movement,[884] here an attempt is being made to reconstruct the political aspects of the movement mainly on the basis of Mughal Court chronicles such as – *Akbarnama, Muntakhab-ut Twarikh* (a critical and secret account of Akbar's reign), *Tabaqat-i-Akbari, Tuzuk-i-Jahangiri, Badshahnama, Alamgirnama* and *Ma'asir-ul-Umara* together with the *Halnama* (a work from Bayazid's pen).[885]

Mirza Hakim's reign of thirty years in Kabul is remembered for the rise of the Raushanai movement of Bayazid Ansari, which diverted the attention of the Mughal Emperors to the north-west frontier region for about half a century.[886] It was in fact, the Mughal political interest in the north-west frontier region which brought both the Mughals and the Raushanais face to face. K.A. Nizami says that "the Raushanai sect had an apparent religious facade but definite political motivations".[887]

The Raushanai movement was founded by Bayazid Ansari (1525-1572), who called himself *Pir-i-Roshan*, the apostle of light, but was by the Mughal chroniclers bitterly referred to

---

[884] S.A.A.A. Rizvi, *Raushanai Movement,* reprinted from ABR Nahrain ed. J. Bawman, Leiden, 1967-68.

[885] *Dabistan*, p. 345. Bayazid Ansari was the son of Shaikh Abdullah. He was born in Jalandhar, just a year after this event, Babur defeated Ibrahim Lodi.

[886] For a fuller discussion on Mirza Hakim see Munis D. Faruqui, in *JESHO*, pp. 487-523; Jamal Malik, "16th Century Mahdism: The Rawsaniya Movement among the Pakhtun Tribes", in *Islam and Indian Religions*, eds. A.L. Dallapiccolla and S. Zingel-Ave Lallemant, Stittgart, 1993, vol., I, pp. 31-59.

[887] K.A. Nizami, *Akbar & Religion*, New Delhi, 1989, p. 61.

as *Pir-i-Tariki,* the apostle of darkness. In all official Mughal documents they are referred to as *Tarikis.*[888] He was born at Jalandhar in the Punjab and was brought up in Kanigoram in the heart of Waziristan. His doctrines are embodied in his famous work *Khair-ul-Bayan* (Goodness of Narration), written in both prose and verse and contains a call to high ethical standards in life.[889] Besides, detailed accounts of Bayazid Ansari's doctrines and the role of his followers are available in many other works. Most of these works are cited by K.A. Nizami.[890] Among his critics, the works of Abdul Karim, known as Akhund Darweza, particularly *Makhzan-ul-Islam*[891] *(Treasure of Islam), Tazkirat-ul-Abrar Wa'l-Ashrar*[892] and *Irshad-ut-Talibin* furnish information about the public resentments to Bayazid's doctrines. In his works Akhund Darweza attacked Bayazid's claim.

According to teachings of Bayazid Ansari the spiritual guide had a divine status and it was obligatory to carry out his orders implicitly. The spiritual guide was to decide what was 'permitted' and 'prohibited' for his disciple. He thought that

---

[888] *Tabaqat-i-Akbari,* II, p. 368; *Akbarnama,* III, pp. 509, 513-14, 521, 525-26, 531-32, 607, 625-26, 639-40, 70, 776. He gives a detailed account of this movement and the Mughal operation against them. Cf. *Akbar & religion,* p. 65. Akhund Darweza termed Bayazid as *Pir-i-Tariki.* The Mughal chroniclers took the hint from him.

[889] *Dabistan,* pp. 345-346. *Khair-ul-Bayan* is in four versions – Arabic, Persian, Hindi and Afghani. His other work is *Khurpan.* These works were once very famous but on account being heretical, were later on banned by orthodox decree.

[890] *Akbar & Religion,* p. 62.

[891] MS. India Office Library, cited in *Akbar & Religion,* pp. 61-62.

[892] MS. Riza Library Rampur, cited in *Akbar & Religion,* pp. 61-62.

Farah Abidin

the concept of *Imamat* was an effective mean in mobilizing the Afghan tribes. He projected himself as if he was divinely inspired and declared that he reached a stage where he had become one with Almighty.[893] He believed in the theory of transmigration of souls. He propagated his teachings and soon attracted a large number of followers. Their number so greatly increased that Akhund Darweza bitterly states that the whole region was overrun by infidelity.[894] Bayazid's doctrine was criticized by the orthodox Muslims.

The Raushanai had a strong base of support among various Afghan tribes who provided him man power on whose support Bayazid proclaimed himself as the divinely inspired *Mahdi* and exploited them for establishing his political prestige in the Kabul region.[895]

Bayazid converted to his faith many of the tribes inhabiting between Peshawar-Khaibar Pass and Kabul. He had many followers in Orakzais, Afridis, Karlanari Afghans, Mahmands in Ningnahar, Mohammadzais and the Yusufzais. But he soon met with an opposition in the latter's territory where the followers of Pir Baba (Sayyid Ali Shah of Tarmiz strictly orthodox in the straight Hanafi Sunni way) in Buner with his champion Akhund Darweza opposed him. Bayazid them transferred his headquarters to Tirah,[896] where Afridis,

---

[893]   *Halnama*, MS. 920/37 Subhanullah Collection, M.A. Library, ff. 65 b- 66 a, 276 b, 278 b, 326 a- 333 b.

[894]   *Tazkirat-ul Abrar*, p. 146. cited in *Akbar & Religion*, p. 65.

[895]   *Ibid.,* pp. 61-62.

[896]   *Ma'asir-ul-Umara*, II, p. 247. Tira was a hilly area some 32 *kos* in length and 12 in breadth; Elphinstone, II, p. 401. Teera or Khaibar range commences a little below the fort of Attock from the right bank of the river Indus, on the opposite side from the fort, and runs in a westerly direction till it meets the Soliman

Orakzais, Khalils, Mohmands and Bangash flocked to his standard. It was here in Tirah that he started mobilizing the tribes to overthrow Akbar's authority and issued drafts on the treasury of Mirza Hakim whose decision to suppress the Raushanais was prompted by their continuing attacks on trading caravans passing through Kabul to Hindustan and vice versa. In 1571-72, Mirza Hakim launched offensive operations against the Raushanais in order to push them out of Kabul Nilab region. Under the intense pressure from the Kabul government, he was arrested but was later acquitted, really because the Kabul government feared his tribal support.[897]

After Bayazid's death (he had five sons – Shaikh Umar, Nuruddin, Khairuddin, Kamaluddin and Jalaluddin) his son Jalaluddin continued the movement which took the forum of quasi-nationalist uprising. In 1581 when Akbar was on his way to Hindustan from Kabul, he gave assurance to Jalala, who aged only 14 at that time, and his followers that they had liberty to follow their religion.[898] Farid Bhakkari the author of *Zakhirat-ul Khwanin* states that even this liberalism by Akbar was not able to calm the Raushanai and Jalala without the imperial permission left the court and marched to Tirah.[899] He had a band of four hundred followers who had been attracted to him by hope of plunder and revolution.[900]

---

ridge, south of *Saffaid Koh* separately the valleys of Kohat and Peshour.

[897] M.D. Faruqui, pp. 498-99.

[898] *Halnama*, p. 332; Monserrate, pp. 141-142. Monserrate states his Majesty cared little that in allowing everyone to follow his own religion he was in reality violating all religion.

[899] Farid Bhakkari, *Zakhirat-ul-Khwanin*, ed. Saiyid Moinul Haq, Karachi, 1970, II, pp. 223-24.

[900] Monserrate, pp. 141-142.

Jalala proclaimed himself the king of the Afghans and began to preach violently like his father. He started mobilizing tribes inhabited the areas in and around the Khyber Pass. His followers blocked up passes between Kabul and Hindustan. They raided and plundered the caravans passing through the Khyber Pass and openly defied the Mughal authority. They even killed Sayyid Hamid Bokkari, the Mughal *jagirdar* of Peshawar with forty of his relation and besieged the fort in 1585.[901] Their success over Sayyid Hamid Bokhari emboldened them.

The disturbances created by these heretics around the Khyber Pass jeopardized Akbar's political interest in this region, adversely affected commercial activities and encouraged both the Safavids and the Uzbeks in their anti-Mughal designs.[902]

Akbar sent Zain Khan Koka, Shah Quli Khan Mahram and Shaikh Farid Bakhshi and a large number of other officers to redress this disaster and to extirpate the Tarikis. Man Singh, who was in charge of the Kabul *suba* after the death of Mirza Hakim, was ordered to move to the Khaibar from Kabul. There took place a great tussle between Man Singh and the Tarikis. The Tarikis and the Afghans appeared in large hordes and carried on a fight. At this time Madho Singh, the brother of Man Singh, who was with Ismail Quli Khan at the *thana* of Ohind, arrived with a well-ordered army, to reinforce Man Singh. After that the Raushanais were defeated and many of them were slain.[903]

---

[901] *Tabaqat-i-Akbari*, p. 371; *Akbarnama*, III, pp. 510-511. He was one of the loyal servants of Akbar, and was posted at Peshawar for crushing and destroying.

[902] *Akbar and Religion*, pp. 65-66.

[903] *Tabaqat-i-Akbari*, II, p. 371.

From 1586 onwards all the experienced generals of the Mughal army like Man Singh, Zain Khan Koka, Hakim Abul Fath, Abdul Mutlab Khan, Asaf Beg, Mahabat Khan, Sayyid Khan and Lashkar Khan were sent to suppress the Raushanais and their Afghan allies.[904]

After the recall of Man Singh by Akbar, Mutlab Khan was sent into the Bangash country in 1587. Zain Khan himself returned to the charge undertook various campaigns during 1587-1592, but without any real or lasting success.[905]

In 1588 Sadiq Khan the new commander reconciled the Afridis and Orakzais, who agreed to keep the Khyber Pass open. Jalala therefore, lost trust in these tribes, and went to Turan.[906] It appears that Jalala approached Abdullah Khan Uzbek to help him against the Mughals but the latter refused. During 1592-93 Jalala again came to the scene and inspired the tribes to take up arms against the Mughals. Akbar ordered the frontier forces and the *subedar* of Kabul Qasim Khan and Asad Khan to attack the Raushanais.[907]

Jalala fled to Tirah and Qasim Khan was ordered to go back to Kabul. Soon after this he was assassinated and Qulij Khan was appointed as the new *subedar* of Kabul and dispersed

---

[904] *Ibid., Akbarnama,* pp. 510, 525-26, 607, 626, 639-41; *Tuzuk-i-Jahangiri,* pp. 263-64, 311-12; Lahori, II, pp. 3-4, 190-191; *Amal-i-Salih,* I, pp. 372-79; *Ma'asir-ul-Umara,* II, pp. 247-50.

[905] Raverty, pp. 257-258, 261.

[906] *Akbarnama,* III, pp. 527-528. From Tirah Jalala went into the defiles of the Yusufzais country and then to Turan. An order was also given to the *faujdars* of Jamrud and Bangash that every one should apply to the capturing of the leader of the Tarikis; *Maasir-ul-Umara,* II, pp. 724-29.

[907] *Akbarnama,* III, pp. 526, 651-652.

the Raushanai.[908] Zain Khan, who once again in 1597 was sent to set the affairs of Kabul in order captured Walidad (the son of Khairuddin and Kamal Khatun, the daughter of Bayazid) and other with all the tribesmen.[909] According to the *Halnama*, "Wahdat Ali, Walidad, with some other Raushanais were sent to the fort of Ranthambore by Akbar. Kamaluddin was already there and all the three were put to death at the royal order. Kamal Khatun, with her sons, was given in charge of Qasim Khan, the *Mir Bahr*. Ahdad along with his mother were under the custody of Asaf Khan. Later on Jalala recalled them through Ava Bakr."[910]

The Mughal succeeded only partially in their attempt to win over these tribes against the Raushanais and were unable to force Jalala to submit who remained a source of constant trouble till his death in 1601. In 1600 Jalala was founded at Ghazni, who had gone there to support the Lohani tribes against the Shadmani Hazaras but the latter opposed him. He wanted to get out of the city and fled to Aq Rabat mountain. Murad Beg pursued him and put him to death.[911]

Thus by 1601, the position of Akbar in the north-west frontier was quite strong but next year Ahdad (Shaikh Umar's son), Jalala's nephew and son-in-law once more stirred up strife

---

[908]   *Ibid.*, p. 654.

[909]   *Halnama*, f. 345 a.

[910]   *Ibid.*, f. 347 b.

[911]   *Akbarnama*, III, p. 776; *Ma'aasir-ul-Umara*, II, p.246; *Halnama*, f. 440. The author reports that hearing the news of Jalala's death, Ava Bakr was so shocked that he died at Mednipur, where he was posted as *faujdar*, under Baqar Khan, the *subedar* of Orissa.

in Tirah and rallied to his support the tribes such as Afridis, Orakzais and Bangash.[912]

Under the leadership of Ahdad the Raushanais defied the imperial authority and fought a number of battles during the reign of Jahangir. Jahangir refers to them in his memoirs that they remained a source of danger and constant threat for the Mughal state. He reports that in 1611 Ahdad attacked on Kabul in the absence of Khan Dauran, the *subedar* of Kabul.[913] Muiz-ul Mulk, the commandant of the town resisted the Raushanais in which several of them were captured and killed.[914]

Khan Dauran was replaced with Qulij Khan. The former, however was sent to Peshawar to check the activities of the Raushanai there.[915] In 1613, Qulij Khan died, Ahdad finding

---

[912] *Halnama*, f. 370. His name was Ahdad but people called him Ahad; *Dabistan*, p. 311; *Ma'asir-ul Umara*, II, p. 246. The author wrongly puts him as Jalala's cousine. Ahdad is said to have some super-natural power and few of them believed that he was divine.

[913] *Ma'asir-ul Umara*, II, pp. 642-645. In 1607-08 Shah Beg entitled Khan Dauran was appointed the governor of Kabul (Tirah Kabul, Bangash, Swat and Bajaur). He served there for a long time.

[914] *Tuzuk-i-Jahangiri*, pp. 96-97. Muiz-ul Mulk displayed measure of activity and the Kabulis and the other inhabitants specially the Qizalbashis (Farmali according to Roger) barricade up the streets and fortified the houses.

[915] *Iqbalnama-i-Jahangiri*, p. 53; *M'aasir-ul Umara*, II, pp. 642-645. According to its author, Khan Dauran, as a result of old age lost his physical strength and became incapable of carrying out forced marches—which were essential for a governor of Afghanistan. He was recalled and appointed the governor of Thatta; *Akbarnama*, III, p. 397. It is wrongly put as that he was transferred to Patna.

it a good opportunity attacked Kot Tirah and next year again with a large number of horses and army he attacked and slaughtered several of its people. But Mutaqid Khan together with Khan Dauran successfully routed him and his followers.[916] In the 10th R.Y. of Jahangir, Ahdad again with the support of his followers created disturbances in Kabul. The Mughal forces under Khan Dauran compelled him to confine to the fortress of Charkh. He however, managed to escape towards Qandahar. Many of his followers were killed and hundred of them were taken prisoners.[917] In the meantime as a result of the family disputes, Ilahdad, the son of Jalala, migrated to the Mughal court and joined the imperial service.[918] Ilahdad was honoured by the Emperor and the title of Rashid Khan was conferred upon him.[919] Shah Beg (Khan Dauran) was ruling the hilly region very well by avoiding a test of strength but the entire scene changed when in 1617 Mahabat Khan was appointed as the *subedar* of Kabul, Raja Kalyan, son of Raja Todar Mal was sent to act as his chief lieutenant in Bangash.[920] Mahabat Khan demanded Rashid Khan's dispatch from the court. Jahangir though agreed upon it but his son and brother were kept in the custody as hostages.[921] The author of the *Halnama* states that Rashid Khan was reluctant to go to that region.[922] His reluctance was due to the fact that he was

---

[916] *Tuzuk-i-Jahangiri*, pp.128-129.According to it Kot Tirah was 8 *kos from* Jalalabad but Tirah is farther away. In the Br.Mus. MS. it is referred as *Kotal-i-Tirah* i.e. the Tirah defile.

[917] *Ibid.*, pp. 152-153.

[918] *Ma'asir-ul-Umara*, II, pp. 246-48.

[919] *Tuzuk-i-Jahangiri*, p. 193.

[920] *Ibid.*, p. 196.

[921] *Ibid.*

[922] *Halnama*, f. 411 a.

deputed against his own relatives. He himself revolted against the Mughals but was pardoned by Jahangir on the request of Itmad-ud Daullah. He rendered valuable services to the Mughal State till his death in 1648.[923]

Mahabat Khan sent a force under the command of his son Amanullah[924] to capture Ahdad. Meanwhile towards the close of 1619 or early in 1620, Mahabat Khan came to know that Ahdad's chief supporters were mainly among the Orakzais of the Daulat zai branch, inhabiting around Kohat. He invited them and after feasting them and getting them to give up arms, under the pretence of conferring honorary dresses upon them, killed them to the number of three hundred.[925] After this act of treachery, Mahabat Khan believed that he had broken the backbone of the resistance in Tirah. He ordered, Ghairat Khan along with other officers to march against Ahdad in Tirah by way of Kohat. Ghairat Khan at the head of a large force advanced and on reaching the crest of pass, he was encountered with Panju, a Firoz Khel Orakzai. A fierce fighting took place and both fell rolling one over the other. Panju cried out to his tribesmen, strike, kill me also, but let him not go! Consequently both of them were slain. The disaster on the part of the Mughals was quite large; the

---

[923]   *Tuzuk-i-Jahangiri*, p. 196; *Ma'asir-ul Umara*, II, pp. 242-250.

[924]   *Ibid.*, I, pp. 740-748. He received the title of Khanazad Khan when he was appointed his father's deputy in Kabul. During the reign of Shahjahan he received the title of Khan Zaman. Also see vol., III of the same text, pp. 385-409.

[925]   Raverty, p. 391. It appears from Khushhal Khan's account that Mahabat Khan at the instigation of some Goriah Khel and Karlanari Bangash did this.

Raushanai captured 5000 horses besides other booty. All this led to Mahabat Khan's recall to the court.[926]

In the account of the 15th R.Y, Jahangir writes "among the events of this period were the death of the Sayyid Izzat Khan entitled Ghairat Khan. Ghairat Khan who was one of the hottest temperament, and ever ready to rush upon his enemies, did not approve of Jalala Khan the Gakhar's prudent advice and determined upon attacking the Afghans forthwith. He began the ascent and the Afghans like ants and locusts, collecting from different parts, completely surrounded the attacking force …"[927]

Six years after this disaster in 1625-26, during the term of office of Khwaja Abul Hasan that Ahdad was besieged in the fort of Nawagarh and killed by the governor's son Ahsanullah Zafar Khan, who was managing the *suba* as the deputy of his father. Zafar Khan sent his head, staff and signet to Jahangir and was honored by the emperor with the title of Muzaffar Khan and from the position of deputy was made the *subedar* of Kabul.[928]

After the death of Ahdad, the leadership of the Raushanais passed into the hands of Abdul Qadir. A year after this Jahangir died and was succeeded by his son Shahjahan. Lahori

---

[926] *Tuzuk-i-Jahangiri,* p. 160. Mahabat Khan never returned to Kabul as its *subedar.* Jahangir's description of Mahabat Khan's recall is more honest than the other Mughal chronicles, who explains that he was recalled for other important reasons, as he was the only capable noble to oppose the prince Khurram, who had put down his father's order in proceeding to Qandahar in 1622, when the Uzbeks attacked Kabul it was Khanazad Khan who defeated the invaders.

[927] *Ibid.*

[928] *Dabistan*, p. 310; *Ma'asir-ul Umara*, II, pp. 246-47.

states, when Muzaffar Khan was on his way to Kabul from Peshawar, the beast of prey like Orakzais and Afridis occupied the Khaibar road in his front and began to plunder Muzaffar Khan's force, his baggage and the ladies of the *harem* fell into the hands of Afghan, but his wife, Buzurg Khanum was saved and ransomed by the efforts of Said Khan, the *faujdar* of Bangash.[929] This attack was organized by Bibi Alai (wife of Ahdad and the daughter of Jalala) and her son Abdul Qadir.

Lahori states that during the 1st R.Y. of Shahjahan Muzaffar Khan was the *subedar* of the Kabul *suba* but the same year, he was removed from that position and Lashkar Khan was appointed.[930]

Muzaffar Khan's failure emboldened the Raushanais. All their Afghan allies assembled in great numbers under the leadership of Abdul Qadir and marched towards Peshawar. They entered the city and killed the deputy of the *subedar*. It was a general rising of all the Afghan tribes round the north-west frontier region with one accord to rise against the Mughal State, only with the exception of these three – the Khalils,

---

[929] *Halnama*, pp. 460 a-462 a; *Badshahnama*, I, p. 125; Amin Qazwini, *Badshahnama*, transcript of the Riza Library MS (Rampur), in the Department of History, Aligarh, p.1 59l.

[930] *Lahori*, I, p. 213, II, pp. 190-191, Shahjahan discovered that Muzaffar Khan was strongly advised by the most experienced person not to proceed to Kabul but he did not pay heed to them. The Afghan tribes who were ever ready to plunder and molest, occupied the road in his front and began to plunder the baggage of his force. As he left no experienced officer to guide his rear, a deal of property was carried of and he did nothing to remedy this disaster and did not turn back to aid them. On this account Lashkar Khan was sent as the new *subedar* with a force of 15,000.

Mahmands, the Daudzai round Peshawar; the Khattaks (under Shahbaz Khan, father of Khushhal Khan and grandson of Malik Akoroy) and the Daulatzai.

The Mughal garrison of Peshawar had to throw themselves into the citadel and the city was completely invested. Said Khan the *faujdar* of Bangash prepared to march to relief of the garrison.[931] At first Abdul Qadir and his force undertook the investment alone, but when a large number of other Afghan tribes assembled to aid him, they became jealous and suspicious of him. Abdul Qadir, himself became suspicious of their intentions and thought that they would in probability intrigue with the Mughals and would hand over him to the Mughals. He thus retreated to Tirah and the tribes were dispersed.[932] Said Khan had by now arrived at the scene along with the forces and attacked the Afghans that had remained and slew a large number. In this affair a great number of Yusufzais and Gagianis were also killed. Shahjahan was so pleased with Said Khan that he made him the *subedar* of Kabul and was promoted to the rank of 5000 *sawar*.[933] Khushhal reports that after this affair, "the Mughal authority began again to be recognized in the province of Kabul".[934] Subsequently, Said Khan with his usual tacts was able to bring to terms Abdul Qadir and Bibi Alai. *Halnama* informs that "Said Khan

---

[931]	Qazwini, p, 131 b.

[932]	*Halnama*, f. 463 a. Thus, "with their usual stupidity and wrong headedness of Pashtun (Afghans) they became jealous of him, whom they came to support, thinking that he will take all the credit to himself"; Raverty, p. 394.

[933]	Lahori, I, p. 400; Qazwini, p. 238 a; *Ma'asir-ul-Umara*, II, p. 435.

[934]	Cited in Olaf Caroe, *The Pathans: 550 B.C. – A.D. 1957*, London, 1965, p. 229.

accompanied Abdul Qadir to the emperor, who gave him a horse and robe of honor and asked him to join Mughal service offering him the rank of 3000; and if he wished to leave Kabul the rank was to be 2000."[935]

Said Khan asked the emperor to leave for Kabul as he had promised to Bibi Alai to bring Abdul Qadir back to Kabul. Consequently he was deputed to Kabul along with Said Khan. They arrived at Peshawar but soon after that Abdul Qadir died a natural death.[936]

Meanwhile some of the tribes around Naghz recalled Karimdad (s/o Jalala) who was living in the Lohani territory with his disciples and followers. He raised the standard of revolt and brought Bangash territory under his control.[937] Said Khan sent a force against them and some of them came to the terms with the Mughals. Karimdad who had taken shelter in a valley was spared, while his brother was put to death.[938] The royal troops entered the territory of Naghz, captured them and destroyed their property. Karimdad with all his family surrendered to the Mughal and was to put to death.[939]

---

[935] *Halnama*, f. 4676; *Ma'asir-ul-Umara*, II, pp. 246-247. He received the rank of 1000 and services at Kabul in 1633-34; *Amal-i-Salih*, III, p. 466. His rank, according to him was 1000/600.

[936] *Dabistan*, p. 311

[937] *Badshahnama*, II, p. 12; *Amal-i-Salih*, II, p. 267; *Halnama*, p. 482 a. Karimdad (s/o Jalala) was the uncle of Ahdad. His mother's name was Bibi Begum.

[938] Raverty, p. 397. The brother of blind Karimdad who was creating sedition and rebellion in that quarter (Naghz) at the instigation of Yalingtosh on behalf of the Nazr Muhammad, the ruler of Balkh.

[939] *Dabistan*, p. 311.

His mother Alai, with one of her brothers, Rashid Khan, and a number of Raushanais appeared before Shahjahan in Delhi. He treated them kindly and they were sent with honour and ranks to the Deccan provinces. Bibi Alai received *farrukhi* and a Doshala; other ladies accompanying her also received shawls. Rest of them were treated well and joined State services.[940]

Rashid Khan governed Telingana and was made *subedar* of Nandair during the late years of his life. He died in 1648.[941] Even after his death his younger sister Bibi Nur Khatun was well treated by the emperor. After the death of Rashid Khan she requested the king for *Madad-i-Maash* grant for her maintenance and increments in the allowances of the *jagir* of his son and her request was granted.[942]

The Shamsabad documents refer to some land grants conferred upon the family of Rashid Khan by the Mughals. The Document No. 39 informs that Rashid Khan's wife wanted to transfer her property to her daughter, Bibi Khair Khatun, "my entire possession, a village of 180 *bigha* and Bagh-i-Shamsabad which according to the *Farman-i-Shahjahani* is in my name, including all household articles, cash and kind will be hers, as I have none except her; the other sons of Nawab Sahib will not be entitled to this."[943] Another document shows that the Bangash Afghans had killed Bibi Khair Khatun's (d/o Rashid Khan) son Abdul Baqi, when this news reached Ilhamullah

---

[940]   *Badshahnama*, II, p. 34; *Halnama*, ff. 480 b, 483 a; *Ma'asir-ul-Umara*, II, p. 248; *Dabistan*, p. 311.

[941]   *Ma'asir-ul-Umara*, II, p. 250.

[942]   *Halnama*, p. 485 b.

[943]   *Shamsabad and Blihor Documents*, No. 39, p. 54. A transcript is in the Department of History, AMU, Aligarh.

(son of Rashid Khan), who was an imperial servant, he issued orders to hand over Abdul Baqi's property to her mother.[944]

The author of *Ma'asir-ul-Umara* informs that after the death of Rashid Khan his sons Ilhamullah and Asadullah and his brother Hadidad continued in Mughal services. In the 28th year of Shahjahan's reign, Asadullah was made the *thanedar* of Chandor and increased his rank to 1500/1000 horses. After the death of Hadidad Khan in 1657 his fief was granted to Ilhamullah who was promoted to the rank of 15000/15000.[945] In the war of succession Ilhamullah sided with Aurangzeb. After the battle of Dharmat, Aurangzeb honoured him with a dress and a flag and his rank was raised to 3000/3000. The emperor also conferred upon him the title of his father "Rashid Khan".[946] All through his life he remained the recipient of Royal favours and rendered valuable service to the Mughal state.[947]

Thus under Aurangzeb and his successor, the descendents of the *Pir-i-Raushan* received special favour and from then onwards we hear no more of the Raushanais.

---

[944] *Shamsabad and Bilhor Documents*, No. 54, p. 70 a.

[945] *Ma'asir-ul-Umara*, II, pp. 250, 303-305.

[946] *Alamgirnama*, p. 76. Out of 3000 *sawars,* 500 were *do-aspa* and *se-aspa*; *Ma'asir-ul-Umara*, II, p. 304.

[947] *Alamgirnama*, pp. 44. 150. In the 5th year of Aurangzeb's reign he was appointed as the *faujdar* of the *sarkar* of Kamrup and then as the *subedar* of Orissa. During 1676-77 he was appointed to the Deccan campaigns.

Bibliography

The bibliography only contains the documents, books and articles cited or referred to in the thesis. The bibliography is divided into two sections. Section A is based on sources. There are many sub-sections in this and a rough chronological order has been followed based on the date of the original preparation or publication. Section B is based on modern works which is arranged alphabetically on the basis of the names of authors. The British museum, Bodleian, Ethe, India Office, Royal Asiatic Society, cited are those for which microfilms, photocopies and rotographs are available in the Research Library, Department of History, Aligarh Muslim University.

A. Sources:
1. Unpublished Persian Sources:

1. *'Ain,* MS, Add. Br. Mus. Add. 7652 and Add. 6552, CAS, Deptt of History, Aligarh, R. Nos. 297-298.
2. Muhammad Sharif Najafi, *Majâlisu-s-Salâtðn,* pre 1627, Or. 1903, R. No. 19.
3. Anonymous, *Bayâz-i-Khwushbøð,* written before 1647, MS. I.O. 828, R. No. 194.
4. Muhammad Sadiq Khan, *Shâhjahânnâma,* Br. Mus, Or. 174.
5. *Dasturø-l-'Amal-i-Navðsandagð,* c. 1646-48, Add.6641.

6. *Kaifiyat-i-Subajât-i-mumâlik-i-mahrusah-i-Hindustan,* B. M. Or. 1779.

7. Jagat Rai Shuja-i-Kayath Saksena, *Farhang-i-Kârdânð,* 1679, Aligarh, Abdus Salam Farsiya, 85/315.

8. *Zawâbit-i-'Alamgðrð,* Aurangzeb, Or. 1641, British Museum, Add. 6598 R. No. 62, CAS, Aligarh.

9. Munshi Nand Ram Kayastha Srivastava, *Siyâqnâma,* Lithographed, Nawal Kishor, Lucknow, 1879.Khulasatu-s Siyaq, [AD 1703], Add. 6588, Aligarh, Sir Sulaiman 410/143.

10. *Dasturø-l-'Amal-i-Shâhjahânð,* Add. 6588, MS. Sir Sulaiman, Aligarh, R. No. 56, In Deptt of History. Aligarh.

11. Muhammad Tarin bin Abil Qasim, *Ajaibu-l Tabaqat,* and MS. R. A. S., 179

12. Jagjivan Das, *Muntakhabu-t-Twârikh,* Add. 26, 253.

13. *Dasturø-l-'Amal-i-Alamgðrð,* British Museum, Add. 6598.

14. Shaikh Muhammad Baqa, *Mirâtu-l-'Alam,* Ghost writing for his patron, Bakhtarwar Khan MS. No. 314/85.

15. *Daturø-l-Asr-i-Alamgðrð,* Aurangzeb's 3rd R. Y. R. No. 53, CAS, Deptt of History, Aligarh.

16. *Dastør-al 'Amal Shahjahânð wa Shuqqajât-i 'Alamgðrð (1701-2),* MS. Add. 6588.

17. *Kitab Shujaratum Nihâl or Risalâ-i Mazruat,* Lindesiana, No. 484, Br. Mus., Add. 1771.

18. Muhammad Kabir, *Afsan-i-Shahân:* British Library, Add. 24, 409.

19. Rai Chaturaman Saksena, *Chahar Gulshan or Akhbar-i-Nawadir*, MS Bodl. Eliot 366. Portion trans. J. N. Sarkar, in *The India of Aurangzeb*, Calcutta, 1901.

20. Rizqullah Mushtaqi, *Waqiāt-i-Mushtāqī*, MS Br. Mus., Or. 1929, R. N. 3, Deptt of History. Trans. Iqtidar Husain Siddiqui, New Delhi, 1993.

21. Abbas Khan Sarwani, *Tarikh-i-Sher Shāhī*, Ms. India Office, I. O. 218 (Ethe 219).

22. Muhammad Waris, *Badshahnāma,* transcript of Riza Library Rampur, MS. In the Department of History, Aligarh, Nos. 86-87.

23. Amin Qazwini, *Padshāhnāma*, Or. 173; Add. 20, 734; transcript Riza Library, Rampur, in CAS, in Deptt of History, Aligarh, No. 19-21.

24. *Hālnāma,* MS. 920/37 Subhanullah Collection, Maulana Azad Library, Aligarh.

25. *Shamsabad and Bilhor Documents*, No. 39, p. 54. A transcript is in the Department of History, AMU, Aligarh.

2. Published Persian Sources:

26. Zahiruddin Muhammad Babur, *Babørnāma*: (I) Chaghtai Turki text: Hyderabad Codex, facsimile ed. A.S. Beveridge, London, 1905, reprinted, 1971; (II) Persian translation by Abdu-r Rahim Khan-i Khanan (1589) Bombay, 1308/1890; (III) English translations: i) A.S. Beveridge, 2 vols., London, 1921; (ii) Leyden and W. Erskine, revised by L. King, Oxford, 1921; (iii) Wheeler M. Thakston, New York, 1996.

27. Bayazid Bayat, *Tazkira-i-Humayøn-o-Akbar*, ed. M. *Hidayat* Hosain, Bib. Ind., Calcutta, 1941.

28. Arif Qandahari, *Tarðkh-i-Akbarð*, ed. Muinuddin Nadwi, Azhar Ali Dehlawi, and Imtiyaz Ali Arshi, Rampur, 1962; trans. Tasneem Ahmad, Delhi, 1993.

29. Nizamuddin Ahmad, *Tabaqât-i-Akbarð*, ed. Nawal Kishor, 3 vols., Lucknow, 1875.

30. Abdu-l Qadir Badauni, *Muntakhabu-t Twarðkh*, ed. Ali Ahmad and Lees, Bib. Ind., 3 vol., Calcutta, 1864-69.

31. Abul Fazl, *Akbarnâma*, ed. Agha Ahmad Ali and Maulvi Abdu-r-Rahim, Bib. Ind., 3 vol., Calcutta, 1878.

32. Abul Fazl, *Â'ðn-i-Akbarð*, ed. H. Blochmann, Bib. Ind., Calcutta, 1867-77. I have collated this edition with the two 17th century MSS, Add. 7652 and Add. 6552 for the revenue figures of the *suba*.

33. Alauddin Ata Juwaini, *Tarikh-i-Jahan Gusha*, ed. Mirza Abdul wahhab Qazwini, Gibb, Memorial series, 1911-1912.

34. Mir Khwand Shah, *Habib-us Siyar*, ed. Ghyasuddin, Bombay, 1857.

35. Iskandar Beg Turkman, *Tarikh-i-Alam Ara-i- Abbasi*, Tehran, 1314.

36. Muhammad Bin Khwand Shah alis Mir Khwand, *Rauzat-us Safa*, Tehran, 1339, V.

37. Khwaja Ni'matullah al- Harawi, *Tarðkh-i-Khânjahânð* or *Makhzan-i-Afghani*, ed. S. M. Imamal-Din, 2 vols., Dacca, 1960 and 1962.

38. Jahangir, *Tuzuk-i-Jahångðrð*, ed. Saiyid Ahmad, Ghazipur and Aligarh, 1863-64; transl. A. Rogers and H. Beveridge, 2 vols., London, 1909-14.

39. Mutamad Khan, *Iqbalnâma-i-Jahångðrð*, ed. Abd al Haiy and Ahmad Ali, Bib. Ind., 3 vols., Calcutta, 1865.

40. Kamgar Husaini, *Ma'asir-i-Jahangiri*, Or. 171; ed. Azra Alavi, Bombay, 1978.

41. Abdul Hamid Lahori, *Badshåhnåma*, Bib. Ind., 2 vols., Calcutta, 1866-72.

42. Farid Bhakkari, *Zakhðrat-ul-Khwånðn*, [completed in 1650] Aligarh MS Habibganj Farsi 32/74; ed. Saiyid Moinul Haq, 3 vols., Karachi, 1961, 1970, 1974; vol. 1 trans. Ziyauddin Desai, Delhi, 1993.

43. Yusuf Mirak, *Mazhari-i Shahjåhånð*, ed. Sayyid Hasamuddin Rashidi Karachi, 1962.

44. Mobad", *Dabistån-i-Mazåhib*, litho. Pub. Ibrahim bin Nur Muhammad, Bombay, 1857 facsimile reprint, Tehran; trans. D. Shea and A. Troyer, Lahore, 1973.

45. Salih Kanbu Lahori, *'Amal-i-Salih*, ed. G. Yazdani, Bib. Ind., 4 vols., Calcutta, 1912-46.

46. Muhammad Kazim, *'Alamgðrnåma*, ed. Khadim Husain and Abdu-l Hai, Bib. Ind., Calcutta, 1865-73.

47. Sujan Rai Bhandari, *Khulåsatu-t Twårðkh*, ed. Zafar Hasan, Delhi, 1918.

48. Saqi Mustaid Khan, *Ma'åsir-i-Alamgðrð*, Bib. Ind., ed. Calcutta, 1871.

49. Muhammad Hashim, Khafi Khan, *Muntakhab-ul Lubåb*, ed. Kabir al- Din Ahmad and Wolseley Haig, Bib. Ind., 2 vols., Calcutta, 1860-74.

50. Ali Muhammad khan, *Mir'åt-i-Ahmadð*, ed. Nawab Ali, 2 vols. & Supplement, Baroda, 1927-28 and 1930.

51. Shahnawaz Khan, *Ma'åsir-ul-Umara*, Abdu-l Haiy's recension, ed. Abdu-r Rahim and Ashraf Ali. Bib. Ind., 3 vols., Calcutta, 1888-91.

52. Sharfuddin Ali Yazdi, *Zafarnâma,* ed. Maulvi Muhammad Ilahabad, Asiatic Society of Bengal, Calcutta, 2 vols., 1887-88.

53. Inayatullah Khan Kashmiri, *Kalimat-i-Tayyibât,* Salar Jang, MS. ed. S. M. Azizuddin Hasan, Delhi, 1982. 1871.

54. F. M. Qawwas, *Farhang-i-Qawwâs* [c. 1342-3], ed. N. Ahmad, Tehran, 1974. (Dictionary)

3. Contemporary European Accounts:

55. Marco Polo, *The Book of Ser Marco Polo,* tr. and ed. Henry Yule and Henri Cordier, 2 vols., Delhi, 1993.

56. Sidi Ali Reis, *The Travel & and Adventures of the Turkish Admiral, Sidi Ali Reis in India, Afghanistan, Central Asia and Persia during the years 1553-1556,* tr. A. Vambery, London, 1899.

57. Fr. A. Monserrate, *Commentary on his Journey to the court of Akbar,* tr. J.S. Hoyland, annotated by S.N. Banerjee, Cuttack, 1922.

58. J. H. van Linschoten, *The Voyage of John Huyghen van Linchoten to the East Indies,* from the old English translation of 1598, ed. A. C. Burnell (Vol. I) and P. A. Tiele (Vol. II), Hakluyt Society, Vols. 70-71, London, 1885.

59. *Early Travels in India (1583-1619),* collection of narratives of Finch (1-47), Mildenhall (48-59), Hawkins (60-121), Finch (122-87), Withington (188-233), Coryat (234-87), and Terry (288-332), ed. W. Foster, London, 1927.

60. Thomas Roe, *The Embassy of Sir Thomas Roe, 1615-19, as Narrated in his Journals and Correspondence*, ed. William Foster, London, 1926, New Delhi, 1993.

61. *The English Factories in India*, 1618-69, ed. W. Foster, 13 vols., Oxford, 1906-27.the volumes are not numbered and have, therefore been cited by the years allotted to each.

62. Samuel Purchas, *Hakluytus Posthumus* or *Purchas his Pilgrims*, London, 1625, Glasgow, 20 vols., 1905.

63. Francois Pelsaert, '*Remonstrantie*, c. 1626, tr. W.H. Moreland and P. Geyl, Jahangir's India, Cambridge, 1925.

64. Francois Pelsaert, '*Remonstrantie*, tr. by B. Narayan and S. R. Sharma, '*A Contemporary Dutch chronicle of Mughal India*', Calcutta, 1957.

65. Joannes De Laet, '*De Imperio Magni Mongolis*' etc. 1631, tr. J.S. Hoyland and annotated S.N. Banerjee, *The Empire of the great Mogul*, Bombay, 1928.

66. Peter Mundy, *Travels,* vol. II 'Travel in Asia, 1630-34', ed. Sir R.C. Temple, Hayluyt society, 2nd series, xxxv, London, 1914; and Vol. V (including accounts of travel to India, 1655-56), ed. L.M. Anstey, London, 1936.

67. Fray Sabastian Manrique, *Travels, 1629-43*, tr. C.E. Luard assisted by H. Hostoen, 2 vols., Hakluyt Society, London, 1927.

68. Jean Baptise Tavernier, *Travels in India*, 1640-67, tr. V. Ball 2nd edtion revised by W. Crook, 2 vols., London, 1925.

69. Francois Bernier, *Travels in the Mughal Empire:1656-68*, tr. On the basis of Irving Brocks version by, A. Constable, with notes, 2nd edn. revised by V.A. Smith, first published, London, 1934, reprinted, New Delhi, 1983.

70. Jean de Thevenot, *'Relation de Hindustan, 1666-67;* A. Lovell's tr. of 1687, reprinted with corrections, notes and an introduction by S.N. Sen in *The Travels of Thevenot and Careri,* New Delhi, 1949.

71. Niccolao Manucci, *Storia do Mogor or Mogul India: 1656-1712,* tr. W. Irvine, Indian Text Series-1, Royal Asiatic Society, Calcutta, 1966.

72. C. Wessels, *Early Jesuit Travellers in Central Asia: 1603-1721,* first published, 1924, reprinted, New Delhi, 1992.

4. Travels:

73. Thomas Watters, On Yuan Chwang's *Travels in India 629-645 A.D.,* ed. T.W. Rhys Davids and S.W. Bushell, London, 1905.

74. Alberuni, *Kitabu-l Hind,* tr. E.C. Sachau, 2 vols., Delhi, 1964.

75. Ibn Battuta, *The Travels of Ibn Battuta,* tr. H.A.R. Gibb, reprinted, Delhi, 1993.

76. Mounstuart Elphinstone, *An Account of the Kingdom of Caubul and its Dependencies in Persian, Tartary and India,* 'new and revised' edn., London, 1839.

77. William Moorcroft and George Trebeck, *Travels in the Himalyan Provinces of Hindustan and the Panjab, in Ladakh and Kashmir, in Peshawar, Kabul, Kunduz and Bokhara.....from 1819 to 1825,* ed. H.H. Wilson, 2 vols., London, 1837.

78. Alexander Burnes, *Travels into Bokhara, Together with a Narrative of a Voyage on the Indus* [1831-33], 3 vols., London, 1834.

79. G.T. Vigne, *Personal Narrative of a visit to Ghazni, Kabul and Afghanistan,* London, 1840.

80. Charles Masson, *Narrative of Various Journeys in Balochistan, Afghanistan and the Panjab: 1826-1838,* 3 Vols. London, 1842.

81. Mohan Lal, *Travel in the Panjab, Afghanistan and Turkistan to Balk, Bukhara and Herat, and a visit to Great Britain and Germany,* 2nd ed. S. Hasan Ahmad, Calcutta, 1977.

82. Sir John Chardin, *Travels in Persia 1673-1677,* Reprinted, N.Y., 1988.

83. Jenkinson Anthony, *Early Voyages and Travel to Russia and Persia,* ed. By Delmar Morgan and C. H. Coot, 2 vols., Hakluyt Society, 1886, London.

84. Sir John Chardin, *Sir John Chardin's Travels in Persia,* tr. E.M.D. Lloyd, London, 1720, ed. Percy Sykes, 2 vols., London, 1927.

85. James B. Fraser, *Narrative of a Journey into Khorasan in the years 1821 & 1822,* with a new Introduction by Edward Ingram, OUP, New York, 1984.

B. Modern Works:

86. *Afghanistan: Ancient land with modern ways,* Produced by the Ministry of Planning of Royal Government of Afghanistan.

87. Anatoly M. Khazanov, *Nomads and the Outside World,* tr. Julia Crookenden, London, 1994.

88. Angus Hamilton, *Afghanistan Description and Travel,* London, 1906.

89.   Anotoly M. Khazanov and Andre Wink, *Nomads in the Sedentary World*, Great Britain, 2001.

90.   Arnold Fletcher, *Afghanistan: Highway of Conquest*, New York, 1965.

91.   Beni Prasad, *History of Jahangir*, Allahabad, 1962.

92.   Brian Robson, *A road to Kabul*, London 1928.

93.   Chetan Singh, *Region and Empire: Panjab in the Seventeenth Century*, Delhi, OUP, 1991.

94.   Christine Noelle, *State and Tribe in the nineteenth century Afghanistan: The reign of Amir Dost Muhammad Khan (1826-1863)*, 1997.

95.   Denzil Ibbetson, *Panjab Castes*, Delhi, 1993.

96.   Donald N. Wilber, *Afghanistan: Its People, Its Society, Its Culture*, New Jersey, 1962.

97.   Edward Thomas, *Revenue Resource of the Mughal Empire: 1593-1707*, London, 1871.

98.   G.A. Grierson, *Linguistic Survey of India, Eranian Family*, Vol. X, Delhi, First Published, 1921, Reprinted, 1990.

99.   G.A. Grierson, *Linguistic Survey of India, Indo-Aryan Family North-Western Group*, first published, 1919, reprinted, 1990, VIII, Part, II.

100.   G.P. Tate, *The Kingdom of Afghanistan: A Historical Sketch*, Bombay and Calcutta, Times of India Office, 1911

101.   George B. Cressey, Crossroads: *Land And Life in south-west Asia*, New York, 1960.

102.   H. K. Naqvi, *Urbanisation and Urban Centres Under the Great Mughals*, Shimla, 1972

103.   H. M. Elliot and John Dowson, *The History of India as told by its own Historian*, in 8 vols., first published, 1867-77, reprinted, New Delhi, 2001.

104. H.H. Wilson, Judicial and Revenue Terms and of useful words occurring in official Documents relating to the administration of the Government, Delhi, 1968.

105. H.W. Bellew, Afghanistan: *A Political Mission in 1857, with an Account of the Country and People*, First Published, London, 1920, first reprint, Lahore, 1978.

106. H.W. Bellew, *The Race of Afghanistan*, Delhi, 1980.

107. Hamid Sulaiman, *Miniatures of Baburnama*, Tashkent, 1970.

108. Henry Yule and A. C. Burnell, Hobson Jobson, *a glossary of Colloquial Anglo-Indian Works and Phrases*, ed. William Crook, London, 1903.

109. *History of Civilization of Central Asia from 16th century to mid-19th century*, ed. Chaharyar Adle and Irfan Habib, Unesco, publication, 2003.

110. *Hudud-i-Alam*, V. Minorsky, trans. *The Regions of the world*, London, 1937.

111. I. H. Siddiqui, *Sher Shah Sur and His Dynasty*, Jaipur, 1995.

112. Iskandar Beg Turkman, *Tarikh-i-Alam Ara-i- Abbasi*, Tehran, 1314.

113. J.A. Robinson, *Notes on Nomads Tribes of Eastern Afghanistan*, Quetta, 1934.

114. J.N. Sarkar, *Mughal Polity*, Delhi, 1984.

115. Jamal Malik, "16th Century Mahdism: The Rawsaniya Movement among the Pakhtun Tribes", in *Islam and Indian Religions*, eds. A.L. Dallapiccolla and S. Zingel-Ave Lallemant, Stittgart, 1993.

116. James D. Tracy, *The Rise of Merchant Empires Long-Distance Trade in the Early Modern World, 1356-1750*, New York, 1990.

117. Johannes Leon Gommans, *Horse-Traders, Mercenaries and Princes: The Formation of the Indo-Afghan Empire in the Eighteen Century,* Brussels, 1993.

118. K.A. Nizami, *Akbar & Religion,* New Delhi, 1989.

119. L.W. Adamec, *Historical and Political Gazetteer of Afghanistan,* Vol., 6, Graz (Austria), 1985.

120. Le Strange, *The land of Eastern Caliphate, Mesopotamia, Persia and Central Asia from the Moslem Conquest to the time of Timur,* Cambridge university Press, 1930.

121. M. Athar Ali, *Mughal India, Studies in polity: Ideas, Society and Culture,* New Delhi, OUP, 2006.

122. M. Athar Ali, *The Apparatus of Empire Awards of Ranks, offices and Title to the Mughal nobility: 1574-1658,* Delhi, OUP, 1985.

123. M. Athar Ali, *The Mughal nobility under Aurangzeb,* 2nd edn. Delhi, 1997.

124. M.F. Lokhandwala, tr. *History of Gujarat,* Baroda, Oriental Institute, 2 vols. 1970, 1974.

125. Mohibbul Hasan, Babur Founder of the Mughal Empire in India, Manohar, Delhi, 1985.

126. M.S. Randhawa, *Paintings of Baburnama,* National Museum, New Delhi, 1983.

127. Mary Bradley Watkins, *Afghanistan Land in Transition,* New York, 1963.

128. O.H.K. Spate & A.T.A. Learmonth, *India and Pakistan, a General and Regional Geography,* London, 1954.

129. Olaf Caroe, *The Pathans: 550 B.C. – A.D. 1957,* London, 1965.

130. Percy Sykes, *A History of Afghanistan,* London, 1940.

131. Rajat Kanta Ray, "The *Bazar*: Indigenous Sector of the Indian Economy", in Dwijendra Tripathi, ed., *Business Communities of India*, New Delhi, Manohar, 1984.

132. R. G. Mukhninova, *Sotsialnaya Differentsiatsia Naseleniya Gorodov Uzbekistana*, Tashkent, 1985.

133. S.A. Mausavi, *The Hazaras of Afghanistan*, Great Britain, 1998.

134. S.A.A.A. Rizvi, *Raushanai Movement,* reprinted from ABR Nahrain ed. J. Bawman, Leiden, 1967-68.

135. S.P. Verma, *Art and Material Culture in the paintings of Akbar's Court,* Delhi, 1978.

136. Sarkar, *Mughal Polity*, Delhi, 1984.

137. Satish Chandra, *Essays on the Medieval Indian History,* Delhi, 1987

138. Satish Chandra, *Parties and Politics at the Mughal court: 1707-1740,* Delhi, 1979.

139. *Sikh History from Persian Sources*, ed. J.S. Grewal & Irfan Habib, Delhi, 2001.

140. Simon Digby, *War-Horses and Elephant in the Delhi Sultanate A Study of Military Supplies,* Oxford, 1971.

141. Sir George Robertson, *Kafirs of Hindu Kush,* London, 1896.

142. Sir John Chardin, *Sir John Chardin's Travels in Persia,* tr. E.M.D. Lloyd, London, 1720, ed. Percy Sykes, London, 1927, 2 vols.

143. Stephen Fredrick Dale, *Indian Merchant and Eurasian Trade: 1600-1750*, New Delhi, 1994.

144. Stuart C. Welch, *The Art of Mughal India Painting & Precious Objects*, New York, 1964.

145. *The Chahar Gulshan*, J. N. Sarkar, trans. *The India of Aurangzeb*, Calcutta, 1901,

146. *The Imperial Gazetteer of India*, XIV, Haryana, 1908.

147. *The Indo-Aryan Language,* ed. Gordan and Dhamesh Jain, London, 2003

148. *The Rise of Merchant Empires Long-Distance Trade in the Early Modern World, 1356-1750,* ed. James D. Tracy, New York, 1990.

149. Thomas Holdich, *The Gates of India Being An Historical Narrative,* London, 1910.

150. W. Irvine, *The Army of the Indian Moghuls: Its Organisation and Administration,* Delhi, 1962.

151. W.H. Moreland, *India at the death of Akbar,* London, 1920.

152. Walter Hamilton, *Geographical Statiscal and Historical Description of Hindustan and the Adjacent Countries,* Delhi, 1971.

153. William Irvine, *Later Mughal,* Delhi, 1971.

154. Wayne E. Begley, "*Four Mughal Caravansarais Built During the Reign of Jahangir and Shahjahan*", ed. Muqarnas, New Haven, Yale University Press, 1983.

155. William T. Couch, *Collier's Encyclopedia,* Twenty Volumes with Bibliography and Index, New York, 1957.

156. William Erskine, *History of India Under Baber,* New Delhi, 1994.

157. Zahir Uddin Malik, *The Reign of Muhammad Shah: 1719-1748,* Delhi, 1977.

158. Ebba Koch, *Mughal Architecture,* Munich: Prestel, 1991

5. Maps:

159. *A Map of the Kingdom of Caubul and some of the Neighbouring Countries, altered from a Map constructed in the year 1809* by Lieut. John Macartney, London, 1838.

160. Official Map of Afghanistan, compiled mainly from the 1957-60 survey. Separate political & Physical versions, legends in English and Persian, issued by Afghan Cartographic Institute, Kabul, 1968.

161. Irfan Habib, An Atlas of the Mughal Empire: Political and Economic Maps with Detailed notes, Bibliography and index, Delhi, 1986.

6. Journals:

162. Iqtidar Alam Khan, The *Karavansarays* of Mughal India: A Study of Surviving Structures', in *Indian Historical Review*, vol. xiv, no. 1-2, July 1987-Jan 1988

163. Iqtidar Husain Siddiqui, 'Evolution of the *Vilayat*, the *Shiq* and the *Sarkar* in Northern India (1210-1255)', in *Medieval India Quarterly*, ed, K. A. Nizami, vol., V, Aligarh, 1963.

164. Irfan Habib, 'Changes in Technology in Medieval India', *Studies in History*, vol. II, No. 1, 1980.

165. Irfan Habib, 'Technology and Economy of Mughal India', *The Indian Economic and Social History Review*, vol., xvii, No. 1.

166. M. Athar Ali, 'Provincial Governor under Aurangzeb An Analysis', in *Medieval India A Miscellany*, vol., I, Delhi, 1969.

167. *Medieval India—A Miscellany*, Aligarh/Bombay, 1969.

168. *Medieval India—A Miscellany*, Aligarh/Bombay, 1969.

169. R. W. Ferrier, "An English View of Persian Trade in 1618", *Journal of the Economic and Social History of the Orient XIX/2* (1976)

170. Muzaffar Alam, "Trade, State Policy And Regional Change: Aspects of Mughal-Uzbek Commercial

Relations, C. 1550-1750", *Journal of the Economic and Social History of the Orient, Vol. XXXVII, Part I,* 1994.

171. Munis D. Faruqui, 'The Forgotten Prince: Mirza Hakim And the Formation of the Mughal Empire in India', in *Journal of the Economic and Social History of the Orient, Vol., XXXXVIII, Part 4/*2005.

172. Thomas Edward, 'The Revenue of the Mughal Empire in India', *Journal of Asiatic Society of Bengal,* 1881.

7. Proceedings:

173. Irfan Habib, 'Evolution of the Afghan Tribal System', in *PIHC,* 62nd session, Bhopal, 2001.

174. Ravindra Srivastava, "The distribution of *Sarais* and Mughal trade-routes in Uttar Pradesh", paper presented at the Indian History Congress, 1976, Paper on Medieval Indian History, Calicut, 1976.

175. Sumbul Halim Khan, 'Rajputs in Afghanistan- The Amber Rulers services in *suba* Kabul (1676-88)', *PIHC,* 56th session, 1995.

176. Surendra Gopal, "Indians in Central Asia 16th and 17th Centuries", *PIHC,* 52nd Session, New Delhi, 1992.